THE LIVING MASTER

THE LIVING MASTER

By
Katherine Wason

RADHA SOAMI SATSANG BEAS
Punjab, India

Published by
Shri K. L. Khanna,
Secretary,
Radhasoami Satsang Beas

1st Edition—1966
3,000 Copies
2nd Edition—1971
3,000 Copies
3rd Edition—1975
3,000 Copies

Printed at the Rekha Printers Pvt. Ltd.,
New Delhi-110020.

MAHARAJ CHARAN SINGH JI

PROLOGUE

This book is about the Master, the Living Master. But it could have been written in any age from the beginning of time. There would be very little difference in its contents. For there has always been a Living Master.

Told from the personal experiences of a disciple with a Living Master of the present day, Maharaj Charan Singh, the following is a story which has been re-enacted since man has walked upon the face of the earth...

CONTENTS

CHAPTER ONE

A QUEST

The Boston night was bitterly cold, unusual for mid-October. A raw, chilling wind tore at our clothes. But they had all come with me to the airport—my mother and father and two close friends. I could sense their despair and concern at my undertaking a journey half-way around the world in search of a mysterious "holy man" in India. This despondency crept into my own mind, too, and I had a lost, hopeless feeling as I boarded the plane. What was I doing? Where was I going? And why? I had waited so long for this moment, and now that it had finally arrived, I tasted the bitter poison of doubt and uncertainty in myself, and wondered if all my hopes and efforts that had led to this end would be any more fruitful than the rest of my life's undertakings had been. Was this, too, to be a disappointment, another futile search for the end of the rainbow, that would again leave me alone in tears? I sank down into the seat and pressed my face against the small port window of the plane. There on the flight deck they stood; four small shadows huddled together against the wrath of the old night wind. I watched them until they became tiny specks, soon vanishing into the night as the plane's wing lifted and sped forward into the blackness.

Then the reflection came. As my mind wandered over the past, the despondency began to be replaced by a quiet resignation, even eagerness. There was no other way. The answer could not be found by escaping into the world's deceitful game, nor could it be found in blind adherence to dogma, nor in the endless maze of philosophical speculation, nor in the sand wall of atheism. And this I knew, not from hearsay, but from the strict and lasting instruction of personal experience. For I had plunged rapidly into one golden promise after another and tested almost every answer life could offer, it seemed. And every road had led to a dead end. I had poured through libraries of philosophical, psychological, metaphysical, and religious literature, finding only a confused mass of contradictions. But somehow I kept on searching though I knew not why.

Then my thoughts settled on the memory of the day that marked the turning point. The decision had been instantaneous. From that moment on there was never a shadow of a doubt that what I wanted was the spiritual life and only the spiritual life. It was a warm morning in August in the backwoods of Maine and I had been sitting on top of a hill in a sunny glade since early dawn. For days before I had been leaving the farmhouse from morning till night to ponder and question over the meaning of life and the ultimate source of all existence. I felt that I was on the edge of a discovery, that something was just a fingertip way, waiting to be unfolded and known. Nature's atmosphere surrounded me. The wind moved the trees above as a kind hand, birds sang and played among their leafy arms in the sheer joy of living. The tall, unmown hay covering the breast of the hill rose high around me, sweet with the smell of life. A place of virgin, untouched beauty, it inspired a burning desire to know its Creator and Sustainer—to leave the realm where one is only an outsider observing the Artist's creation and enter the Kingdom where one may know the Artist.

There had always been an interest, always a restless curiosity in my heart after truth, but suddenly, in that instant, my whole being became athirst for spiritual knowledge. A longing to know and understand poured through me. It lingered on for many precious moments, and left in its wake the unspoken vow that I would not stop until I had found the answer.

For many years before this time I had been reading through books on the many approaches to this ageless question. Religion had been a household word from my earliest childhood, my father being a minister of the Christian church. And as most children reared in a religious environment, I had the accompanying faith. At the age of six I can recollect vividly having wept with some of my friends in Sunday school after having been told the story of the crucifixion of Jesus. But not long afterwards, doubt began to set in. How could one be sure of all the stories about Jesus told in the Bible? How could one be sure that He really performed all those miracles and that he was the only begotten Son of God? There was nothing in the way of proof to substantiate all this. "Read the Bible", I was told. "Have faith in God". Follow the teachings of Jesus and He will love you." And so I read the Bible, attended church, and tried to believe. But somehow that lurking doubt crept into my mind in even my strongest moments of faith.

When in the early teen years, I found a book on spiritualism in the public library, and assiduously devoured every word. Here was evidence of consciousness existing in a far higher and more real plane— evidence of life after death. From the pages of that book came my first introduction to the concept of

God's all-embracing oneness, and the idea that consciousness is the only reality. The book told of how
the material world in which we as mortals exist is not
what it appears to be; that "matter," as such, is only
a lower manifestation or extension of a higher energy.
We therefore live in the "obstructed" aspect of the
universe, but this same universe is in its essence "unobstructed." After shedding one's physical body at
death, the book said one could move about in this
higher plane of consciousness, manipulating the
unobstructed *essences* of time and space and motion.
And it told of how "thoughts are things," and that
nothing is as important to an individual as what the
individual thinks about it.

All was not understood by me at that time, but it
offered a new channel in which to direct my thinking.
It offered something which I could believe, which was
rational. But most of all it initiated that restless
curiosity for truth.

As the years went by, I drifted into the study of
many forms of religion and philosophy. The transition
from spiritualism to Indian yoga occurred via the study
of extra-sensory perception, or scientifically conducted
research into the psychic possibilities of man's mind.
This research was receiving a great deal of publicity and
the interest of scholarly as well as spiritualist circles was
directed toward these experiments. Dr. Joseph
Banks Rhine, the originator of the research and a well-
known psychologist of Duke University, set out to
prove that there exist faculties of perception in man
which are beyond the limited range of the five senses—
faculties which can foresee the future, read the thoughts
of others telepathically, perceive objects and events
beyond the reach of normal vision, and faculties power-

ful enough to control the material surroundings, or "mind over matter".

This research was born in 1933, and over the years increasingly air-tight experiments were conducted. Dr. Rhine pioneered the first recognized explorations into the validity of "witchcraft" and "fortune-telling," and brought the crystal ball of the gypsy into the laboratory for scientific enquiry. Thus far he has been successful, since he has proven beyond mathematical and scientific question that such faculties do exist. The severest critics and skeptics have had to sit up and take notice, reluctantly admitting that his experiments are valid. A stumbling block, however, stands in the way of further research, for these psychic faculties are not under the conscious control of the mind. The person being tested has no knowledge of the operation of his extra-sensory powers. Only after a significantly long series of experiments with cards, dice or numbers and the application of strict mathematical formulae does the existence of extra-sensory perception become evident to the scientist. Though a giant step forward in man's search for himself, scientific proof of his psychic nature is not an answer in itself.

A book on yoga (union), the age-old Indian science of the method of joining the subconscious man and the conscious man with a higher consciousness by which direct perception of one's true nature and relationship to reality is attained, led me to hope that here might be a possible gateway to further research and knowledge. If these methods could be successfully practised, then these extra-sensory powers latent in man's subconsciousness would be automatically under conscious control. The next step, it then seemed to me, would be to find someone who had attained this "union," and bring him into the scientific laboratory as had been done with psychics and mediums.

More years went by. As my studies went deeper into the many branches and phases which broadly come under the category of "yoga," the study of extra-sensory perception became unimportant and faded away into the background. It became clear to me that those who were advanced in yoga did acquire great control and power over their surroundings, but that they were not, as a rule, interested in applying these powers to this material world. Apparently, misuse of psychic abilities and powers for selfish reasons or for personal advancement would result in the loss of them. But as I progressed in the study of these subjects, new, deeper and far more fascinating possibilities than the development of psychic powers were revealed. Theosophy, Rosicrucianism, Christian Science and many other fields became the target of my studies. Frequently I would visit a large book store in the center of Boston and spend hours skimming over and selecting from a variety of books on the many different ways to discover truth. It gave me great delight to read those books. Each would open up a new vista of thought, and I found myself eagerly anticipating what treasures might lie hidden within the covers of each new purchase.

During this search, however, certain unresolved problems would at times come to the surface. So many different "answers" were set forth, so many claims were made in the name of Truth which contradicted and opposed one another. I can clearly remember my struggle with one doctrine which I had carefully over-looked and tried to avoid studying at all. It was reincarnation—a "bitter pill" to the western mind. For some time I would skip over the pages that dealt with reincarnation, almost as if afraid to be convinced of what I thought to be a radical departure from truth. But there came a day when I knew that the question had to be squarely faced, and accepted or rejected before I could continue much longer in my studies. With determination I turned to a book devoted to this subject alone, and soon wondered why I had waited so long. Very clearly the "bitter pill" of reincarnation was explained, so that I had no other recourse but to accept it gladly. I learned of the complementary law which is at the foundation of reincarnation—the law that says, "As ye sow, so shall ye reap."

But what is reincarnation? I had always understood it to be the belief that one's soul takes on life after life in this world, including the animal and plant kingdom as well as the human form, which, looking at the surface picture, was correct. But it had always seemed to be more like an imaginary fairy tale contrived to suit the mind in its quest to explain life's mystery and to justify the poverty-stricken plight of the East. And it was only a surface picture. Actually, a thorough study of this subject revealed a cosmic plan or system that is far more logical and acceptable than any other.

Since reincarnation depends on the law, "As ye sow, so shall ye reap," or as it is called in the East, karma, an understanding of karma is needed before one can even glimpse the truth of reincarnation. The law of karma states that every doer shall receive the exact result, reward or loss, of his actions. Comparable to the unbendable laws of physics, it is the law of cause and effect, of action and reaction. When one performs right actions he will receive good results. When one performs bad or wrong actions he creates future bad effects for himself. The law further states that one must account for his actions in the same circumstances in which he created them. In other words, one cannot pay for having stolen a sum of money anywhere else but in this world where the act was committed, whether the payment is made in one's present life or in a future life. In addition, the desires and longings which one harbors for things of this world— such as money, power, beauty, and so on—all these desires must eventually be fulfilled. And they can only be fulfilled in this world; they are desires of this world.

The totality of experiences and desires and attitudes one has in his lifetime, along with those accumulated from past lifetimes, determines his position and experiences in the following lifetime. A child is born with a twisted leg, yet has the sweetness of an angel. Her distraught parents weep and ask why, blaming God and calling Him merciless. "What did she ever do to deserve this fate?" they cry. And how to explain why one person may be born a genius while another is an idiot? How is it that at the age of four years a child may sit at the piano and play a difficult classical work with a talent that ordinarily would have taken years to develop?

Where do these "gifts" come from? Where do "misfortunes" come from? An innocent man is hanged; why is there such injustice? Could it be that God is so unjust that He will allow one soul to enjoy good health and happiness and refuse to look upon another who is torn with misery and suffering? No. Because every individual is reaping the results of his own behavior from far back in the past. The talented child may have spent a lifetime devoted to the study of music, or even longer. What she attained then was not lost when she was reborn into another life. If an individual is suffering untold miseries, it is only because he inflicted such miseries upon others in some past life. And he had to be reborn to fulfill the law by undergoing from others exactly what he once gave to them. On and on it goes—one can never escape from this law of justice. For as one reaps the results of his past actions, he is likewise creating more karma to be worked out in the future.

But there were those who said in their books that through their own spiritual studies and experiences they had found that one does not return to this earth, but goes to a higher heavenly region and progresses from there. This presented an unsolvable contradiction, or so it seemed, until I learned that *both* concepts are true. For a soul may spend as long as a millennium or more enjoying the sweet fruits of the heavens before returning to this world in another life and another form. And during this time he would not himself be aware that he would one day return unless he had believed in rebirth during his earthly life. In some cases, on the other hand, the interval might be a mere instant before the return, but the return is always inevitable.

In response to my previous belief that reincarnation was born in the East to justify the poverty-stricken conditions there, I learned that knowledge of this truth was in existence long before the East suffered as it does today. In fact, it was known and accepted as a fundamental reality in times when India was considered the wealthiest and most progressive land on earth.

But there were still other points of contradiction which remained unsolved, and questions that remained unanswered—until the week spent on the hillsides of Maine. During that week every phase of spirituality then known to me was carefully restudied and compared. All seemed to promise that their way was the correct road to salvation. With close study, however, it became apparent that there are definite basic similarities in the so-called "opposite" schools of thought. As a rule, the birth of each school originated with the life and teachings of a particular individual. With very few exceptions, at the back of every occult form or faith is the name of one who formed it first and made it live. From Zoroaster to Krishna, Buddha to Guru Nanak, Moses, Mohammed, and even Jesus Christ—the list could go on and on. Moreover, there are prophets who have come from time to time to interpret the teachings of these Great Ones, forming new branches or divisions within a faith. Some of these branches would themselves grow so far apart that strife and discord would arise, although each would still claim to be faithfully adhering to the same original teachings. In the Christian religion this has particularly been true. There are perhaps as many versions and variegated doctrines attributing themselves to Christianity as there are major religions of the world.

It was most amazing to me, however, to find that the differences existing among openly opposing schools of thought are not really differences at all. Under careful study, points of contradiction are easily reconciled by discovering the reasons behind them. The "differences" seem to be only those of interpretation, those stemming from the individual mind rather than from Truth itself. The interpreter projected his concept of Truth as he saw it, but inevitably his own mental and emotional framework would cloud the message, merely giving the Truth a different garment.*

*I have given much thought to the possibility of describing

As the mystery began to unfold itself with such clarity and simplicity, I wondered why I had been so blind. There was only one Truth—only one answer to the ultimate, all-important question. There could not be any other than the one Truth. And the key to understanding was there, lurking behind the next corner, waiting only for the corner to be turned for the Truth to be personally experienced.

Firstly, the human being stands at the top of the ladder of material creation. There is no other form on this earthly plane which he can perceive to be greater than himself. For man is "made in God's image" and has dominion over all the countless myriads of forms of life and matter around him. His degree of consciousness is able to reason, to search, to deduce—it is that distinctive quality above all others which strives to know and understand. It is a unique gift given to the human race alone.

It could not be, I began to see more clearly, that man's purpose is to behave as do the animals over which he has dominion, to plod through his allotted years seeking only his comfort and pleasures, perceiving the world through his five senses alone and limiting him-

---

in detail these innumerable paths and how they prove to be valuable stepping stones in one's spiritual development. But it is obviously true that to adequately present such a study, a volume in itself would be necessary. A religion, philosophy, or occult path cannot be properly understood with a few brief, cursory pages of description. Here is where misinterpretation will creep in—the surface picture is often a harsh and incorrect view where conclusions are drawn and judgments made from an improper understanding of the single truth at the foundation. The few instances where these various religions and philosophies are touched upon are elected only for the purpose of narrating how the Path unfolded itself in one individual case.

self to the material confines of his body. It could not be that he exists merely to broaden the intellect, build unbelievable machines penetrate into the mysteries of the atom. To what avail? For what does he so frantically and intently seek?

And it could not be that because man is unable to readily conceive of a degree of consciousness greater than his own that there is nothing beyond him, or higher than himself, even though many of today's scientists and people of the world seem to hold this opinion. In actuality, nothing could be more limiting to one's consciousness than this idea. For example, the consciousness of a dog cannot conceive of a consciousness beyond its own; it is an obvious impossibility for the limited awareness of a dog to comprehend the greater consciousness of a man. The dog cannot even conceive of it. But this does not change the fact that a greater consciousness does exist. For *man* knows that it does. Man knows that he has dominion over all the creatures of the earth because his consciousness embraces and exceeds that of any other creature. He does not have to turn to his books to find this out.

And just as it is impossible for the dog to conceive of an awareness greater than his own, it is also impossible for man to have a true knowledge of a level of reality existing beyond his thinking mind. He speculates, he theorizes, he prays, he philosophizes— but these alone can never take him out of the confines of his mind, the limits of his own sense of "I" ness. I began to understand that apparently the only way one could, with genuine authority, make statements about a higher degree of consciousness would be by *oneself* expanding *into* that degree, by personally attaining to this consciousness, and crossing the boundaries of body, mind and intellect which are governed by the senses and reason. The distinction of intellect, common only to man, is a faculty which merely leads him to this discovery, and all the books scriptures and religions are the stepping stones—the means and not the end. The real understanding is transcendent and will not dawn until one not only attains to the higher consciousness, but also becomes *united* with it. For he must veritably transform his consciousness and awareness into a greater dimension of reality.

As evidenced by their written words, all the Great Ones throughout the ages had experienced this transformation. They had discovered that within man is Truth or Spirit to be found, and had thus perceived that this Spirit is Reality and the central core of all things; is all in all, and yet eternally and universally One. Their messages sprang from their personal, joyous union with this all-embracing Consciousness which we call God.

It was the immortal words of Lord Jesus Christ that finally gave me this realization. *"Behold, the Kingdom of God is within you."** How much wisdom was contained within that brief phrase! A whole new world opened up when the real meaning of that phrase began at last to dawn within, and I was flooded with joy. Christ is to be taken literally in this respect. The Kingdom of God *is* within. Truly man himself is the "temple of the living God."

*Luke 17-12.

CHAPTER TWO

A QUEST FULFILLED

Soon after leaving the wooded hillsides of Maine and returning to the city, I stumbled on the key. I was selecting books from the paper-back department of my favorite bookstore, avoiding the shelves of more expensive, hard-covered books. As usual, a long and delightful period of time passed before the final selection was made. But when this had been done and I was on my way to the cashier, I could not help wandering over to those treasured rows of books in the corner. Caught by some unexplainable something, I put the paperbacks down and took a large, dusty volume from the topmost shelf. Perhaps it was the title, *The Path of the Masters*, which attracted me, or even the simplicity of its plain gray binding, for I hardly glanced at its contents before purchasing it alone. And all the way home I asked myself why I had done such a foolish thing. Certainly there were plenty of books waiting to be studied at home as it was. How little did I know that a treasury of spiritual wisdom lay hidden between its simple covers.

From the moment I began to read, there was no putting it down. How those pages sang to me then; it was almost too good to be true. Never before had I read a book like it. There was no question of analyzing the message it carried or comparing it with others. When the Truth clearly stands before one, there is no time for anything but rejoicing. All the missing links, the unanswered questions, fell into place—why we are here, how our spiritual progress within is to be accom-

plished, what super-consciousness really means—the
full, logical and satisfying explanations were all given.

The accounts I had previously read of the experiences of those who had reached a state of higher
consciousness described feelings of intense bliss and joy
...revelations of the entire universe and its workings
in an instant...union with the very fountainhead of
light and knowledge...intoxicating rapture beyond
human understanding. Their super-conscious states
so surpassed the one they had left behind in purity and
wisdom that without hesitation they would exclaim,
"I have found the Ultimate; I have become one with
it!"

But when searching for a system of meditation which
could lead one to this super-conscious state, I had had
no success. There had always been some indefinable
something missing. It seemed that spiritual experiences
would either come to a person spontaneously, arising
from a loving and devotional heart; or they would come
only after long and difficult years of practising certain
exercises or breathing methods—oftentimes requiring
constant supervision.

The Path of the Masters, however, written by Dr.
Julian P. Johnson, an American surgeon who had lived
for many years in India, told of a spiritual science called
the Radha Soami Path (the Path of the Lord of the
Soul, or Supreme Being), also called Sant Mat (the
Teachings of the Saints), which offers the disciple all
these experiences at will. And it does not end there
for the disciple on the Radha Soami Path is led on and
on to increasingly higher states of consciousness and
spirituality—to heights undreamed of by those on other
Paths. In fact, the very first step, and in a few rare
cases the second step, of this Spiritual Path is the ultimate

goal of all other systems.   Yet it denounces none, but embraces them all.   The final stage is described as a great Ocean of Light and Love completely beyond our imagination or comprehension, and so intense that the entire physical universe of countless trillions of suns could not equal a trillionth part of the Light there.   The physical universe would appear as but a tiny speck of darkness in comparison.   Not only were these unimaginable heights of Spirituality, which had been secretly guarded from the world by sages in the past, introduced openly, but also the method was described of the way to personally attain them *while yet living in the human body.*   And this method is so revolutionary—and yet so simple—that I could think of nothing else.

To begin with, before one can start on this Path, *he must find a living Teacher of the spiritual journey,* one who had Himself attained the Highest Realm and who, in His essence, has thereby become one with God. Intense love for a past Master and an overwhelming desire to meet God face to face may alone be the impetus to carry a devotee to the first stages on the pathway to the Infinite, but without having contact with and obtaining Initiation from a living Master on this plane, he would not be able to go any higher, nor would he even be aware of the existence of the higher realms.

A spiritual Master, once found, connects the disciple with the vehicle or power which will carry him to the fulfillment of his goal—God-Realization.   That power— the infinite Power behind all other powers—is the keynote of the Radha Soami Path.   It is the projection of God which continuously emanates from Him through all the regions of spirit and of mind, and through all the heavens until it reaches the material plane—as if it were a giant river from the God-Ocean. It is the life-breath and sustenance of all that is, and was, and will be. *It is the Word of God.*

But the work of the Master does not end at this point. For by the power of the Word He has become one with the Supreme Consciousness in His inner being and He is therefore able to take upon Himself the entire responsibility of guiding the disciple throughout his spiritual journey. When the disciple reaches the first stage of higher consciousness, he becomes aware of this guidance; for then he meets his Master, manifested to him in a radiantly illumined form and waiting to receive him with a great love beyond the disciple's dreams or imagination.

In addition to its message, *The Path of the Masters* also gave the name of a present living Master in India, Maharaj Charan Singh Ji, of Beas Punjab, and the names of His representatives in other countries of the world. I immediately got in touch with the American representative, adopted the required vegetarian diet and, after receiving word of acceptance from the Master in India was initiated on this Path one snowy day in January. And now, some months later, I was in a plane high over the Atlantic Ocean, soon to be at the end of a very long journey. The steady drone of the engines gradually quieted my wandering thoughts, and my next impression was the pilot announcing the approach to London.

By pre-arrangement I met a friend, another initiate, in London, Joseph Leeming—a writer who had recently retired from the United States Information Agency. Mr. Leeming had become a disciple of the present Master more than eight years before. A

deeply devoted and respected Satsangi*, Mr. Leeming
had written a number of books on the Radha Soami
science. Fortunately, he was now making his third
trip to the Radha Soami Colony in Northern India,
and we continued the rest of the way together.

After landing in New Delhi, we traveled by train
to the Punjab State of Northwest India, finally arriving
after night had fallen in the little city of Jullundur.
There we were met at the railway station by Khanna
Sahib, an Indian gentleman from the Colony. To
reach the Dera (camp or colony) as the Colony is
called, it took an hour by car along the famous Grand
Trunk Road, and I have never lived through a longer
hour. The closest I had ever before come to experiencing this unique state of mind had been once just
before walking onto the stage in a theater. Those
few moments appeared to be eternally long. It
cannot really be termed as outright fear or nerves, but
a terrible sense of inadequacy and incompetence.
One's faults and shortcomings stand before the mind
like mountains, and one has to fight the wish to run
away before the curtain rises.

The only difference between the way I felt during
that hour-long drive and the way I had felt just before
a curtainrise was that I didn't want to run away. But
the rest of it, the feeling of inadequacy and incompetence,
seemed to assail me with hundred-fold intensity.
An infamous array of faults and shortcmings, every
wrong deed I had ever committed, paraded before my
eyes with merciless persistence.

As if to seek some solace I looked out of the car
window, but there was only an answering blackness,

---

*Disciple on the Radha Soami Path.

faintly relieved by the pale solitude of moonlight.
There were no familiar street-lamps lining the road;
no flashing headlights of approaching cars. And my
thoughts raced on and on as the miles sped past and the
minutes ticked away. How unbelievable it all was !
How absolutely incredible ! My eyes would soon rest
upon the physical form of the Master, upon the Supreme
Father in human form. I had heard of those who had
fallen at His feet when first meeting Him, of those who
had burst into unrestrained tears, and of those who
had seen great and overpowering light emanating from
Him. Some had been so intensely aware of the Power
of the Word of God that they could not even speak.

After a period of speeding through the darkness
that seemed to me as long as an entire night, Mr.
Leeming leaned forward in his seat and pointed to
something outside his window. "There they are,"
he said. "The towers of the Satsang Ghar !"*

With a start I turned and followed his gaze. We
had just driven onto a long bridge. My eyes traveled
over the moonlit waters of the Beas River and far up
its western bank. And then I saw them, the beautiful
domed towers of the great Satsang Ghar building,
telling us that the Dera and the Master were not far
away. High and majestic they soared aloft from the
flat plain lands of the Punjab. The light of the new
moon cast an unreal shimmer upon the seven towers,
and at that distance they seemed to be only a hopeful
mirage. But as we passed through the village of Beas
and drew nearer, the ghost-like quality changed to that
of solidarity, and I was able to recognize them from the
pictures I had seen. Then the inescapable truth

---

*Meeting hall at the Radha Soami Colony.

dawned upon me. I was here at last, here at the long hoped-for spot of earth where the Light of the world walks daily. No more counting the weeks and months.

A few minutes more and we entered the Dera gates and were driven through the center of the Colony to another gate, where the driver stopped the car.

"Here is the entrance to the Master's compound," Khanna Sahib told us. "He is waiting for you now. Come."

My knees were unsteady, my hands were icy cold and clammy, but I felt myself getting out of the car and walking with Khanna Sahib and Mr. Leeming through the gate and into the Master's garden. We sat down on a terrace outside a lighted room.

"The Master is in there," Khanna Sahib pointed out. "Wait here." He entered the room and a minute passed. Then he reappeared and gestured for us to come forward.

And then...then I saw the Master for the first time. He met me at the door and took both my hands in his. I looked upon His face, a kind, beautiful face, unlike any other. My throat constricted and I couldn't speak; but He looked into my eyes and said, "I'm so glad you've come." At that moment the world was mine! The love and the warmth and the power emanating from Him filled me with joy. His eyes—so kind and full and luminous. He invited us to sit down on a couch and He sat in a chair next to us. In the conversation that followed, the Master talked mostly with Mr. Leeming about his previous visits to the Dera, much to my gratitude. It would have been very nearly an impossibility to speak coherently at that first meeting.

During those five minutes, or half an hour or hour—how long we were in His company I have no idea—I involuntarily kept my eyes down and stared at the flowered Persian carpet on the floor. Occasionally I would look up at Him and again be overcome by what I saw. Perhaps the photographs of the Master resembled him somewhat, but no portrait could ever begin to reveal the radiance and beauty of His face.

The time spent with Him was like a dream—and how is it possible to describe such a dream? Only vivid, unconnected fragments of those moments remain in the memory. But that inward, restless hunger which accompanies so many of the seekers after Truth, effortlessly dissolved into a new sense of peace. With the Master one becomes aware, without realizing why or how, that one is in the Presence of the Highest.

As soon as we left the Master that evening, we were shown to our rooms. My memories of those moments are vague and indistinct, but I can recall having wept with relief and joy. There is, though, one tangible remembrance of that night—a short entry in my diary which reads:

"I have just met the Master. Ah, but the dream has finally come true. How wonderful and beautiful He is. Words cannot describe His glory. I wish now only to be alone and not think or work but just be happy. Is it really me?"

And so, the path trodden in this world to reach the Master was at its terminus at last. The quest was finally fulfilled. And yet the real journey was just beginning.

CHAPTER THREE

FIRST DAYS AT THE DERA

At three the next morning the sound of a siren filled the air. But it was welcomed and expected, for I knew that it was used every morning at the Radha Soami Colony to waken the disciples. For then the most important hours of the day begin—the hushed, quiet hours of meditation before dawn when one is engaged in the greatest service he can give his Master.

But first, on this October morning, I quietly stepped for a moment to the terrace outside the room. All was still in the deepness of the night but for an occasional, distant cry of a wild dog on the plains, or the song of a bird who had forgotten to sleep, or the gentle rustling of a breeze playing among the branches of a nearby tree. But the Dera's outward stillness was deceiving at three in the morning, for the Colony was not asleep. In fact, those living within its boundaries were then more intensely awake than at any other time. For all were in meditation, many very deeply, their spirits traversing the upper regions of light and glory and love. Still elated from the night before. I looked over to the Master's bungalow nearby. Its shadowy outline was heightened by a single, bright bulb at an uppermost corner, signifying the Master's presence in the Colony. There, I thought, just a few steps away is the One who leads them all, the King of kings and Lord of all the realms. And, as if it were a reminder, the thought turned me back to my room to begin the hours of meditation.

Three hours later there was a knock on the door.

A young Indian boy entered carrying a tray with my
morning tea. "Radha Soami", he smiled at me in
greeting. Leaving a steaming teapot and a cup, he
departed with another "Radha Soami" to take tea
to another guest. The stillness that had accompanied
the deep night was now replaced by the stirrings of a
busy morning. I could hear the voices of the servants
from across the Guest House compound, and the sound
of footsteps running up stone stairs and across a terrace;
the birds were awake and started their chorus to greet
the morning; the rattle of pots and pans could be heard
from the kitchen where breakfast was being prepared,
and the young Indian boy sang out with the verses of
a song in praise of the Master and the Lord.

Slowly sipping my tea, for the first time I really
looked at my "ashram" room. It was not typical of the
idea that most westerners have of such lodgings. There
were no cement floors and damp stone walls with a
hard, wooden cot. Instead the guest rooms at the
Colony were surprisingly lovely, decorated in a modern
style. The colors of green, rose and beige were used,
combining with the deep mahogany furniture and
woodwork. At one end of the room and on either wall
were bay windows accented with forest green draperies.
The walls were painted a pale beige and the full-sized
rug wove these colors into a typical Indian design,
adding brilliant touches of rose. Well furnished, the
room contained a large closet, a bed, two comfortable
chairs, and a small, compact desk and chair. There
was even a vanity table with a long mirror. But it was
not the external surroundings that were so pleasing.
The room seemed to be filled with invisible "welcome"
signs, and one experiences the same comfortale feeling
as when entering the home of one's childhood after a

long absence. I looked outside my window into the magic of the day as a brightly-colored bird sat on the windowsill and watched the new stranger cautiously.

Breakfast was announced at 7:30 by the sounding of a small gong, and I went to the special dinning room provided for foreign guests within the Guest House compound. There were only a handful of us at that time, and we were told that we could have anything we wished for our meals; in fact we might plan our entire menu to fit in with our accustomed habits. And the Indian boys who looked after us could never do enough to see to our comfort.

At that time, however, I gave little notice to all the new and unexpected surroundings at the Dera. Thoughts of the Master, and of seeing Him again at morning Satsang* crowded out everything else. Satsang was held at nine o-clock every morning, and from what little I had read, I knew that it was a beneficial part of one's spiritual life. At this time the Master is said to be "directly linked" with the Infinite, and the spiritual currents and power that radiate from Him are said to be stronger than at any other time. I had also been told that during the time of Satsang one should look continuously into His eyes. Dr. Johnson's book had said that there is nothing that will help a person more in his inward progress than attentively looking into the Master's eyes. When this gaze is met by even a glance from Him, it is said that "the sins of countless lives are erased" for, in effect, it is a divine glance direct from the Supreme Father Himself.

---

*Literally, true association. The term is used when referring to a meeting of a group of people to discuss the spiritual Path, and more particularly, as in this instance, it refers to lectures or discourses given by the Master to His congregation.

At 8 :45 the siren again was sounded, this time as the first call to Satsang. My anticipation mounted as we started out for the Satsang Ghar, and it seemed an endlessly long walk from the guest house that first morning, though it probably took us no more than five minutes. On the way, I could not help but notice how well arranged and clean the surroundings were. The village streets were clean-swept, and the tracings of brooms formed criss-cross patterns on the cream-colored earth. But why, I wondered, did they seem to be deserted. There were no great multitudes thronging the streets as I had been told was to be expected at this time of the year.

But when we reached the Satsang Ghar my breath was taken away. High above us the gold-tipped domes of the towers reflected the bright morning sun. From inside the great hall itself the strange and haunting sound of a melodious Indian hymn chanted by an untold number of voices drifted out to meet us. Following the Indian custom, we took off our shoes and left them in a small enclosure just outside. My heart pounding, I walked up wide, marble steps and entered the building through one of its many doors. And immediately I knew why the streets had been so empty. There were multitudes of people at the Dera all right! Here they all were, seated on the floor and waiting for their beloved Satguru* to come. All eyes followed the "new foreigners" as we were beckoned to sit with other guests on large, thick cushions just in front of a small raised platform.

Once seated, my eyes quickly scanned the interior. The spacious white walls reached a height of a hundred

*Perfect Master.

feet, and their spotless surface was accented by the deep, cherrybrown woodwork of the casemented wooden windows and the single, narrow balcony lining the whole interior, half-way between the floor and ceiling. A medley of mosaic designs was inlaid on the marble floors. On the platform itself sat two men, cross-legged, the pathis or chanters. Both were serene and distinguished in appearance with their turbans, impassive countenances, and white, flowing beards. Before them there was a small, low table upon which a heavy volume of scriptures lay open.

Soon a murmuring wave of "Radha Soami" passed through the crowd, and hundreds of eager eyes were turned toward a side entrance. And suddenly there He was. The Master had come.

A shining transformation came over the faces of the people. Joy and unmasked devotion were written in their expressions as He walked to the platform, and another ripple of "Radha Soami" passed through the seated crowd when He placed His hands together in greeting to them. Before sitting in the cross-legged posture, the Master touched His forehead to the clean, white cloths spread over the platform. This He did, I was told, in remembrance of His own Master.

And the people—it is useless to attempt to describe their joy. I had read about it, this spontaneity of worship pouring from the hearts of His people when He came amongst them, but between reading of it and actually experiencing it there can be no comparison. For this love is beyond the grasp of intellect. This quiet wave of spiritual joy and elation which fills the hearts of thousands of people at the Master's presence can only be understood by being a part of it. It is not like the excitement that grips a theater audience at the entrance of a celebrated actor. It is significantly different. For the feelings of the theater audience are expressions of the emotions, of the mind. But the joy and love expressed for the Master are of the soul.

A hush settled over the crowd as the bearded pathis chanted verses from the scripture. Then the Master began to speak, and there was another, softer murmur as those present settled back to listen. Though I could not understand the language, it was evident that the Master was explaining in detail the verses which had been chanted. The entire discourse continued in this pattern of melodiously chanting verses from the scripture with a following explanation from the Master.

When the Satsang drew to its close, the Master with folded hands said "Radha Soami" to all and left the platform. My eyes followed Him until He disappeared through the distant doorway. Then I felt a tap on my shoulder. It was Mrs. Nan Ross, a Scottish lady who had come to the Master from South Africa. Her eyes were filled with tears from the sublime and other-worldly wonder of Satsang. "Come," she said. "We don't want to miss a single minute of the time He gives us." She was speaking of the daily visits which the guests from other countries have with the Master following each morning's Satsang. And so we made our way as swiftly as we could in and out through the crowd and down the broad steps to where we had left our shoes. There we met Mr. Leeming who had been sitting on the other side of the hall during Satsang (in India it is customary to separate the men from the women), and the three of us walked together to the Master's compound.

On the way I asked Mr. Leeming about the scriptures which were quoted in Satsang. He told me

that many of the great Indian Masters of past decades
and centuries who practised and taught the spiritual
method of the Word had written poetry and prose of
amazing beauty, and that their words had been an
inspiration to countless millions throughout India.
But unfortunately, as has often happened, misinter-
pretations had crept in after the mortal death of the
author and the real, esoteric meaning had eventually
been lost beneath the inevitable covers of dogma.   The
Master, in His Satsangs, would tear away these covers
and give the true interpretation of the verses.

"The verses themselves are called shabds," Mr.
Leeming added, "and scores of them are known and
loved by the Indian people—something like the hymns
we sing in the West but with an even higher spiritual
significance."

By this time we had reached and were entering the
Master's gate. And quite different it was from the
strangeness of the night before. I remembered something the Master had said to Mr. Leeming while we were
sitting with Him then. "She will feel much less strange
tomorrow when she knows this is home. After all,
you are here." Then He added, smiling directly at
me, "And I am here."

The gates to the compound opened on a wide walk-
way covered overhead by an arched trellis interwoven
with vines of roses. The scent of late summer flowers
and roses sweetened the air. Beyond the archway on
our left was a lawn fringed with bright-colored blossoms;
on our right we saw the Master's house. A wide
terrace in the midst of a rose garden served as the front
yard. Further on in the compound another building
with an arched veranda could be seen, and a circular
pool where white and purple lotus blossoms floated

on beds of leaves. I had heard that the Master's family and relatives often stayed in this compound, and that during Bhandara times more than eighty children and adults were sometimes given room here.

Then I heard the words "Radha Soami" and turned to see the Master walking from His house to the terrace. He greeted us with a radiant welcoming smile, and after happy exchanges of more "Radha Soamis," we seated ourselves in wicker chairs arranged on the terrace in a circle. I thought then of how many of our brother and sister initiates had spent unforgettable moments of their lives on that very terrace. Here, in the Master's rose garden, people from all over the world and from all walks of life have gathered. From royal families to diplomats, government ministers and politicians; businessmen, doctors, lawyers, generals and judges; writers, artists, teachers and students—all these and more have come to sit at His feet. It has been said that "before a True Master even kings and angels do bow down." And nearly all parts of the globe have been represented—the United States, South and Central Africa, England, Canada, South America, Germany, Scandinavia, Switzerland, Greece, Scotland, Australia, to name but a few. There at His feet, the world which lies outside the Dera gates and beyond is forgotten, and differences of social standing, of race, of politics, even of nations, fall away as dead leaves.

The group was small that day, however. Another American lady, Miss Louise Hilger, Mr. Leeming and I had come from the United States, and Mrs. Nan Ross from South Africa. We were introduced to some Indian guests also present—the Raja and Rani of Sangli and the four princesses, their daughters. Soon our number would grow, as a special day at the Dera was approaching. It was then Tuesday, and on Sunday, October 29th, the anniversary of the death of Sardar Bahadur Jagat Singh Ji was to be remembered. He was the Master who had preceded our present Master and who had left this earth eleven years before. Such commemorations are held four times during the year, in remembrance of each of the previous Radha Soami Masters of this particular line.

There was some conversation, but most of the time, as if by common consent, was spent in quietness. From the very beginning, one seems instinctively to know when to remain silent in His Presence.

Following our visit with the Master, tea was served in the garden of the Guest House, and we were visited by a handsome elderly man, a Sikh with a long, flowing white beard. He was in charge of agriculture at the Colony. With him, he brought his grandchild, a small boy with black curls framing his face and the loveliest, most luminous brown eyes I had ever seen in a child. The third member of this delightful trio was a plain, brown dog, a spaniel, who immediately made friends with all of us. The old gentleman laughed often, and was full of fascinating stories of the Masters who had gone before—many of them were stories which he had personally experienced.

"Tell us some stories about the Present Master," I requested him after a little while.

We waited eagerly for him to answer, for this gentleman had lived at the Dera for more than a decade, in fact during the entire time that the present Master had been at the helm of its affairs.

He was silent for some time and a faint smile played over his face as if he had a secret. "Look here," he said at last, throwing up his hands, "I cannot say

anything....He is too great!" And with that we had
to be content.

Lunch was at 12 : 30. We had insisted that we
would be only too happy to eat whatever the cook
wished to serve us, though I must honestly admit that
I had not expected very palatable food. This was
chiefly because before leaving for India, one is usually
told that India's food is difficult for a westerner to
enjoy and digest, and there was little doubt but that
one would become ill from it. But quite the opposite
was true. The pungent and subtly spiced preparations
were a delight to eat, and though the vegetarian diet
of the Radha Soami Path is strict, an amazingly wide
variety of dishes was served. And, as far as I could
discover, no one had ever become ill from the Dera
food.

On an after lunch stroll around the Dera, we
wandered through narrow village streets lined on either
side with small, brick buildings, and then along a wide
avenue with a lane of trees down its center—the avenue
along which one travels when he first centers the Colony's
main gates. Rather than cars and traffic lights, one
would see an occasional train of mules carrying
bricks on their backs, or a man trundling a wheelbarrow
laden with earth. I wondered how I would ever
remember my way around the next day, not to mention
how I would recall the scores of people to whom I
was introduced. Everywhere we went they would
speak to us with welcoming smiles and cheery "Radha
Soamis."

When we returned to the Guest House, one of the
servants handed us a message which read, "You are
invited to a tea in Maharaj Ji's (the name by which
the Master was most often addressed) garden at 3 : 45

p.m." Again we were off to spend more treasured
moments in His company.

And so passed the day—that incredible first day.
So much activity and so many new impressions were
crammed into it that it might have stretched across
a week or more. But all days spent at the Dera are
incredible when the Master is there—some merely
stand out in the memory more than others.

The following day was highlighted by an evening
buffet dinner at the Dera home of the Raja and Rani
of Sangli and their family. To an outsider it might
well have looked like any other dinner party being
given in India that evening. His eyes would have
first taken in the tables of elegantly prepared dishes,
the exquisite surroundings—and he might even have
recognized the Raja and Rani of Sangli and their
family as the hosts. But if he were to look a little
closer and a little longer, he would have seen that
there was present a certain guest, one who stood out
unmistakably from the others. This strangely distinguished personage singled no one out for His
company, but moved about, speaking to each one
in the same quiet, smiling manner. The faces of those
to whom He spoke would light up with a special
delight, and each one in the group would often pause
and gaze for long moments at this guest's remarkably
beautiful face, though He might at the time be in a
distant corner of the room. Perhaps our observer
might even have detected a few tears gathering in the
eyes of some of the beholders. And he would whisper
to himself, "What strange thing is this? What happy
secret do these people keep and cherish?"

Possibly, if he had been listening carefully, he
would have heard one of the ladies in the group speak

privately to the special guest. "You look after us so well, just as a father watches over his children," she said. "It is my duty to look after you," He replied, smiling.

Yet this man was not the Raja. Rather the Raja seemed to be more humble towards this extraordinary personage than anyone else.

Our make-believe, wondering friend would have found a clue if he had himself approached the guest and looked directly into His eyes. In fact, it is quite certain that he would have then become a sharer of the "secret."

And it was without doubt an evening that would astound the eye of one who had not before seen the Master, or was not acquainted with the Radha Soami Path. It passed far too quickly for us all, and soon the Master was leaving. We followed him in a little band; it was just too difficult to say good-bye. Some of us were going his way, though we could have taken a much shorter route. When He heard us behind Him, He turned and started to smilingly protest. "But it is on our way," we chorused.

The Master laughed. "Just like little sheep you are," He said.

This entirely destroyed our attempts at seriousness about the matter. We broke into laughter, and it continued all the way to the Guest House entrance. I think we were laughing more from happiness and gratitude than anything else. I had the strong feeling that everyone in the group was very glad to be one of His little sheep.

At our gate, He turned and smiled at us, pressed His palms together and said a final "Radha Soami." We stood silently and watched Him walk away into the darkness. How is it, I wondered, why is it that He inspires such overpowering love and devotion in us?

It was the very next afternoon when we saw this same devotion manifested again, but on a much larger scale. It was late in the day, and soon we would be preparing for the regularly scheduled hour of meditation before supper at 7 : 30. We had just climbed to the roof of the Guest House from where we looked eastward across the mile-wide, shallow bed of the Beas River, which at that season of the year was nearly all dry land. The area immediately before us was now dotted with the moving figures of people, thousands of them, for late afternoon was *seva* time for the entire Colony and for all the other disciples who were visiting.

Seva means service to the Master of any kind. On this particular day it consisted of cutting and carrying bundles of hay-like grass, measuring six feet or more in length, which covers the land in the river bed. In a long, winding procession the people were carrying the grass to the Dera proper where it was being stored for use as oven fuel in the winter.

We watched the people as they finished their work for the day. Behind us the sun was setting. A magical, golden hue tinged the air and bathed the scene below us. We saw the people gathering together in a huge mass; we heard their joyful voices singing shabds in praises to the Master; we watched as in a long procession they reverently made their way back to the Dera. And walking before them, leading them, was the Master. He walked as only a Master can—with the noble bearing of a king and the humility of a saint combined. For both of these the Master is, and unimaginably more. The moment brought to mind a phrase heard long ago.... "And He shall lead His flock like a shepherd..."

CHAPTER FOUR

BY THEIR FRUITS

On a sunny afternoon a few days later, after some other foreign guests had arrived, a small group of us decided to investigate a large juniper tree far out on the edge of the river bank. We had often noticed this tree, particularly when looking out from the Guest House roof, since it was the largest one on the western bank of the river, and it stood alone against the horizon. It was under this very tree that Dr. Julian Johnson, author of *The Path of the Masters*, used to write and meditate. A disciple of the late Baba Sawan Singh Ji, our Master's Master, he came to the Dera in 1933 and lived and studied by the side of the Great Master until his death nine years later. During that time he wrote two books. One of them, called *With a Great Master in India*, is an inspiring collection of letters which he wrote to his fellow disciples in America. The other, *The Path of the Masters*, is the most widely read book of all the Radha Soami literature and is a volume that has brought many a sincere seeker to the Path.

From the roof of the Guest House, the tree seemed to be only a short distance away. But once we started to walk slowly toward it, we found quite the opposite to be true. We had not counted on the deep ravines and gullies that cut across our path. The Indian sun was unkind to us as we trodged along, and the tree seemed all the time to be growing farther and farther away. Finally, after nearly an hour of plodding and climbing, we reached our destination, and I could well understand why Dr. Johnson had chosen this lovely spot. There is a certain intimacy and peace about this juniper tree which invites one to quiet thought and meditation. Its branches separate and spread out wide and low giving a large cool area of shade on the ground. From beneath it, when looking back towards the Dera, one sees the seven serene and lofty towers of the Satsang ghar silhouetted against the pale blue sky. From the ridge of the steep river bank on which the tree stands, one looks out over the river bed, golden with acres of tall wheat. Then the eye travels across the river bed to the river itself, and beyond to the Indian jungle on the eastward side.

On our way back to the village, we took a closer look at the many deep ravines we had to cross. Two of us climbed down into one of the steeper ones and to my surprise and delight we discovred some old caves hollowed out of the ravine walls. These small caves even had separate rooms in them, and one was very "modern," with mud plaster on its walls! But I wondered what had happened to the ascetics and sadhus (holy men) who lived in them.

Later I discovered the answer. An old resident of the Dera told me that several years before, Maharaj Ji had gone to the caves and had urged the old ones to leave their hermitags and take an active part in Dera life. In fact, special quarters were built for them which stand today as open not only to those who once lived in the caves, but to all other sadhus and devotees who may wish to use them.

A lesson was learned here. For the Masters of the Radha Soami Path have taught that one cannot find true God-Realization by escaping into a hermitage. One should rather live in the world but at the same time keep his heart and soul and mind steeped in devotion to God—*in* the world, but not *of* the world.

As the days went on, we found this principle living in the hearts of all the people of the Dera with whom we were in close daily contact—they radiated the devotion for God they had within them to all those who were around them.   One example, out of countless others, was that afforded by my visit to Lilavati, the lady who served as the Dera's ladies' tailor.   Soon after arriving at the Dera, I was told that oftentimes, particularly when one planned to stay for some time, the western ladies adopted the Punjabi dress.   It is useful and comfortable, consisting of bloomer-like trousers called a salwar, and a tunic to the knees with slitsides called a kamiz. The costume is not complete unless one wears a large, filmy piece of cloth known as a chunni around the shoulders or, when in the Master's presence, over the head.

To get such a costume made, I went one morning to Lilavati's home, taking with me some newly purchased yards of material, as in India ready-made clothes are rarely found.   On entering the narrow courtyard of the small brick cottage on the outskirts of the Colony, a smiling, beautifully radiant Indian woman greeted me.   Her hair was snow white, but her face looked as fresh and smooth as that of a woman of twenty-five. We exchanged the familiar "Radha Soami'" greeting, and she ushered me into the single room of her cottage. It was very clean, having a small foyer, a bathroom, and a neat cooking area.   And surprisingly enough, there sat a sewing machine in the middle of the room.

She could understand no English, nor could I speak her language with the exception of one or two of the basic words soon learned by all foreigners—

words such as *tikh hai*, meaning "correct," and *achchha*, meaning "good". But I showed her the material, and she seemed to understand what I wanted after a series of gesturings punctuated with frequent laughter. During this "conversation," others began drifting into the small room, all eager to help and offering suggestions as to how the finished garments should look. Lilavati produced a yardstick, and everyone present began to participate in the task of measuring, designing, and planning, amidst more gesturing much laughter, and with the aid of a most eloquent sign language. The Indian girls who had joined us showed me a variety of styles to choose from by having me examine the outfits they were wearing. Finally, after nearly an hour had passed, a decision was reached as to what style would be most becoming. Some how the message was conveyed to me that I should come back in two days for the finished work.

Then a young Indian girl with a single, long braid of glossy black hair down her back came forward and took my hand. "Guest House?" she asked. Her bright sparkling eyes accented a friendly smile.

"*Tikh hai*", I replied, and we left together. I felt I had known her all my life—but that was not unusual. One feels this way about everyone that one meets at the Dera. It brought to my mind that invisible yet unbreakable Cord which binds us all together. And the ever-conscious devotion to God and the Master keeps it securely tied.

This invisible Cord is felt even more strongly when one participates in seva himself, as I discovered that same day. From the moment when I joined the people at their work. I had the same, overwhelming feeling of shared happiness that I had found in the daily Satsangs.

Right from the first one carries the heavy bundles of grass centered on one's head. But surprisingly enough, it is easier this way as more wieght can be managed at once, and one's, balance is maintained evenly.

It was an inspiration to be a part of the endless procession of people all laden down with the heavy grass, trudging along in service to the Lord, their voices ringing out with the sweet sound of shabds. No thought does one have of being tired from the task. It is rather the other way around. One takes on the heaviest load possible; one works as quickly as one can. Rather than being tiring it is refreshing and uplifting. A disciple beside whom I was walking told me that once, when he had seen an old crippled woman moving along slower than the others under a particularly heavy bundle of grass, he asked the Master, "How can this be? Such a poor, crippled soul who can barely walk—yet taking on this heavy load?"

"It is love," the Master told him.

And one has only to look around him at the faces of the people to know that this is true. Their countenances reflect the love in which their hearts and minds and souls are steeped—not a blind love, but one that springs naturally and spontaneoulsy from the realization of His presence within them. One sees the very poor and lowly working shoulder to shoulder with those of wealthy, even royal standing. For the Master teaches that God does not honor one more than another, and that when one enters the Kingdom of God within one's own being, one knows that we are all united in our essence, and that love is the axis upon which we all revolve.

It was all still so new and incredible! This place,

this small spot of land in India, presented a living, daily demonstration of the ideal that sincere religious leaders have been trying for centuries to achieve with people all over the world.   When I carried the bundle of grass on my head, I felt I was a part of something—something that was intensely real and vital.   As I moved along in the stream of people, it seemed as if we all belonged to the same unbelievable happy family, as children of the same father.   And there, standing on a nearby rise of land, was the Living Master Himself.

We worked until the Indian sunset began to color the western sky, announcing that darkness would soon be upon us.   The crowd following the Master back to the Colony proper that evening was larger than the one we had seen a few days before from the Guest House roof, for now it was the evening before Bhandara day.   It was also the eve of *Diwali*, the festival of lights, a great day of celebration in India.

Diwali...a day as meaningful in India as is Christmas in the West. In the cities and in villages in all parts of the country, the people celebrate it every year with millions upon millions of lights.   Even at the Dera we could see little lights glimmering here and there as we walked about in the evening, though we knew that here it was not done for the traditional reasons. Throughout India it is an occasion that has been celebrated for countless centuries in honor of the Indian hero Ram Chander, whose trials and adventures are recounted in the epic poem called the *Ramayana*. Every Indian child by the time he is able to talk knows the story of the wandering, exiled prince Rama who finally returned home to claim his rightful throne. The millions of lights signify the celebration of his return.

At the Dera, however, those who lit a few of these lights understood a different and deeper interpretation of the *Ramayana*. For the Masters have explained that it is a parable which tells of the journey of the soul away from the Home of its Heavenly Father. For countless ages the soul wanders loveless and lost, entirely forgetful of its true origin. But finally there comes a day when the soul realizes its mistake, and a rebirth takes place when the upward journey of the soul, its return to its true Home, begins. The lights of Diwali symbolize the realms of radiant glory which greet the soul within. So at the Dera, rather than observing Diwali with a profusion of dazzling lights and loud celebrations, we saw small groups of people quietly sitting together holding Satsangs, or singing shabds in praises to God. And often we came across those who were sitting quietly in meditation and themselves beholding the transcendent glory of the inner Kingdom.

Bhandara day itself passed in a blur of activity. There were two Satsangs, morning and afternoon, in honor of the Master Sardar Bahadur Jagat Singh Ji, who had died on that date eleven years before, October, 23, 1951. The multitudes doubled and redoubled themselves as a floodtide of people poured through the Dera gates. It was a joy to see them. Some were bare of foot and clothed in rags. Some carried small bundles of bedding upon their heads, for the ground would be their sleeping place at night. Many faces were lined and worn from hardship and poverty, but radiantly alive in the knowledge that they would soon see their beloved Father.

When the day was over, the evening dinner at the Guest House was quieter than most other meals had been. All seemed to wish to remain silent with their own thoughts as they pondered over the wealth of experiences that were being so freely given by the Master day after day. For increasingly one feels that most of one's own personal experiences are either too sacred or too difficult to describe. So these treasures are kept harbored deep within the heart as the Master's gifts.

My eyes involuntarily filled with tears as I slowly walked to my room for the night. Could it be only a dream? But no, that was impossible. For every minute of every day that one spends at his Master's feet is more real than all the rest of his lifetime put together. Rather than a dream, it is an awakening. An incredible sense of peace and wonder flooded over me—and anticipation too, for the morrow would dawn a new joy.

CHAPTER FIVE

CLOSER THAN BREATHING

"Maharaj Ji, do you know everything?" I asked Him bluntly. It was my first private interview with the Master, and I had been sitting in His living room for about ten minutes. There was so much I wanted to say to Him. In fact, as is the experience common to many disciples, I wanted to burst ito tears, to fall at His feet, to let out every problem inside all at once. But somehow I sat very still, and we just chatted together quietly. He asked if the food was good, if everything was being attended to properly, if my room was comfortable, and so on. In spite of my inescapable feeling of awe, however, I had to know if He really could see what was in one's heart.

The Master laughed. "Do you *want* me to know everything?"

"Yes," I said quickly. "Because then I won't have to tell you everything."

There was an unfathomable look of kindness on His face. But He did not answer the question just then. He simply looked at me for a long moment—a look which needed no words. Of itself it seemed to say, "Be still... and know."

As I soon came to realize, the Master never leaves a question unanswered. During the coming months He answered that first question day by day in a hundred little ways. He would speak of things which I knew He had no way of knowing externally. Perhaps He would make a casual remark which at the time I would not recognize as being an answer—but later upon reflection, it would become clear that He was teaching me something of importance, and slowly revealing His divine Self.

As day after day goes by in the Master's presence, one can almost watch, as if an outside observer, the reactions and changes taking place inside oneself. Not many days had passed by, for example, before I began to feel an undefinable anxiety whenever I was not in His company. A certain gnawing inner restlessness persisted and stayed with me from the time my foot-steps led me away from Him until they again found their way back to His side. I became increasingly aware of this feeling, and irresistibly began to follow Him whenever He was anywhere outside His compound or walking about the Dera. In fact, at every possible moment, for it filled me with so much growing pleasure to be with Him. No matter where under what circumstances, I found that the nearness of His physical form radiated an aura of peace and love that could not help but uplift and elate anyone who was nearby.

But gradually, almost imperceptibly, I began to have misgivings about the prudence of my behavior. Meaningful glances from others first started this uncer-tainty. And at times Maharaj Ji Himself would give me long, deliberate looks. Finally, one or two of the older disciples mentioned to me that one should try to avoid running after the Master, that He had his own work to do, and that one should honor this. Though these hints were very mildly put, and the Master Himself said nothing to indicate that He wished me to be somewhere else than in His presence, still the uncer-tainty grew until it finally became a problem.

At last I took the question to Ramji Das Ahluwalia, the Dera secretary. He told me that instead of expressing all the longing and yearning one feels for the Master by seeking Him out in His physical form, one should rather sit for meditation and search for Him within. It is, in fact, this very longing for His vision that enables one to see the Radiant Form of the Master inside, and eventually to merge in the Lord.

The following morning I awoke with a new resolution. That day, I told myself, I would exercise restraint. A respectful distance would be kept, and the Master would only be seen at the regular times of Satsang and in His garden. All day long the resolution held firm. And it appeared that the endeavor was going to be successful. Most of the day was spent typing in my room, but at 5:30 I found myself automatically walking towards the seva area where I knew He would be sitting. "What are you doing?" I asked myself. "What has happened to your resolution?"

After coming within sight of Him, I sat on a small rise of ground some fifty yards away and looked at Him intently. "Well," I assured myself. "This is all right. Just as long as you don't go too close to Him."

The Master was alone. He was sitting in a lawn chair on the ridge that marked the highest point in the seva area, so that all might look up at Him as they passed by. And as usual He was the very picture of beauty and light. A short distance away from Him stood Manohar, His personal attendant, and another Western guest.

But my contentment at this distance lasted no longer than a short fifteen minutes. Then I felt that I was again being helplessly drawn closer to His side. Again those persistent feet of mine were taking me directly to the Master. He looked at me when I arrived.

"Maharaj Ji?" I said with a questioning look.

He smiled and motioned for me to sit on the ground at His feet. (There is no place on earth a disciple longs to be more than sitting at his Master's feet. As a rule, the Master discourages it, but fortunately for me there was no other chair beside Him that afternoon.)

"Do you want me to go?" I asked outright.

"Why, what's wrong with you?" He asked, still smiling.

"Well, I made a resolution this morning Maharaj Ji. I told myself that I wouldn't follow you around today and...well, here I am," I finished haltingly.

Then He laughed in his sweet, gentle way and said, "Well, perhaps *you* made a resolution this morning, but I didn't. You may have made up your mind about it, but I made mine up quite differently." His smile broadened. "But if you don't feel..."

"Oh no, Maharaj Ji," I said quickly, "But..."

"Well," he said as if deliberating. "We'll compromise—fifty-fifty."

And again, as in that first interview, He gave me one of those very special looks, the kind of look that makes one feel that one is the Master's sole concern and that the Master knows each and every hidden nook and corner of one's being.

"Thank you, Maharaj Ji," I whispered and walked away from His chair to sit on the ground beside the other two. Tears of happiness were trying to push their way to the surface. How much that short interview had conveyed! Just those few words had held in their meaning a mountain of love coupled with the Master's unfailing tenderness. Because He had, by the way He spoke those words, told me that it is He who calls one to Him, that it is His wish when one is drawn to His feet. And that He knows every step one takes. "Closer He is than breathing; nearer than hands and feet," are the words of a poet who had a discernment of things that lay deep beneath the surface of existence.

The days at the Dera had all too quickly turned into weeks when suddenly, it seemed almost abruptly, the Master's physical form was no longer present. All of us gathered in His compound on the morning when He left for a month-long tour to visit disciples in a number of major Indian cities. Few words were said, for it seemed as though a blanket of silence had settled down over us all. Quietly we stood there and waited until He came from His house. And when He appeared, something electric went through each and every one of us who stood there. Had I ever seen Him look as He did then?

Instead of His usual vest worn over the traditional Indian tunic and pajama trousers of white cotton, this morning the Master was dressed in a beautiful, lightweight Indian coat with the oriental high collar. When He first appeared and stood for a moment in the doorway of His bungalow, a lady who was standing next to me said in a voice that was barely audible, "He is immaculate perfection." And that He is, for when God sends forth His Sons to carry out His work, He gives them the most supremely beautiful forms that the material universe can offer.

Perhaps some readers may wonder why a description of the Master's earthly form has not yet been given. Actually, when faced with opportunities to do this in earlier chapters, I discarded them immediately. For if a picture—a picture which is said to be worth a thousand words—cannot begin to convey the radiance and beauty of the Master, then a few words here are poor instruments indeed.   Yet this day, on the morning of His departure from the Dera in November, the earthly vision He gave us of Himself was so breathtaking that it cannot be kept entirely to oneself.

Our beloved Master, now in His middle-forties, is tall and straight of stature, but not over bearing.   He wears a turban on His head at all times, usually of pale yellow, but this morning it was pure whiteness. Descended from the ancient Aryan race, the Master has a noble face with high cheekbones and a fine, straight nose; His light gray beard is full and flowing; His skin is light tan and smooth, seeming to glow with warmth.   In His countenance one sees youth combined with ageless wisdom, and majesty with gentle compassion, inspiring both peace and trustfulness to those around Him and inducing a reverence that cannot be defined.

And the Master's eyes—oh! the compassionate, peaceful depths of His eyes.   Not of this world they are; how can one describe them?   Sometimes they are as gentle and soft as deeply brown velvet, and sometimes they radiate with such intensity and power that they probe every corner of one's heart and uncover and lay bare one's innermost thoughts.   There are times when He allows one to gaze long and deeply into His eyes, and for this one would gladly cross the oceans again and again.   For all the heartache and tears of a lifetime are atoned for in those supreme moments.   One feels that all the kingdoms of the world would be but a poor price to pay for an instant of meeting the Master's eyes.   The whole world fades away, even one's very self, and becomes non-existent.   It is as if the impatient soul, hungry and irresistibly drawn, were trying to leap out of its bodily prison and pour itself into those eyes.

And on that November morning, the Master's eyes were glancing from one to the other of us gathered there to bid Him good-bye. We knew He read our feelings as the last "Radha Soamis" were said. As He got into the car, a rose which had just been plucked from the garden was handed to Him. And how easily the tears came to our eyes as we watched the car being driven away; the Master's head was bowed and His eyes were closed. The stem of the rose was held between His folded palms with its tiny, delicate petals unfolded towards His face. And then He was gone— for a moment the sense of loss was almost unbearable.

No one could speak as we slowly made our way back to the Guest House. The mind would not stop its thinking. There was so much to comprehend, to understand. But as He had told us many times, the real understanding and love would not come until one was able to go within himself and there behold the Radiant Vision of the Master waiting to receive him. And yet even that would be only the beginning, for His power and His radiance and His greatness increase beyond all credibility as one climbs in glory on the inward Path. There, in those higher realms, the devotee sees millions upon millions of souls, all radiantly magnificent in their own light, yet all worshiping the Master, truly the great and august King of all the kings. And He, in His physical form, had left us just a moment ago through those very gates—with a small rose in His hands.

A few mornings later I sat on the Guest House roof waiting for the sun to appear over the Beas River. It was 6:00 a.m. Damp and cool was the morning air; the breeze was soft. Only a bare dimness had as yet replaced the night. But soon pale rays of light appeared, grew in intensity, brightened, and filled the sky with faint auras of color. Slowly at first, the drama of the sunrise began with deep crimson and scarlet appearing just above the horizon, and opened up to intense golden hues fringed with pink, blending into the deep blue canopy overhead. The sweet melody of a bird winging a pathway across the sunrise lingered in the air as if to announce the entrance of the monarch sun, which suddenly penetrated through its cloak of dust high above the earth's eastern rim. For a brief moment, its red-gold sphere intensified and illuminated the colored auras of the rays it had cast before itself. But soon it no longer allowed the naked eye to look upon its brightness, and the breathtaking pageantry of dawn quickly gave way to daylight. And yet, incredibly so, this temporary glory cannot in a millionth part reflect the Glory which lies within for those who have opened their inner eye to behold it. Such is the mystery of this Path of paths.

That morning, though the sun rose on a far more empty Dera than that of a few days before, and no one cared to appreciate its daily pageant. The tens of thousands who had populated the small village vanished as if the crowded, active days of the Bhandara had been no more than a dream. No longer did the air ring with shabds chorused by thousands of eager voices; no longer did one's entire thinking revolve around where and when one would see the Master that day, eagerly planning every moment so as to spend as many of them as possible in His presence. Smiles seemed to have lost their radiance; happy laughter had quieted, and joyful tears did not flow as bountifully. Only those with the eye to behold His Radiant Form within were in the full

conscious knowledge that He never really leaves one
alone for an instant. But for the rest, it was as if a
master light switch had been turned off. There was
nothing one could do but hold on to one's memories of
Him, strive intensely during the hours of meditation,
and long for the day of His return.

How often I thought at that time of a certain
passage from Dr. Johnson's book, *With a Great Master
in India*. At one time I had wondered at such strong
expression, but by now I had found from personal
experience that it minimized rather than exaggerated.

"The Master has gone. His gracious Radha
Soami has been said, and we are once more left alone
with our meditations and our holy memories...Men
come and go like ships passing each other in the night.
Only in Bhajan (meditation) is there life and light; for
the Master's Radiant Form is always there, if the scales
have fallen from our eyes, that we may see...."

But then, just as the fleeting sunrise had seemed
to almost speak aloud, the Master's goodness and love,
in fact the Master's very godhead, sustains all and gives
life to all. Not that He is entirely contained within His
physical form, but rather that His physical form is the
material expression of the inner Master, the Holy Word,
which dwells within every blade of grass and every
beating heart.

CHAPTER SIX

FROM A BARREN LAND

On a cold but sunny November day shortly after
Maharaj Ji had left the Dera, several of us took a
thorough tour of the great Satsang Ghar. Generally, it
is not in use when the Master is away, since those who
then attend Satsang rarely number more than three or
four hundred. At these times the Satsangs are given
daily by various appointed members of the Colony and
are held out of doors in the area in front of the Dera
library. We therefore could roam about the great hall
to our hearts' content.

It stood outlined against the cloudless sky as we
entered the gates, and I wondered if I would ever cease
to wonder anew at its magnificence. The structure is in
the shape of a giant "T", with a series of wide marble
steps, stately rows of pillars, marble terraces, and tall
arched windows on all eight facades. Covering the
interior there is a great plateaued roof around which the
seven gold-tipped towers rise, one tower at each corner
of the "T", and a central rear tower crowning all with
the loftiest, grandest dome. The entire picture seems
almost to belong to another world, in such rare beauty
is it arranged. At a quick glance, the hall with its
seven soaring towers seems to form a majestic golden
flower, reaching its petals towards the sun. What
great forbearance, what love was needed to erect such
a structure in the face of so many material obstacles!
How many pairs of strong hands joined together in its
construction! How many eager hearts watched and
labored as the spires slowly climbed to meet the sky !

After spending some time exploring the interior, we found a small doorway at the base of the rear tower which gave entrance to a winding stairway of stone. There we began our ascent to the loftiest point, bypassing all the other balconies and plateaus on the way up. It appeared an easy enough climb at the beginning, but after a good quarter of an hour of mounting steadily upward in circles, it seemed as though we would never reach the top. But just then the stairs terminated and a door led us out to a small platform at the foot of the big dome. The panorama that met our eyes left us speechless. In fact, I felt that I should tiptoe to the railed edge lest the vision that lay spread out before us would vanish. For one sometimes feels the need for extreme quiet when confronted with the startlingly beautiful.

Our eyes looked over the six towers beneath us to the Dera Colony. From that awesome height, the whole village seemed to be a handful of neatly arranged toy houses. It was hard to imagine how it could take in and shelter two hundred thousand people at one time—this little spot of earth so separate from the life beyond its gates. Could I venture to call it the world's real capitol? This small Indian village where the Light of the world walks daily? So unobtrusively and quietly it lay there! But no, the people of the world would ask for something far more spectacular to the eye than a simple village. And the Dera would happily remain as it is, an oasis for the thirsty spirit, growing in size only to give more shelter to those who in their hearts call it home.

When we had caught our breath after the strenuous climb, our eyes looked beyond the flat roof and the six spires below us, beyond the gates enclosing the fields

around the hall, to row upon row of small red brick
bungalows, some under construction and others newly
finished.   A wide expanse of land soon to be used for
more building stretched out beyond the cottages.
To the right stood the now unused house of the late
Baba Sawan Singh Ji, our Master's Master.   We
recognized the Dera library, the offices, the old Persian
well, Maharaj Ji's newly built house, the rich green
vegetation and colored splashes of the gardens, and our
own Guest House compound with its fruit garden and
papaya trees and velvety expanse of lawn.   And there,
beyond the Colony on the far right, the Beas River
looked like a tiny ribbon fallen across a golden carpet of
hay, sparkling in the afternoon sun and colored by the
deep blue of the sky.   Slowly we walked around the
small balcony circling the dome.   On the other side and
to the left lay a patchquilt of vegetable gardens and
wheat fields—all of which yielded food for the Colony.
Beyond the Colony gates and across the fields, the outline of a mud village could be seen, its pale, tawny-
colored houses blending with the earth.   The whole
panorama before us resembled a page torn from a
Biblical story-book.

It wasn't until we had descended the circular
stairway within the tower and were walking through the
gates to leave the Satsang Ghar behind that we were
able to speak.

Later I learned that the bricks which form the walls
and towers of the Satsang Ghar, and for that matter the
brick bungalows and other buildings of the entire
Colony, were all wrought from the very earth upon
which they stand.   Being from the West, my tendency
was to take many things for granted and it never
occurred to me to wonder how the large quantity of

material needed for these buildings was made available. All around the Dera for miles there are either primitive mud villages or wasteland, even jungle, with no great factories to supply bricks or other kinds of building materials. When the Dera first began to grow, there was no road leading to it upon which the necessary amount of bricks could be brought in from the nearest cities. And bullock carts were hardly sufficient to transport the needed supplies.

One day I noticed two rusty smokestacks standing far out in the field behind the Guest House. Curious, I asked what they were, and was told that they were the smokestacks of the Dera's brick kiln. That afternoon several of us recruited Sardar Balwant Singh, the agriculturist who had visited us during morning tea on the first day, to take us there and show us how it worked.

We came first upon some men digging up blocked-off portions of the ground, making loose piles of deep brown, rich clay. This dry clay was placed in water holes until it became sodden and muddy. Then it was kneaded with a spade until it had the consistency of dough. Small quantities of this dough were then packed into brick-shaped wooden molds and powdered with soft sand to prevent the mud from sticking to the sides. Then the mold was removed.

A deeply browned Indian was rapidly making the clay-dough bricks and placing them in neat rows. We stood and watched his dark, skilled hands deftly turn out finished bricks at the rate of nearly four a minute. He seemed unaffected by our attentive presence, continuing his work without breaking pace while we timed him with the second-hand of a watch.

The top-soil dust swirled about our feet as we walked toward the brick kiln itself, in which the bricks were being fired. Shaped like an oval ring with twelve-foot wide sides, the kiln was entrenched eight feet deep into the ground. The smoke stacks were at one end. Molded bricks were placed inside the oval in criss-cross layers so that air could freely move through them. Kerosene was spread throughout, and when one end of a block of layers was lighted, the chimneys at the opposite end drew the air through, supplying the fire and coals inside with oxygen. Wood fuel was fed into the block from iron lids in the hardened, temporary protective cover placed over the block of bricks under fire.

On the day when the brick kiln is put into operation for the coming season, the Master Himself strikes the match which sets the kerosene aflame. From then on it becomes a continuous process, some half a million finished bricks or more being produced each month.

Thus, incredibly so to my western mind, every structure, every brick building including the great Sastsang Ghar itself had come from the earth upon which we walked every day. But where and when did it begin? What was the real story behind the birth and growth of this beloved Colony?

The answer unfolded itself as I questioned and talked with the old ones at the Dera—those who had watched it grow almost from infancy—listened to their store of legends and memories, and as I read the brief historical sketches of the Colony written in various Radha Soami books.

In the beginning, the Dera was but a wasteland, and the firm ground upon which it now stands was criss-crossed with deep hollows and ravines with only a few lean shrubs to break its barrenness. It was an area which had never been populated and had always been unquestionably avoided by those seeking land for their farms and homes.

But poor land was only a small part of the reason why the area had remained uninhabited. The largest part was played by fear, for the land was believed to be haunted by evil ghosts and goblins. It was here, on the west bank of the River Beas, that the army of Alexander the Great rebelled at the intense heat of the plains and the great commander was forced to halt his eastward march of world conquest and begin his long retreat to Persia. Perhaps it is only a legend which says that the retreat began at the very spot where the Dera stands today, but perhaps, too, this was the Lord's method of preserving the land through the centuries, keeping it untouched and waiting for His Sons.

But long before it was born as a spiritual colony, before the first mud hut was erected, there was foreknowledge of its future in the mind of at least one highly-evolved soul. This holy man would gather stones from far and near and carry little bundles of them to the bank of the river where he would methodically place them in small heaps and piles. The people laughed and called him Kanhom, the half-witted. They jeered at him when they asked him to tell of his "mission," but he would quietly answer, "One day this will be a flourishing community. Splendid houses will be built upon this land and its population will equal that of a city."

The people would then look around at the barrenness and waste of the land to which he gestured when he spoke, and would walk away in laughter. They did not know that their good fortune had brought them into the company of a mastana, one "intoxicated" by esoteric revelations and who had attained inner knowledge of the divine intent for this particular plot of land.

His elation had compelled him to serve the land,
although nearly a century would pass before his predictions were to materialize.

Today, when wandering through the village streets,
one does find a flourishing community, and one that is
continuously expanding.   There is an excellent, up-
to-date library at the Colony where one may select
from thousands of books on nearly every religious and
philosophical subject in the world.   With only a few
exceptions, it is one of the largest collection of books on
comparative religions that I had ever seen.   There is
also a small hospital or dispensary under the able charge
of Dr. Maluk Singh, a retired Civil Surgeon.   Its doors
are open to all members of the Colony and to the people
of many neighboring villages as well.   And every kind
of physical illness and disability is cared for here.   In
one year over 350 minor operations and 15 to 25 major
operations are performed in this hospital, not to mention
the thousands who receive other necessary medical care.

Recently a thirty-ton water tower was erected in
order to supply sufficient water for the hundred thousand
or more devotees who come to the Dera at Bhandara time.*
Now electricity and running water are part of every home.

But how could all this be possible when the Dera is
so far from any industrial center and is surrounded by
Indian villages which may be as much as two thousand
years behind the rest of the world?   Such is the power
of the beloved Masters who have guided its growth
from the very first mud hut.   And so, to the story of the
Masters' lives one must look, for They are the beginning
and the end, the cause and the effect, the sole power behind the miracle which was wrought from a barren land.

*The number of devotees at Bhandara time now runs into
several hundred thousand.

CHAPTER SEVEN

IN THE BEGINNING...

"Where may I find one who can enlighten me on the mystery of the five Holy Sounds?" asked a strange young pilgrim of an old man one hot summer day. His feet were tired and his clothes were dusty, for he had been travelling through many villages during the weeks just past. His question was directed to a venerable and saintly-looking sage, one who might at last know the asnwer.

"I cannot help you, my son," the sage replied. "It is true that there are five Sounds which reverberate within man, but I myself know only of two which my guru has revealed to me. I know not how to find the others."

Strange words? Yes. But stranger still the young pilgrim, barely seventeen years of age, to whom they were spoken. A lad who was not an ordinary boy, who never had been one. Born in 1839 in the village of Ghoman, Jaimal Singh had been fired with a thirst for spiritual knowledge since earliest childhood. When only seven years old he had read the writings of the Sikh Gurus, or Masters, who had long since passed away. But the verses they had written had become immortal and had been compiled in the eighteenth century to form the *Adi Granth*, the holy book of the Sikh religion. The boy studied these verses eagerly with the help of Baba Khem Das, a spiritual man of his village. But it was the boy himself who perceived that the sacred book told of five Melodies within man which, he concluded, were inner spiritual emanations from the

Supreme Father and the Essence of all creation. He was sure that the great Gurus were not referring to external musical songs and instruments. And so, with that pure faith born in children, Jaimal Singh began to search for someone who could explain this enigma to him. Perhaps, he thought, he might learn the secret of how to hear these mysterious, holy sounds. There had already been times in his young life when a pure, white light would open up within him, and he hoped with all his heart that his search would not be in vain.

He had asked his teacher about the Melodies, but to no avail. Baba Khem Das did not know the answer. As the years went by, his search had taken him to an untold number of holy men and mahatmas and sages in many parts of India. But time and again he was disappointed, finding only the same blank faces, the same incredulous stares. What on earth, he wondered, was so odd, so strange, about one who only wished to explore a mystery? And where, by whom was the mystery to be solved? There must be someone, he persisted in believing, who could give him the answer.

But now, on this hot summer day, desperate and almost at the point of giving up hope, the tired and dusty pilgrim listened with eagerness as the sage quietly spoke to him in response to his question. "It is true that there are five Sounds which reverberate within man...."

And Jaimal Singh was elated! What did it matter that the learned one himself could not give him the secrets of the five Sounds. Now, at last, he had heard spoken aloud from another's lips the belief he had held for so many years in his heart. And furthermore, this sage personally knew of two of the five Holy Sounds. Never had he felt so encouraged. Now, surely his footsteps were being guided and he was coming closer to the end of his search.

With a lighter heart and new hope, he began his journey homeward. But when he reached Beas, a village only twelve miles from Ghoman, he met a group of sadhus (holy men) on a pilgrimage to Hardwar and couldn't resist joining them. For at Hardwar, many of India's most spiritually advanced sadhus and mahatmas (greatly advanced souls) were to be found. There Jaimal Singh listened eagerly and talked with many holy men, but after several months his hopes once more began to fade. It was of no use. No one at Hardwar knew the secret of the five Sounds. But just as he was about to leave Hardwar in despair, he was told that there was a very old sadhu who dwelt alone in the jungle some fifteen miles away. "But he lets no one near him," his informer said in warning

Again almost without hope, but determined to leave no stone unturned, the young pilgrim found himself approaching the forbidden glade where the sadhu lived. As quietly as possible he made his way through the thick underbrush of the jungle until he came to a small clearing. And there he saw a very old, very thin man standing next to a tree. The sadhu's stance was supported by a cloth tied to one of the tree's low, sweeping branches : His eyes were closed as if in deep meditation. Jaimal Singh moved closer to him.

The sage opened his eyes and frowned at the boy. "What brings you here? Do you not know, O foolish one, that you are in danger for your life? Do you not know that tigers and bears stalk these jungles?" His voice seemed strong and vibrant for his aged body.

"If you have not been harmed by them, then I am not afraid," replied Jaimal Singh quietly.

The sadhu's old, wrinkled face softened and he smiled at the youth before him. "You have spoken well," he said. "I shall help you if I can. What is it you wish to know ?"

Jaimal Singh told the old sadhu of his years of searching, his hopeless disappointments, his pitifully few encouragements. He trusted this strange old man more than he had ever trusted anyone. Somehow he knew that he was speaking to one who understood what he was trying to say, what he had tried to say so many countless times before.

"Do you know the secret?" Jaimal Singh implored him. "Can you impart this knowledge to me?"

The sadhu studied him and sighed. "My son, I can only tell you what my inner vision has revealed to me. Yes, you are right, salvation will come only through the Shabd, the spiritual Sound Current, the Celestial Music. I have seen that there is a great Mahatma of the highest order who had been in solitary meditation for some seventeen or eighteen years. And He has just emerged from His secret place to give this knowledge to the world. Go to Him, my son. You may find Him at Agra."

"But will you not come with me?" Jaimal Singh asked him.

"I cannot walk on these legs now; they are heavy and difficult to move, for I have stood on them for many years in my particular spiritual practice. Though I have attained miraculous powers, I yearn for this knowledge as you do. I shall go to Him one day, but sometime after you."

The aged holy man's eyes were misty as he looked penetratingly at the boy for an instant. Then he closed them again, as if in dismissal.

Impelled by a very great longing and a most impatient joy, Jaimal Singh wasted no time in going to Agra. This time, surely this time he would not meet with disappointment.

Agra....home of the world-famous Taj Mahal. The young, travel-weary pilgrim wandered down its streets and spoke to many of its people. He entered many temples and inquired of the priests and religious scholars, but to no avail. Foolishly, in his haste he had forgotten to inquire of the old sadhu where he might find the great Mahatma. But his footsteps were well guided, for one afternoon while bathing in the River Jumna and, as always, pondering over where he might possibly search next for the Mahatma, he overheard a conversation. Two men had just come to the river bank and were talking about a great Master named Swami Ji Maharaj. At once Jaimal Singh asked them for the Mahatma's address and the two disciples gladly directed him to Panni Lane in Agra.

Jaimal Singh ran nearly the whole distance. He could not get there fast enough. His whole being was on fire with anticipation. When he arrived at the given address, it was time for afternoon Satsang. And there his eyes drank in the sight of the great Mahatma for the first time. Without a word, Jaimal Singh fell at His feet.

"From where have you come?" asked Swami Ji of the boy.

"From the Punjab," Jaimal Singh replied.

"He has arrived—my old, old friend," said Swami Ji, half to Himself.

Surprised, Jaimal Singh wondered at the strange words of the great Mahatma. He had never seen Him before, he knew.

After several months of attending Satsangs, Jaimal Singh was convinced that there was no greater Master in all of India than Swami Ji. He listened attentively to every word that Swami Ji spoke. And he delighted in those words, for they answered all his questions and fulfilled all his dreams. Yes, this greatest of Mahatmas could give him the secret of the Holy Sounds. In fact, the Shabd* (Holy Sound, Word) was the foundation of Swami Ji's teachings. Jaimal Singh learned that the five Melodies are actually manifestations of the one Word of God which emanates from the Supreme Father and sustains all planes and creation, all universes, all realms of spirit, mind and matter. He learned that this Holy Word is the transcendent, dynamic, all-powerful Presence and force of God, and that it is the only means by which the soul can return to its most Supreme Origin. It is referred to as "Sound" and "Melodies" for lack of a better expression in mortal language. And Jaimal Singh had been right—the Word is not "heard" by the physical ears; and in fact, cannot be experienced at all unless a finer, higher sense is developed in the disciple by his Master. It is sweet beyond all earthly comprehension; it is enrapturing beyond all dreams; it purifies the soul and draws it upward. All these things Jaimal Singh learned at the feet of his Master during those first few months.

The great Mahatma, as Jaimal Singh was told by His devotees, had been steeped in spirituality since His birth in August 1818. He was named Seth Siv Dayal Singh, later becoming known as Swami Ji Maharaj. Born into a deeply religious family, Swami Ji showed a great depth and understanding of the scriptures and

*Shabd as used in referring to the Holy Word should not be confused with the other meaning of the word, i.e., Indian hymn.

the written words of the great ones of the past. Through the years he had also had some contact with Tulsi Sahib—a great sage of the highest order who had forsaken His kingdom in central India in order to carry on a life of meditation and spiritual practice, and who had settled not far from Swami Ji's birthplace at Agra.

Those early days pointed the beaconway for what was to come. When He was a young man in his early twenties, Swami Ji Maharaj devoted Himself to secluded meditation in a small, back room of His family's home. Seventeen years He passed in this manner, and as the old sadhu in the jungle had envisioned, He had just emerged from His place of meditation in order to present the Path of the Holy Word of God in a simpler, clearer, and more direct approach than had ever before been done. He held Satsang in the privacy of His own courtyard, but already word of His wisdom had begun to spread, and a number of disciples had come to sit at His feet.

Jaimal Singh's only concern was that Swami Ji was not a Sikh, as it was from the *Adi Granth*, the writings of the Sikh Gurus, that he had first learned of the Holy Word, the Heavely Sound. One day he found himself alone with Swami Ji after an afternoon Satsang. Swami Ji asked him if he had resolved his problem of Sikh or non-Sikh. The young devotee's eyes were filled with tears. He could not speak. How clearly this greatest of Saints looked into his heart and uncovered all that was there.

Swami Ji needed no words from the boy to understand. For the remainder of the day He talked with Jaimal Singh as would a father. He explained that the Radha Soami Path transcends all religions; that creed, class, or religious heritage count not at all in the Court of the Lord and have no bearing whatsoever on one's spiritual journey. That scriptures and teachings and discourses alone cannot carry one back to merge in the Lord. For how could it be otherwise? "How can the blind lead the blind," said Swami Ji.* "Hence the insistence upon seeking a Perfect Master. So long as He is not found, the Inner Secret of the Path cannot be known. Satguru is He who is enraptured in the Word within, reveals the Inner Secret, and shows the way to the soul's real home through Shabd.... The Satguru does not depend upon discourses or teachings or scriptures. He Himself *is* the Supreme Being in human form.

"The aim and object of all religions and of all ancient seers has been to take the soul, by one means or another, back to its source. Perfect is he who, by practice and meditation, lifts his soul to its real abode, freeing it from all bonds, both internal and external, gross, subtle and causal, and thus detaches his mind from the world and its phenomena. The perfect sadhus, real sages, true lovers or devotees of the Lord, are those only who reach the last stage. They who talk only of the Perfect Ones, or read their teachings to others without reaching that stage or practising towards that end are only intellectuals and theorists.

"Sadhus, Sages, Incarnations, Prophets and other holy personages who did not reach the Real Home, all rank much below the Saints. As, in the upward journey, they stopped at different planes, they founded different religions corresponding to their several attain-

---

*No record was kept of the actual conversation that afternoon. But perhaps, by extracting from the *Sar Bachan*, a collection of Swami Ji's discourses and sayings later recorded, we can imagine how He may have spoken to the boy.

ments. The stage reached by any one of them was regarded by him as the final region.... The ecstasy of the moment of realization caused the devotee to lose himself in an indescribable state of eagerness and blissful intoxication.

"The soul attains to a different state at every stage that it reaches. At each stage it feels as if it controls and pervades through everything below.... Only the Sant Sat Guru (Most Perfect Master) knows of the higher stages. Had these teachers been instructed by a Sant Sat Guru, those higher regions woud have been revealed to them Then they would have been shown the way and helped on the inward Path.

"Likewise, one who crossed the first, second or third stage in the course of his upward journey, was looked upon as perfect. The fact is that the devotee acquires all power when he reaches the first stage, and on account of that attainment he is regarded as a perfect being or Mahatma. There is no doubt that this first region is much superior to the regions of lower consciousness, and one who reaches this stage is absolutely freed from all personal and wordly dross.

"There are stages of the Shabd down to this point... which can be made known to us by a Perfect Master or Satguru.... It is not possible to give any description, oral or written of the Shabd beyond that. There is no parallel in this world to which that Sound can be compared. The adept realizes that Shabd when he reaches that stage. It is via the Shabd of each stage that the soul can, by degrees ascend from one stage to another, up to the highest stage. The ascent of the spirit is absolutely impossible in any other way, especially in this age of darkness.

"Be it known that in the final region of Radha Soami

there is no form, color or delineation, as we know them here; even the Shabd is not manifested there. No description of the region can be given by word of mouth or by writing. This is the final resting place of the Highest Saints and Perfect Masters.

"From one step to another, the soul beholds strange things which cannot be described in human language. Every region and every thing is utterly beyond words. What beauty and glory! How can I describe them? There is nothing here to convey the idea. I am helpless. All I can possibly say is that Love plays the supreme part. It is all Love. So says Radha Soami."

And so, Jaimal Singh became initiated into the innermost secrets of the Radha Soami Path that memorable day in 1856. Immediately he began the spiritual practice as he had been instructed; and for many weeks he stayed in Agra with his beloved Master. He often performed his meditations in Swami Ji Maharaj's garden just outside the city.

On one particular afternoon, when he was deeply engaged in meditation, Swami Ji entered the garden. But the boy paid Him no heed—neither did he speak nor get up to greet his Master, for his attention was wholly concentrated within in spiritual practice.

Swami Ji, with His own power, drew Jaimal Singh's attention outside and inquired of him, "are you satisfied that what I have given you is the Path of Guru Nanak?"

"Yes", replied Jaimal Singh. "My soul journeys up into high stages even now." "But", he added, "there seems to be some obstacle in my way."

"You have already done it in the previous birth, when you were with me. All this was already done by you," Swami Ji Maharaj told him.

"But what proof do I have of this ?"

"Well, if you want proof, then again take your attention in."

Jaimal Singh closed his eyes; at once he drew his attention within, and Swami Ji Maharaj removed the obstruction which was in his way on the inward Path.

After some time Jaimal Singh opened his eyes. He looked upon his beloved Master. "My life's work is finished," he said. "Yet, let me know, please, at which place of pilgrimage I should sit and practice meditation?"

"In this world, and on this Path, we should take up both worldly and spiritual work, and try to adapt ourselves to both," said Swami Ji. "If one gives up his worldly work, then he would have to depend on others for a living and his spiritual life would suffer because of those who would serve him or worship him as people do when they see a sadhu who has renounced the world. You should take up some work in the world. To make spiritual progress one should live on one's own income."

Desiring only to carry out his Master's wishes, Jaimal Singh joined the army for his worldly work. For three years he remained stationed in Agra, performing his duties to the army, but spending all the time he could at Swami Ji's Satsang and in spiritual meditation.

But then came the day when his regiment was transferred from Agra, and after that from one part of India to another. Jaimal Singh knew, however, that Swami Ji was ever with him, and regularly continued with his spiritual practice, deeply devoted to his beloved Master. Whenever he was granted a few days leave from his regiment, he would engage himself in meditation at the nearest secluded place.

During the years of Jaimal Singh's army service,

Swami Ji's following continued to grow. The small, private Satsangs He had been holding in His courtyard became known among the people, and in January of 1861 He held His first large, public Satsang. From then on devotees and seekers gathered at His feet by the hundreds and, in later years, by the thousands. For He withdrew many of the heavy curtains of secrecy that had kept the internal wisdom of the Word of God hidden from the uninitiated in past centuries.

The teachings of the Great Saint clearly presented the highest degree of Truth to the people— so much so that His devotees humbly asked Him to explain the scope of the Radha Soami Path in full detail so that a record might be made for future study and understanding. Three years before His mortal death, Swami Ji dictated a long volume of prose and poetry called in its entirety the *Sar Bachan*. Great portions of this work have today been translated into many languages and are a treasure to every disciple on the Radha Soami Path.

Swami Ji Maharaj died on June 15, 1878, having drawn more than four thousand initiates into the fold. And in His last earthly moments He assured the devotees gathered there at His side of His everlasting presence by saying, "No Satsangis should in any way feel perturbed. I am with every one of them and in the future they will be looked after even more than before."

CHAPTER EIGHT

PORTRAITS OF THE MASTERS

A figure, a strange and solitary figure, walked along the western bank of a river in North India early one morning in the winter of 1891. The first oblique rays of sunlight rested on His head and cast a long, broken shadow over the rough, pitted land, He wore a high white turban matching the whiteness of His full beard; His face was strong of line; His eyes were deep-set, wise and God-like. He walked slowly, His head lowered and His hands clasped behind His back.

When He came to the only tree on the river bank, the figure paused and dropped to His knees by the flowing waters. With cupped hands He drank deep of the water, and from His pocket He took a round, flat piece of bread which He soaked in the water before eating.

The figure was that of Baba Jaimal Singh Ji who, thirty-five years before, had been a young, travel-weary pilgrim in search of a Mahatma. Now He walked alone upon the banks of the River Beas in the Punjab and was Himself a Mahatma of the highest order. At last His long years of duty in the service had ended, and free from worldly obligations, He would now be able to devote all His time solely to spritual practice.

For many past days and nights He had been sitting in deep meditation beside the silently-flowing river. Stretching out behind Him there were acres of uninhabited, useless land—land which was superstitiously feared by nearby villagers. But Baba Ji* was beyond fear or

---

*Name by which Jaimal Singh became known; signified respect for age and wisdom.

superstition of any kind and saw that no other place could be more ideal for the meditation and service of the Lord. Though He had visited some of India's darkest, most secluded corners, He had always returned to the solitude of that river bank which was only twelve miles from His native village. And on that morning in 1891, Baba Ji built a small mud hut upon the land, and the Radha Soami Colony was born.

Baba Ji's purpose and mission in selecting this land was not for Himself alone. For the torch of Mastership had been given to Him as Swami Ji Maharaj's favored disciple, and in Swami Ji's name He was to give out the teachings of the Radha Soami Path in the Punjab. Inevitably, knowledge of His presence spread to the nearby villages, and the people began to quell their age-long fears about the stretch of waste land and gather there at His feet in small groups. As Baba Ji drew more and more seekers into His fold, more small huts appeared on the land and the Colony started to grow.

For twelve years thereafter Baba Ji remained by the river bank. The small numbers of people who had tentatively sought Him out in the beginning turned into hundreds, and then into thousands, and of these more than two thousand three hundred seekers were initiated by Baba Ji during those years and started on their spiritual journey.

On December 29, 1903, Baba Ji passed on. Today there are records and letters written at that time which have been kept throughout the intervening years and which indicate to a small extent the magnitude of His greatness—in fact, the greatness of all Perfect Masters, for they all embody that great infinte power of Godhood. The following is an excerpt from a letter written by one who had been very close to Baba Ji:

".... For about fifteen days before His passing away such was His condition that whenever any Satsangi went to Baba Ji for Darshan (physical presence) he would become completely unconscious and have no sense of the body or surroundings. He (the person going in for Darshan) had to be carried out from Baba Ji's room by two men who could then take him to another room. He would generally come to his senses after a couple of hours, and if anyone asked him at that time what had happened, he would say, 'There is nothing except Shabd, Shabd and Shabd, and all is Shabd.' This went on continuously for fifteen days...."

And now to introduce the Great Master,* Baba Sawan Singh Ji, the one who was appointed by Baba Ji to further the teachings of the Radha Soami faith and succeed Him as Master. But to describe His infinite capacities in this world, to convey even a single iota of His greatness in a few short paragraphs, is an impossibility. Volumes could not begin to do justice to the incredible way in which He awakened nearly a quarter of a million people from irreligious slumber and transformed them to a life of spirituality; of how He boldly and bravely met tremendous forces of opposition from all sides, injecting humility into many of those who gave the loudest opposition; of how He reached out His hand to the worst of sinners, forgave them, and instilled in them a deathless longing for God; of how, out of unlimited mercy, He quietly suffered as He cleansed the souls of His children, most often without the knowledge even of those closest to Him. One

---

*Today He is lovingly remembered as, and often referred to as, the "Great Master."

could only do injustice to the Great Master in the
attempt to tell about Him.

And so, let us turn to the Great Master's own pen
for the background of his early life and discipleship.
The following paragraphs are extracts from two of His
letters, contained in the book *Spiritual Gems*.

"Although I was born in a Sikh family and at the
age of ten read the *Guru Granth Sahib* and afterwards was
intimately associated with Sikh religious preachers, yet
whenever I read *Gur Bani* (*Granth Sahib*, Sikh holy
scriptures) it struck a strange note in my heart. When
I put searching questions to preachers, etc., none could
give me a satisfactory explanation.

"Gur Mat (Sant Mat) is above all religions. For
a long time I associated with Baba Kahan. He usually
remained in an ecstatic condition, which he developed
after fourteen years of persistent and vigorous practice.
I associated with him for several months and during
that time he showed supernatural powers on several
occasions. When I asked him if he would shower
grace upon me by initiating me, he answered: 'No,
He is somebody else; I do not have your share.' I
then asked him to tell me who that person was so that
I could contact Him. He replied: 'When the time
comes, He will Himself find you......'"

As a young man, Sawan Singh joined the military
service as an engineer, but the desire for spiritual
enlightenment stayed with Him constantly. Continuing His story, He writes.

"When I was stationed at Murrie Hills and in
charge of water supply works, my house was near a
Dharamsala, a free rest house where sadhus, mahatmas,
etc. going on their way to the pilgrimage of Amarnath
in Kashmir, would often stay, and I had the opportunity

of talking to them and discussing religious and spiritual problems with them.

"One day as I was supervising my work, I saw an old Sikh going up a hill along with a middle-aged lady. When I noticed Him, I thought He had probably come in connection with some case in the Commissioner's Court. Little did I think that He was to be my Master. He was no other than Baba Ji Himself and the lady was Bibi Rukko. This I did not know at the time, but found out later that Baba Ji said to Bibi Rukko, referring to me, 'It is for his sake that we have come here.'

"To which Bibi Rukko replied, 'But he has not even greeted you.'

"Baba Ji said to her, 'What does the poor fellow know yet? On the fourth day he will come to us.'

"Baba Ji went to the Dharamsala and started Satsang from the *Granth Sahib*; Babu Sukh Dayal, my friend, came to me and told me of the novel explanations of the teachings of the *Granth Sahib*, which were given out by a Sadhu who recently arrived at the Dharamsala. I was ready to accept the Truth from anyone, and so we went together to listen to the Satsang. In three or four days my doubts were resolved and I got satisfactory explanations to the various questions which I used to take with me.

"At last I asked for Initiation, but requested that I might not be told to accept the name of 'Radha Soami' as I had never heard of it prior to this.

"Baba Ji said to me, 'Radha Soami implies the highest Spiritual Power. What objection have you to the name of Radha Soami?'

"I said, 'It does not appeal to me.'

"Then He asked, 'How many new names of the one God are mentioned in *Jap Sahib*?'"

"I replied, 'Some twelve or fourteen hundred.'

"Then Baba Ji said, 'If you do not object to those names, why do you object to the name of 'Radha Soami?' "

"Thus, my doubts being resolved, I got Initiation.

"At Murrie Hills my house faced Mauj Puri (a place of Hindu Pilgrimage). One day when Baba Ji was visiting me, I pointed in that direction and said, 'Look, Sir, what beautiful scenery.'

"Baba Ji laughed and said, 'I have seen it.' (Implying that He had seen it long ago.)

"I asked, 'Was your regiment ever posted there?'

"He replied : 'My child, you do not understand these things. We saw this place at a time when these hills and valleys had not yet been formed.'

"Baba Ji used to be very kind to me and whenever I came to visit Him, He would give me a place in His own room. Once I got down from the Beas station at twelve o'clock at noon. It was very hot and I sat down under a tree for a while. Then I felt that I had come for Baba Ji's Darshan, yet here I was seeking comfort and delaying that meeting with the Beloved. Even wordly lovers have done much better. The thought troubled me, so I started on foot from the Railway Station to the Dera.

"At the Dera Baba Ji Maharaj, who was very sensitive to heat, came out and began to pace the open courtyard before His room. Bibi Rukko remonstrated and requested Him to go inside His room, out of the hot sun, but He would not. A few minutes before I reached the Dera, He went in and then Bibi Rukko, seeing me coming, exclaimed : 'Oh, now I see why Baba Ji was walking in the hot sun.' (He had Himself absorbed some of that extreme heat so that I would not be overcome by it on the way.)

"There are so many wonderful things about Baba Ji that if I go on relating them for one hundred years, it would not be possible to finish them all.... I am sure, if the Guru wants, He can make even the stones carry out his work...."

And thus He spoke as a disciple always speaks of his Master, though this disciple was destined to become one of the greatest Saints ever to walk upon the face of the earth. In fact, at the time of his initiation by Baba Ji in 1894, Baba Ji said privately to another, "I was holding something for him as his trustee. That trust I have discharged today." And true to those words, months before His passing in 1903 Baba Ji appointed Sawan Singh to be His successor and to work in His place.

It was not long before the disciples of Baba Ji became aware of the divine nature of His successor. To those who had the eyes to see, it was joyously evident from the very beginning. And it became increasingly apparent as the years unfolded. Following His retirement from the service in 1911, Baba Sawan Singh Ji settled at the Colony to which he gave the name of Dera Baba Jaimal Singh in memory of its founder. Under His guiding hand for thirty-seven years, the Colony grew from a small collection of huts by the river bank into a large and flourishing spiritual community.

His greatness was not limited to those boundaries, however, for as the fold ever widened, He began to tour the cities and villages of the Punjab where He knew that spiritual seekers were awaiting Him. The light and force of His wisdom reached into the corners of the spiritually barren towns and villages; it could not be quelled in spite of the opposition and criticism which

at that time kept pushing itself forward.   In the beginning the people who followed Him were named "man-
worshippers," and "believers in ghosts and evil spirits."
Oh! the forces of evil that try to halt the advance of
Truth! The blankets of sleeeping darkness that cannot,
will not, allow the light to be seen when it becomes
manifest.   Yet it is an old story and one that is re-
enacted at every opportunity.   It was told in Jerusalem;
it is told today; and it was being told there in India a
few short decades ago.

But for those who paused, listened and heeded,
theirs was the highest reward, theirs the fullest joy.
Not only did the Great Master teach them that God and
His Kingdom lay within their own being, He veritably
led them to the realization of His words.   Through all
tests and trials these brave ones remained strong, and
the pure spiritual wisdom spread and grew and took root
as if by an ever-continuing miracle.   Satsang centers
and halls in the Great Master's name began to appear
in the cities of the Punjab, and almost as soon
they were erected, they were filled to overflowing.
Eventually the light of the spiritual path spread to
India's other provinces as the Great Master extended
His tours.   Such was the greatness, strength and
magnitude of this light that its call was heard throughout the world—in England, America, Africa, Switzerland, and other countries.   The multitudes streaming
through the Dera gates each year to see their beloved
Spiritual Father multiplied from hundreds to scores
upon scores of thousands; and during His forty-five
years of ministry, He initiated over one hundred
thousand people.   Books were written, distributed, and
read.   As this incredible movement continued to unfold, it seemed that suddenly the Grace of God was

released to the consciousness of His waiting and thirsty souls, and nothing could restrain or curb the force of His calling.

Yet the Great Master Himself was "as simple in manner as a little child, with no sort of pose or air about Him," as described by Dr. Johnson in a letter written at the Colony to American Satsangis. He further wrote,

"He always appeared as if he regretted being the center of an adoring crowd. His spirit of good fellowship is enchanting. You soon feel at home with him and not only that, but you soon come to feel that there is no real home except in His presence. Thus He makes you a part of His own family at once. His manner toward all of us is much like that of a mother comforting her tired children and soothing them to rest. His manifest love is His supreme quality, as it appears to me, and that is also the very essence of His gospel."

On April 2, 1948, a great cry of grief tore through the Colony and echoed throughout India, for no more would His adorable earthly form be seen in this world. As one Satsangi, who had been a devotee of the Great Master for over fifty years, said, "The happy village where only laughter and smiles had been present for a half century, became suddenly a place ridden with sorrow—it seemed lik a ghost town where only memories stalked the forsaken streets in cruel, phantom shapes."

Yet the Great Master did not leave His disciples to bemoan His passing for long. There are numerous reports of how He appeared to His devotees if they had not already been given the eye of understanding in their daily meditations. For a Master never leaves His children, even for an instant. The mere shedding of

His physical form does not alter that fundamental truth concerning the relationship between a Master and His disciples.   This, too, is part of the very essence of the Master's gospel.

As his successor, the Great Master appointed Sardar Bahadur Jagat Singh Ji, an elderly disciple who had been initiated by the Great Master as early as 1909 and who since that time had attained the heights of spiritual advancement.   His worldly life he had lived quietly and simply as a professor of chemistry at an agricultural college in the Punjab.

Sardar Bahadur had always been unusually conscientious and thorough in performing his daily work and had gained the respect and admiration of all—yet he never drew attention to himself in any way and always gave others the credit due to him.   On many occasions he had anonymously given sums of money to pay for the tuition of students who otherwise would not have been able to complete their education.   By students and staff alike, even during his days as a professor, he was known as "Guru Ji" because of the many hours he spent each day in meditation.

Today there are those at the Dera who once had been his students, and from them we hear story after story of Sardar Bahadur's generosity, his unassuming selflessness towards his students, and of his strength and firmness of character throughout the years.   The agriculturist now in charge of the vegetable gardens, Balwant Singh, at the Dera was not only a student of Sardar Bahadur, but had also had the good fortune to live with him for thirty-three years.   In giving an example of the unusual fervor which was a living part of Sardar Bahadur's everyday life, he once said, "I paid close attention to Sardar Bahadur all the time

in the beginning, and noticed that before doing anything—even taking a sip of water—he would for an
instant close his eyes.   Before he would enter a room or
rise from a chair, just for a moment he would hesitate
and his eyes would close.   It was almost imperceptible,
but when you watched closely you could see that he
performed this exercise unnoticeably to others, but
always without fail.   It was not until much later that
I asked the Professor about it.   He said that he would
remember the Master in his mind for a moment before
performing any action.   'After a while it becomes a
habit,' he told me then, 'and eventually it will greatly
assist in seeing the Master's Radiant Form within.' "

And in the Foreword of Sardar Bahadur's book,
The Science of the Soul, we read, "His faith in the Satguru
was so unshakeable that once, while in Lyallpur, he
called on Saint Lasuri Shah, a highly evolved ascetic—
with a message from Hazur Maharaj Baba Sawan
Singh Ji.   He used to carry such messages frequently
between the two mystics.   The ascetic was so pleased
with this particular message that he embraced
Sardar Bahadur Ji and offered to open up immediately
the Inner Vision.   The offer, to which anybody would
have succumbed, was politely but firmly declined with
the words that 'His own Master would do this as and
when he thought proper.' "

In 1943 Sardar Bahadur Ji retired from his years of
teaching and settled permanently at the Dera.   In the
five intervening years before he was appointed to be the
Great Master's successor, he spent nearly all his time in
deep meditation—sometimes for days at a stretch.   He
served as Master from April 1948 until His death in
October 1951, and during his three and one-half years of
ministry He initiated approximately twenty-six thousand

souls into the path of their spiritual journey homeward.

The following notes were taken one afternoon in a conversation with Pundit Lal Chand, another former student of Sardar Bahadur Ji. He too had had the good fortune to reside with the Professor for many years. "Most people thought we were real brothers," he told me that afternoon. "He was most affectionate, had a subtle sense of humor, and the most luminous, piercing eyes."

But most interesting was his account of the death of Sardar Bahadur and the appointment of the present Master. For, as a closing to these portraits of the Radha Soami Masters of Beas of past years, it gives us a glimpse of how that unbelievable humility born of true Saints is manifest even up to the time of their last breath.

"Months before His passing, Sardar Bahadur became very ill, and the Satsangis became anxious to know who would succeed Him," began Pundit Lal Chand. "But unconcerned, Sardar Bahadur would say in very clear words, 'Don't be worried about it. I will make a very good arrangement before my death.'

"As the months passed, He made repeated assurances that all would be taken care of in due time. Finally one Sunday morning, Sardar Bahadur told His doctor to instruct the Dera secretary to write out a will in favor of Charan Singh Ji of Sikanderpur, and also to send him a telegram to come immediately. Puzzled, the doctor asked me later 'Who is this Charan Singh?'

" 'He is the grandson of the Great Master," I told him.

"When Charan Singh's uncle heard about the appointment of his nephew as successor to Sardar Bahadur, he went running to Sardar Bahadur and with folded hands requested, 'Sir, we have been entrusted to your care by the Great Master.   Pray, stay on and look after us."

"Sardar Bahadur smiled at him and raised a quieting hand.   'Look here,' He said firmly, 'Whatever I am saying, I am saying on orders from above.'

"When the will was finished, Sardar Bahadur Maharaj Ji read and signed it in the presence of four of us gathered there at His bedside.   He then smiled peacefully and folded His hands.   'I am grateful to the Great Master that His things have gone back to Him,' He said quietly.

"Later that day He told us that His body should not be given any baths after His death and gave instructions that no expensive clothes should be put on Him.   'Do not keep my body for more than half an hour,' He said. 'Do not wait for anyone before cremation—neither Satsangi nor relative, and after the cremation wash all the ashes down the river immediately."

" 'Gracious Sir, your orders will be carried out,' we told him.

"Then someone said, 'Sir, take care of us and keep room for us up there.'

"Sardar Bahadur smiled broadly.   'Bravo! There is a lot of space.   You will be taken care of.'

"Then He refused to see anybody else on that day. Ordinarily the Satsangis used to come for His darshan upstairs following evening Satsang everyday, but on that day He said, 'No, I am feeling very tired now.' Even old colleagues from the college were not granted entry into the room where the Saint lay.

"At twelve midnight He asked me to sponge His body and change Him into clean clothes.   Ah, what a feeling it was to be entrusted with the care of Him in His last hours—He whom I loved so deeply.   It was only

His grace which kept me from collapsing myself. Such sweet humility was in Him!

"A few moments later He told Gandhi Ji, His attendant who was sitting at the other side of His bed, 'I am going to sleep.' He lay on his right side and wrapped the warm shawl around Himself and ordered me and Gandhi to sleep We obeyed Him, and lay down. But soon we were back at our respective places by His bedside. I was sitting by the window at His right side and Gandhi Ji at His left side. At 2:40 in the morning, when the rest of the Colony was rising to prepare for their hours of devotion, Sardar Bahadur Jagat Singh knocked on the window. At once I took His pulse in my hand, but His wrist slipped out of my fingers. Gandhi Ji immediately picked up His other hand and from His face I knew that He at last slept to waken permanently in the Supreme World.

"His body was brought down in the morning. As soon as the cremation was completed by the river bank, the present Master sprinkled water over the ashes to cool them down. The entire remains were then washed down into the river."

Again, the law was fulfilled as the torch of Mastership was passed on to another. And there lies the Truth which carries the greatest glory of all. That this is not a testimonial written of glories gone by, to be only remembered and visualized within one's heart. For the Living Master is with us now. He walks among us; He encourages our every faltering step towards the Infinite; He gives us His hand when we stumble; He gives us His eternal and never-failing love. What greater glory could there be?

CHAPTER NINE

THE PRESENT MASTER

"Ah yes," the old man's eyes twinkled as he gave an incredulous shake of the head. "The Master is the very highest. His humility is so great, so unbelievable, that He goes to the utmost extremes to conceal Himself— except on rare occasions when it cannot help but come to the surface. Once He said to me, 'Do not look upon me as God; look upon me as His servant only.' "

It was not the first time we had visited the Master's personal secretary and attendant, Dewan Daryai Lal, and listened to his unlimited collection of stories of the Masters. For he had been initiated in 1910 at the Colony, and had spent most of the intervening years in close association with the Great Master, with Master Sardar Bahadur Jagat Singh, and with the present Master, Charan Singh Ji Maharaj. Having retired from his worldly position as a district judge of the Punjab many years before, he was now a permanent resident at the Dera, and spent his time in the constant company and service of the Master. On this particular afternoon, several of us from America, Europe and South Africa were seated with him in his small office.

Daryai Lal leaned forward in his chair. As he began to speak again, his voice was lowered, almost a whisper. "Listen," he said, "Masters are not made, they are born. Some of us knew of His divine destiny when He was only a boy!"

"How?" we chorused.

"I shall tell you how it happened. We were visiting the Great Master in Dalhousie, the place where

He would spend the hot summer months. But this particular summer He had been suffering from a serious illness for weeks. It had come upon Him just after having initiated an unusually large number of seekers into His fold."

The elderly gentleman stopped speaking for a moment. He seemed to leave us as he traced the memory path back many years to light upon one of those incidents which remain in the heart for a lifetime. "My companion, Professor Jag Mohan Lal," he continued almost to himself, "stood by the Great Master's bedside and enquired of His health.

" 'I am quite *tyar bar tyar* (ready to depart),' replied the Great Master.

" 'This came like a bombshell and we were stricken with sorrow. The Professor could not restrain his tears. In a choked voice he asked, 'To whom are you leaving us, Great Lord ?'

" 'Why ? Where am I going ?' the Great Master asked.

" 'You said, Sir, you were "*tyar bar tyar*,' " the Professor echoed the Great Master's words.

" 'Yes. I am *tyar bar tyar*,' said the Great Master. It was then that we realized the Great Master was indulging in a little play upon the words *tyar bar tyar* which, in another Indian tongue, meant that He was quite fit and healthy.

"Soon after," Daryai Lal continued when our laughter had quieted down, "the Great Master recovered very speedily. Only four days later He came from His room to sit on the sunlit lawn of His house for a while. It was a lovely afternoon, and most peaceful as we sat there alone at His feet. Both the Professor and myself thought it the most opportune moment to make a request of the Master—a request which had been on our minds for days.

" 'Maharaj Ji,'' the Professor began, 'You are the Lord of earth and heaven; would you grant us a boon?'

"The Great Master appeared to be saying 'Yes, ask,' but then He suddenly restrained Himself and asked, 'What boon do you want to have?''

"We kept silent for some moments.''

" 'Well, come on, out with it,' said the Great Master, smiling.'

" 'Whatever it is, our Lord promise that you will grant it,' I said childishly.

"At this the Great Master laughed. 'I am not a prophet. How can I grant a request unless I know what it is ?'

" 'Our Lord! You are not a prophet, but prophets come from you,' I exclaimed to Him.

" 'Sir,' the Professor broke in determinedly, 'we wish that we may leave here before you go.''

" 'Yes,' the Great Master replied, chuckling. 'You can gladly leave whenever you like. I intend to stay here till the end of September.'

"An involuntary laugh escaped our lips, but we knew he had understood our real meaning. 'Not from Dalhousie, Sir, but from this earth. Please ordain that we may leave it before you go,' said I.

" 'No. You should neither desire to live nor wish to die. Leave every thing in the hands of Him who is the Lord of life and death,' the Great Master told us.

" 'We do not want to live here a single moment without you,' we implored Him. 'Life without you would be worse than death, our Beloved Lord.'

" 'I shall always be with you. That I promise,' He reassured us.

" 'All right, Maharaj Ji,' the Professor began again. 'Will you tell us in whose hands you will leave us? Who will be the Master after you?'

" 'Even that cannot be disclosed just now. Everything at its proper time.'

"Then the Great Master asked a lady who had come to sit with us a few minutes before to go and bring Him a glass of water. This, we discovered afterwards, was meant to send her away.

"The Professor waited until she had disappeared into the house and again pressed for the revelation of the name of His successor, but the Great Master refused point-blank. 'It would be too difficult to keep such a secret,' He said. 'And there are people who would begin to conspire against him even now.' The Great Master became silent and looked towards the house.

" 'Are they Satsangis Sir? Could any Satsangi conspire against the Master's command?' enquired the Professor.

" 'You will have occasion to see to what lengths an ambitious and unscrupulous person can go. But never mind that.'

" 'Then, Sir, please grant us the abundance of your love that we may not be misled and that our faith and love in the feet of the True Master may always remain permanent and fixed,' I begged Him finally.

" 'My successor will come with ten-fold powers and grace. The Satsang and the Dera have yet to make very great progress. Your love and faith shall also increase, and you will receive greater grace and regard,' said the Great Master.

"Just then the Great Master's grandson, Charan appeared at the corner of the house with a small suitcase in his hand. It seemed as if the Great Master could no longer restrain Himself. 'There he comes,' he said in a whisper, more as if speaking to Himself than to others.

"The boy came and fell at the feet of his Master, who with great love, put both His hands on his head.

" 'I understand your college closed about a fortnight ago,' the Great Master said. 'Where have you been all this time?'

" 'I went to Sirsa* Sir, for a few days,' replied Charan.

" 'How was everybody there?'

" 'Perfectly fine, Sir.'

" 'Well, you must be tired. Go and take some rest now. Where would you like to stay? With me or with the Professor. I know you would like to stay with the Professor.', Then the Great Master ordered the servants to take his luggage to the cottage in which we were staying.

"When he was gone, there were tears in the Professor's eyes. 'Lord,' he said, 'I am grateful for the grant of this knowledge about your successor. This has reassured us very much. He who is to take over from you is so young in years that we hope to be blessed for many years yet to come with your presence and grace,' he said.

" 'Oh! do not depend on that. Wait and see,' the Great Master told him with a smile and quietly went into His room.

"Well," continued Daryai Lal, "that day dear Charan came to reside with us in the cottage. Barely eighteen or nineteen years of age, he was a fine, quiet, handsome young man, and was loved by everyone from his earliest childhood for his sweet nature and pleasant

*Sirsa is the site of acres of farms which the Great Master built up as the home for His family.

manners. But now, in the light of what had been revealed to us, how could we help showing him our special respect, though, of course, we could never say a word about the secret we had just learned.

"The divine boy's sweetness conquered us completely. We were simply overwhelmed by his love and affection. In fact, he became an ideal for us. Even at that early age he would give regular time to meditation both morning and evening. This put us to shame and made us sit in meditation more regularly. Charan prepared our beds, served us tea, read to us from the *Sar Bachan* and other scriptures—in fact, he would not allow us to do anything for ourselves at all.

"Here was a conundrum," Daryai Lal laughed, remembering. "How to solve it? To be served by a future Master? But why future? Masters are always Masters. They are *born* Masters and not made or trained to be so. They simply hide their greatness under a cloak.

"But there are those very rare times when inevitably and involuntarily something happens which proclaims their hidden greatness. Here I am tempted to relate a personal experience of mine with the present Master when he was a small child of five or six years. He was a beautiful child as I have already said. In fact, all of the great Masters are so, for nature always gives the best of material that it possesses for the body of a Saint. It was most satisfying to do anything to please this child, but at that early date I did not know of his exalted destiny, though he gave signs of becoming a very great man. We treated him then only as a small child of the Master's house.

"In those days I was a government officer, and was always furnished with a more than ample supply of pens, pencils, and other similar articles. Whenever I visited the Dera, I would often bring Charan and his brothers and sisters a number of these colorful pen-holders and pencils, small pocket books, and crystal paper-weights with figures of flowers and animals in them. Once I brought a big, six-cornered pencil which was green in color. It was quite a new thing in stationery and had been issued to the officers for the first time since green had become the officers' color. When I presented it to Charan, he announced that he had no pen-knife, and how could he sharpen it without one? I quickly promised to bring one for him the following Sunday.

" 'You will never bring it,' he said.

" 'No, my duckling,' said I. 'You will surely have a beautiful knife with two blades the next time I come.'

"The boy shook his head. 'It is all over. You will never bring us any more gifts,' he asserted.

"This remark of the child did not please my haughty officer's nature, for in those days my word was never controverted by anyone, either in the office or at home. So, the next Saturday I collected two pocket knives, two crystal paper-weights, and two pocket books with small pencils in them and asked my servant to pack them in the suitcase which I was to take with me to the Dera.

"When I arrived the next morning at the Colony, I found the children playing in front of the house where I usually stayed. I beckoned them to me with a wave of the hand, and they all came running—all, that is, except Charan. You cannot imagine my surprise and disappointment when on opening my suitcase I discovered that there were no presents in it! I could not understand where they had gone and was greatly

puzzled and bewildered. Harnam Singh was surely
my most trusted servant, and in fact he had placed the
articles in the bag in my very presence. How could
they have been spirited away?

"On my next visit I myself placed two pen-knives
in my coat pocket—but in vain. For upon reaching
the Dera, I could not find them. I was utterly dismayed.
And again, on the occasion of Christmas one year, I had
purchased some fine toys for the children. This time
I left the box which contained the toys in the compartment of the train in which I had traveled!

"In short, since the very day on which Charan
spoke to me about it, I was not able to bring a single
present to the children—try as I might. It puzzled me
then, but now it is quite clear. For Charan had the
vak siddhi even as early as that. This siddhi (supernatural power)—that whatever escapes one's lips comes
out to be true—is the last of the siddhis which the yogis
achieve after spending ages in yogic practices. What to
say of one who had this power in his childhood!

"It was always true that nobody was allowed to
give presents to the children or to any member of the
great Master's family. They refused point-blank to
accept a single token from anybody. In this way,
perhaps, I was politely asked to stop transgressing this
general rule about which the Masters have always been
very strict.*

"Some years later he again revealed himself to me,"
Daryai Lal continued without a pause. "It was evening

*Today, as it was then, this rule is still in effect. The Master
asks that visitors refrain from bringing gifts of any kind to the Dera;
in fact, no money is acceted at all from those of us who stay at the
Dera from foreign lands—even if the visit lasts for months or years.

time, and I was spreading the carpets on the open ground in front of the library for Satsang. Just then Charan appeared and quickly ran past me. Over his shoulder he called out, 'Hold the Satsang inside!' I tried to catch hold of him, but he slipped away. After half an hour the Great Master came. No sooner had He started His discourse when a fierce storm, with howling, screaming winds accompanied by rain, suddenly burst out with such severity that it was impossible to remove the carpets before they became thoroughly soaked. Yet the sky had been quite clear and the sun had been shining brilliantly the whole day. Just one hour before, one would never have dreamed that there would be a downpour. When the Great Master saw the onrushing clouds, He repeated the words of His grandson, 'Hold the Satsang inside.' "

Daryai Lal then leaned back in his chair and adjusted his glasses. We thought that he would speak no more that afternoon and we were about to leave. But he didn't even notice; his thoughts were still years away.

"Now I would like to mention to you another incident that will show you how meek, humble-minded and full of the spirit of self-abasement this great child was. You seldom find such unprecedented humility and utter freedom from pride and vanity—even in much older and highly developed souls. Most often a man is humble from his sense of imperfection and is modest inasmuch as he puts little value on his qualifications and acquirements. But this divine child's perfections led him to keep his superior excellence under cover. He took his greatness so lightly and succeeded in concealing it so completely that it baffled even the most shrewd and sharp-eyed intelligence.

"I was present on his *Nam Karn Sanskar* (the name-giving ceremony of a child). When he was a few months old his father brought him, clothed in red silk, to the Great Master. In his father's arms he looked like a cherub—only the physical wings were missing. As soon as the Great Master looked towards him, the baby began to smile. And such a bewitching smile it was that the Great Master took him in His lap, though He had never done this before to any child. A triumphant flush made the baby's beautiful face still more beautiful. He clasped the Great Master in an embrace. When the baby let go at last, the Great Master looked into his big shining eyes and said, 'Now tell us, by what name do you want to be called?'

"The babe smiled still more seraphically. His smile was contagious and all the assembly burst out in happy laughter.

" 'All right. We will name you Harcharan,' the Great Master said, smiling at the baby.

"Harcharan means 'God's Feet', and we called him by that name for years afterwards. When he joined the primary school, his name was entered as 'Harcharan' in its registers. But when left to his own discretion upon entering high school, he removed the 'Har' from his name and kept only 'Charan.' From 'Lord's Feet' he changed it to 'Feet of Everybody,' and this is how he signs his name today. There is a saying in Persian that 'everyone is prone to call himself the son of a sultan,' but here was a royal child calling himself 'the servant of all.'

"Yes, truly it is said that the child is the father of the man," Daryai Lal said, smiling at us. He seemed to be really looking at us for the first time since he had begun to speak.

Just then we heard the high tone of the Dera siren announcing the evening meditation hour. It came as a complete surprise, for none of us had been aware that an entire afternoon had passed. It was with reluctance that we exchanged "Radha Soami" good-byes with our friend and left for the Guest House. Already evening had darkened the village streets, and the first bright stars looked down upon us as they began their nightly march across. the sky.

There were many others with whom I spoke who also had experiences to relate about the present Master. They too, like Daryai Lal, had watched him grow up and become a respected and highly-esteemed man under the constant love and attention of his grandfather, the Great Master. Repeatedly one hears them say such things as "He was different from the other children. He seemed to be more quiet, more thoughtful, and more serious. There was always something distinctive about him."

Of his life and activities at the Dera where he spent his boyhood and youth, one would at first thought imagine that he had very special and important duties. But that was not the case. He participated whole-heartedly with the other Satsangis in the various jobs which needed to be done at the Colony, never setting himself apart from the others. "So well he concealed himself," one disciple remarked incredulously, "that it never entered our heads that here was the future Master working by our side. His tasks ranged any-where from carrying bricks with us, to guarding the shoes of Satsangis while they attended the daily Satsangs."

"For the Great Master himself," an elderly Satsangi recalled. "Maharaj Ji used to do what appeared to be

small things.   He took great pleasure in these tasks, for
it is an honor to be in the service of a Master.   When
he was a little child he would bring the Great Master
His slippers or a change of shoes.   In the summer, when
the Great Master would give a discourse at Satsang,
the present Master would stand in back of Him and fan
Him.   In fact, the Great Master would not allow anyone
else to do this job.   One day, the Satsangi went on,
"I took the large, heavy fan in my own hands to try to
do the job myself.   But the Great Master motioned for
me to give it to Charan, saying, 'You will leave it to
him.   It is his privilege.' "

And by a disciple who had gone to school with the
Master and had been a close personal friend in his early
days, I was told, "Of those days I cannot say anything,
for it would only give me a false notion of my own
importance.   It brings to mind the old story of the
prince and his playmate.   Supposing I were a playmate
of a king's son.   Then I would be just a friend to him.
But when the prince becomes king, I then take an oath
of loyalty to him—I become his subject and his servant.
So, too, with our beloved Maharaj Ji."

"Master Sardar Bahadur always praised Charan
very highly as the years passed," said Pundit Lal Chand.
"He would often say to me, 'Charan Singh is *Shah-en-Shah* (King of kings).   He is so good and generous
towards all that he will not take his meals unless all the
sevadars* have eaten first in his presence at the farm in
Sirsa.   The sevadars would actually run from the Dera
to Sirsa to do seva because of Charan's generous hospitality and love for them all.' "

And there were so many more with whom I spoke,
each having a store of fascinating, personal observations
_____
*Those who regularly give service as volunteers.

to make about their treasured experiences with the present Master from His earliest childhood to the present day. In fact, the narration of these incidents of His life could be stretched into a book, or even many books. But at best, these observations would serve only to hint at the external characteristics and attributes of the Master—attributes which are only outer aspects of the Infinite and Eternal Glory which is within Him. And, true to the nature of any Saint or Perfect Master past or present, He does not allow those incidents, which would be most convincing of His divinity to the seeker, to be printed, or even told.

The accounts of His life which now appear in various Radha Soami books cover no more than a few short lines. They tell us that He was born on the 12th of December in 1916, in the small village of Moga; that He is a law graduate, and that "the mantle has fallen on worthy shoulders. Dignity, humility, earnestness and devotion are most harmoniously blended in His expression and demeanor."

When I asked Daryai Lal if he could supply some specific details and dates for the writing of a more inclusive, factual biography, he told me that "the life or biography of a true Saint does not consist of a record of the time and place of His birth, or where He went to school, or the names and genealogy of His parents. What difference would it make," he asked me pointblank, "if the date of His birth, instead of being the 12th of December, 1916, was the 21st of December, 1961; or if His birthplace were Sirsa or some other village rather than Moga. Extensive biographical details of His life are unnecessary; everyone has a history of this kind. As a matter of fact," he added, "the Master would never even permit such a biography to be

written.   One should look to His work in freeing souls
from the bondage of mind and matter and in bringing
them to liberation in the Life and Light of the Eternal."

It was in October of 1951 that He officially under-
took His work as Master.   Since that time, the Dera has
expanded very greatly with Him at the helm of its
affairs.   The entire face and structure of the Colony
has been changed.   The hospital, the library, the water
supply system, new Guest Houses, the electricity,
the plumbing, scores of new cottages and buildings—
all have sprung up from the labors of love of the multitudes who come to His feet.   Not a single portion of it
could have been done without His love and guidance.
He is the axis around which all activity at the Colony
revolves.   His slightest word becomes law, for all His
disciples know that He speaks from Perfect Knowledge
brought down from higher worlds.

Day after day, from the earliest hours of the morning
until late in the night, the Master works unceasingly
and with unstinted love for His disciples.   Very often
are the times when He gives His physical body no rest so
that He may tend to the smallest needs of others.
Constantly in the Master's vision are the hearts
and needs of His devotees—as if before Him were a
giant screen upon which the activities of hundreds of
thousands can be seen at once.

But perhaps the most effective way to describe His
characteristics is to turn from the individual to the
universal. The following are the apparent and objective
signs of Mastership, as adapted from a list given by Dr.
Johnson in *The Path of the Masters,* which are exempli-
fied daily by our beloved living Master.

"1.   First and most noticeable of them all is the
outstanding fact that real Masters never charge for their

services, nor do they accept pay in any form, or any kind of material benefits for their instructions. This is a universal law among real Masters of the Word.... Masters are always self-sustaining. They are never supported by their disciples, by 'love offerings,' or by charity.

"2. True Masters never boast of their mastership, or of their spiritual powers or attainments. If any man claims to have attained the highest in spiritual development, that claim of itself may be taken as conclusive proof that he has not attained so much. True Masters never make such claims, and always show the utmost humility; but they never make their humility obtrusive. They never do anything to advertise their humility or to exhibit it to the public gaze.

"3. True Masters never complain of their treatment at the hands of others. Even if you abuse a true Master, he will not reply angrily, nor will he speak of it afterwards. They never speak of their difficulties, or of the ingratitude of their beneficiaries.

"4. Masters never find fault or blame others, either to their faces or behind their backs, no matter what the provocation. They speak no ill, and they never lecture others concerning their shortcomings. They exalt the positive virtues, keeping silent about evil, except to answer questions or give necessary warnings.

"5. The great Masters never punish anybody, even their worst enemies or those who may have mistreated them.... The Masters' lives are governed *entirely* by the law of love. They give freely of their light and love, even as the sun gives of its light and heat, asking nothing in return.

"6. The Masters are never given to ascetic practices

or unreasonable austerities. This is one quality that differentiates them from many types of yogis. The Masters insist that everyone should give attention to the health of his body, as well as his mind and soul. They always teach that it is a duty to keep the body clean, healthy and well-nourished.

"7.   Masters never go about begging their living. They are always self-supporting. The Master is always the great giver, never a beggar. Neither does he permit his disciples to beg their living, while they sit around in idleness.

"8.   A real Master never performs miracles for public exhibition. He may do them for disciples on special occasions and for particular reasons. But in the case of a living Master, they are kept a secret from the public.

"9.   All great Masters teach and practice the Word of God, the Audible Life Stream or Sound Current. If a man preaches and practices the Life Current, it is presumptive evidence that he is a true Master, although it is not conclusive. That is the central theme of all their discourses, the very core of their meditations. As this Current is the life of the world itself, so it is the life of every True Master throughout all of his daily actions."

But, again, the greatest work of the Master in "bringing souls to liberation in the life and light of the Eternal" lies not in the realm of the physical. The limitless extent of His greatness cannot be evaluated by the limited human intelligence which sees only the human form. It is not possible to confine a true picture of the Infinite Master within the narrow frame of human understanding. One must rise within on the spiritual Path to the realms of higher consciousness before he can begin to comprehend the magnitude of the Master's divinity and before he can say with certain knowledge, "God and the Master are one."

Yet it is the earthly form of the Master to whom we look for guidance and understanding in this world, and it is through His earthly form that we see the presence of the Most High among us. As Joseph Leeming so aptly puts it in his book, *Yoga and the Bible*:

"In the Master resides the great power of God, and through the Master human beings can reach and contact that power. The omnipotent power lives in the Master's body, using it as a vehicle for its manifestations, and thus becomes accessible to mankind."

In conclusion, let us reach back through the annals of time to scores of centuries ago, and light upon an incident in the life of Sukh Dev, a Saint of ancient India. After his initiation his father asked him.

"Tell me about your Master, son. How do you like him?"

Sukh Dev could not answer.

Then his father asked him, "Is he like the sun ?"

"Yes, he has the brilliancy of the sun, but not its heat."

"Is he like the moon ?"

"Yes, he has the coolness and clearness of the moon, but without its shadows."

"With whom would you compare him then ?" his father asked finally.

Sukh Dev was silent for a moment. Then he said, "The Master is like himself." And he could not go beyond.

CHAPTER TEN

SATSANG
IN THE ROSE GARDEN

"Mahraj Ji is back! Maharaj Ji is back!" the young voice of a servant boy rang out exultantly as the sound of footsteps could be heard pounding across the terrace and up the stairs. When he reached my door, his face had that very special look which could only mean that the Master had returned from his November tour. Such an expression of joy! It was as if the Master had been gone for years rather than weeks.

Then sun that morning had risen on a Dera that was far happier than it had been for weeks; birds seemed to sing their songs again, and the air carried a forgotten sweetness. All day the people had been streaming through the Dera gates once again, their faces radiant, their eyes shining. An atmosphere of expectancy was all around; there were ready smiles, and happy "Radha Soamis" everywhere. And now the moment had arrived. The beloved Father had come at last to put life back into our days.

In what seemed an instant those of us from the Guest House were there in His compound. With folded hands we said "Radha Soami" to Him, and an unbelievable feeling of happiness filled each of us. Never did I dream it would be this way. That one could miss Him so much, and experience such happiness at the sight of Him once more. It was almost as if I was once again meeting Him for the first time. To look into those gentle, deeply penetrating eyes is an experience the joy of which cannot be known by memory. And contrary to worldly pleasures, this joy increases and grows into dimensions undreamed of, each time this experience is repeated.

And the days which followed passed as wondrously as those first days at the Dera. The newness and strangeness had gone, but the accompanying happiness kept on growing with each day.

Due to the fact that the number of foreign guests had grown from three to nine persons, the short garden visits with the Master following the morning Satsang became the "English Satsang" hour, and one of our favorite times of the day. As a rule, Khanna Sahib would first read the English translation of the Master's Satsang of the day preceding, and the following are highlights from one of those translations:

"The soul is a drop of that boundless Ocean, the All-Inclusive Soul which we call Param Atma or God. It became separated from its Origin, however, and became entangled with mind and matter. This put the soul in physical chains and made it subject to birth and death. But there is still a constant and inherent desire in all human beings to seek deliverence from this bondage. It is pain and suffering which make us actually aware of our mental and physical subjection. Consequently, it becomes the aim of all of us to obtain eternal liberation from the cycle of birth and death. Therefore, we all instinctively seek union with God and the way back to our Original Home of everlasting peace and bliss.

"The question arises, what is God? The Saints tell us that He is One and the same for all nations, countries and communities. He is the Creator of all and He has no caste, creed, form or color. The next question, is, how can we realize Him? Since He has no physical form, He evidently cannot be found in forests or deserts, on the tops of mountains or in the depths of the seas. The only place where He can be found is within our own selves. If there is any laboratory worthy of our research, it is our own body.* Whoever has found God has done so within himself. If there is any church or temple in which God is realized, it is none other than the human body.

"We are faced with the problem that if God is within us, why do we not see Him? Saints say that He is within us, but we need a Teacher to guide us and show us the way. The Teacher alone has the key, and He alone can disclose the secret. This secret is the practice of Surat-Shabd Yoga, the method of uniting the soul with the Audible Life Stream, for the Lord manifests Himself within us in the form of Shabd, Nam, or Word. He is Omnipresent and is, therefore, never separated from us; but we can realize or be conscious of this only through the grace of the Master, who connects us with the Word.

"The next question to be answered is, what is Shabd, Nam, or the Word? At the outset it may be mentioned that Nam or the Word is of two kinds : Varnatmak and Dhunyatmak. Varnatmak Nam is one which can be read, written and spoken. It is within the bounds of speech. On the other hand, Dhunyatmak Nam cannot be reduced to writing or speech, nor can it be heard with the physical ears. Hazur Maharaj Ji (the Great Master) used to say, 'It is the Unwritten Law and the Unspoken Language.'

---

*In most instances, the Master used the first person plural pronouns in the singular collective sense when speaking to us. It helped keep us aware that we as individuals are one in our essence. This translation, for the most part, conforms to this usage.

"Names given to Him by man, such as 'God,' 'Allah,' 'Radha Soami' and the like, are all Varnatmak and are subject to the limitations of time. The history of all these names can be traced. Many such names have been forgotten and many new ones have taken their place. Many more Saints will arrive in the future and will remember the same One Lord with different names. However, Dhunyatmak Nam is transcendental in character. It is beyond the senses and beyond time and space. This Nam is the Creator of the universe and everything that exists. All creatures, as well as the land, the water, the sun and all the heavenly bodies owe their existence to its Power. Our spoken or written word is only the means, while the unspoken and unwritten Word is the end and object. Names are important till we reach the named One. This Dhunyatmak Nam can be realized through no others save the Saints.

"It is only at the Varnatmak level that we have disputes and dissensions of castes and creeds. These all vanish when we catch or contact the Dhunyatmak Nam, for with its realization is born also the realization of the Fatherhood of God and the brotherhood of man. What does it matter whether that Supreme One is called God, Allah, Parmatma, Osiris, Jehovah, or by any other name? It is the fact that matters, not the form in which the fact is stated. The path is one for all—the means to reach the goal must vary with the pilgrim.

"When once we have the key to this Dhunyatmak Nam, we can trace a uniformity of teaching running like a thread of gold through all religions, ritualism and symbolism. We can discern unity and harmony underneath the diversity of sects and religions.

"It may be emphasized that what is contained in the religious books and Holy Scriptures is not the Nam or Word Itself, but merely a description of it. Nevertheless, these books serve a useful purpose because they instil in us a desire to find the Nam and thus induce us to tread the Path. What we must not forget is that the real Nam is not in these scriptures or in any other writings. Just as the medical books contain the prescriptions but not the medicines; just as the account books contain the accounts but not the cash; even so, the scriptures contain the description but not *the thing*. A prescription, however effective in itself, cannot provide a cure unless we procure it and take it in the right doses. Similarly, the appetite of a hungry man will not be satisfied by reading recipes in a cook book. It is only by eating the food that his hunger is appeased. So also the writings of the Saints simply point out the Way, and unless we actually *tread* the Path we shall never reach our Goal. Cities, rivers and hills are marked on a map. But to locate them on a map is not the same as actually seeing them.

"In this age of Kal Yug the Iron Age, when the life span is shorter and temptations are greater, the method of Surat-Shabd Yoga is the surest and the shortest way by which we, the imperfect, suffering and ephemeral, may become changed into the likeness of the Supreme One, who is above all and through all and in all. As to the practice of Surat-Shabd Yoga, it would be well to quote Guru Nanak:

'Close your sense organs to enable the mind to concentrate without distractions. When concentration is achieved, that is, when the mind does not wander but becomes motionless, then it starts moving toward the Tenth Door, above the eyes. There the Divine Shabd resounds day and night.'

"Once we have contacted the Immanent Power, further study seems barren and useless. The holy books, which were once opened with the eager interest and expectancy as guides to the Reality, as revelations of the purpose of existence, seem a string of empty words. Philosophical and theological speculations seem mere churning of water, which can be kept up indefinitely without any useful results. Words and concepts themselves begin to seem mere sounds and empty symbols.

"Before beginning to build a house, workmen first erect a scaffolding. They stand on this and build the house. When the construction is over, the scaffolding is unnecessary and is taken away. The means are important so long as the end is not achieved. Once the destination is reached, the guide books and maps become superfluous.

"The most delicious Nectar is constantly descending from above within us; but we are engrossed in sensual pleasures through the five gross and five subtle senses, and so remain deprived of this heavenly Nectar. Unless we concentrate our full attention at the point where this Nectar is flowing, we cannot enjoy the bliss of Nam. If a cup is placed upside down, one can never expect it to be filled with water, no matter how much rain falls over it; but if it is placed right side up, then the first or the second rain will fill it. Likewise, so long as the cup of our mind remains extroverted, it cannot be cleaned nor filled.

"When we turn an earthen lamp upside down, we can neither pour oil into it, place a wick in it, nor enjoy any light from it. Similarly, so long as the mind and the senses are extrovert, they can never experience the bliss of the Lotus Feet of the Lord. The first touchstone or test of spirituality is that no desire for sense pleasure remains alive. If even remotely there appears the seed of such pleasure, it should be completely uprooted and destroyed. The tiniest ripple of such cravings can destroy the calm of the sea of meditation and take the devotee farther from his path. Since Nam is the only elixir that can wean the mind away from them, it should be our endeavor to strive for the treasure of Nam.

"Nam or the Word is the key to the mystery of life, the mystery of all planes of existence. There is nothing that cannot be accomplished, there is nothing that cannot be known, by the power of the Word. Therefore, it is the central theme in the Path of the Saints and is absolutely indispensable in God-realization.

"When we go to a temple to worship God, we take with us flowers, sweets or some other donation as an offering. Saints say that all these wordly things are perishable and not worth offering to the Lord. If there is one offering by which we can gain His favor, it is that of our "self" to Him. The way to do this is to resign ourselves to His will. In whatever condition of life He keeps us, we should feel contented and do our best under the circumstances, always keeping in mind that we are to work for the Treasure of Nam. If it is His will to keep us in poverty, there should be no complaint. And if it pleases Him to bestow on us power and wealth, it should not deter us from the Path of Nam. Contentment or complete resignation to His will means that we have to bear karmas, the fruits of our own past thoughts and actions—good and bad—gracefully and cheerfully.

'Happy is he who gladly accepts what is ordained by God. Unhappy is he who craves to get happiness at his own sweet will.'

"If we can learn to be indifferent to pleasure and pain, so that they do not take us away from our path, it would not only lessen the weight of our karmas, but they would also be paid off in much less time.

"If you can take what comes to you through Him, then whatever it is, it becomes divine in itself; shame becomes honor, bitterness becomes sweet, and gross darkness clear light. Everything takes its flavor from God and turns divine; everything that happens reveals God. When a man's mind works that way, things all have this one taste, and therefore God is the same to this man, alike in life's bitterest moments and its sweetest pleasures. He realizes that human joy is little better than pain in disguise, and therefore seeks joys that are not conditioned, that are certain, and that do not fade.

"If you wish to detach the mind from wordly pleasures, you have to attach it to something superior. That 'something' is the Divine Shabd, Word or the Audible Life Stream. When the mind comes within its orbit, it turns its back on worldly pleasures for all time. The true Saints keep their minds in constant touch with Shabd whether sitting, standing or walking, they are completely absorbed in Shabd. Such Saints urge us to do the same and thus lift ourselves up. They teach us to live in this world but 'be not of it'; like a duck that lives in the water but never gets wet. Of course, we have to perform our duties, irrespective of result and without being attached to persons or things. We do everything sincerely to the best of our ability, and leave the results in His hands.

"The next question that arises is: What is our relationship with God, and why should we love Him and worship Him? What are the obstacles in our way and how are they to be removed? What is Shabd, where is it, and how are we to connect our consciousness with this

Shabd, Nam or Word ?

"Man is an individual with two aspects, just like one piece with two ends.   If you look at the ends, it is two; if you look at the rope, it is one.   One end of the rope is limited, the other end of the rope is unlimited. One end is man, the other is God.   Man forgets that end and knows only the end of which he is conscious; and it is the consciousness of limitation which makes him more limited.   Otherwise, he would have far greater means of approaching the unlimited which is within himself—which is only the other end of the same rope, the rope which he calls or which he considers to be himself.

"No recital is better than the Name of God on our tongues; no austerity is greater than the offering of ourselves to His will; no worship is higher than our carrying the Radiant Form of the Master with us; no path is superior to that of listening to the Shabd Dhun; and no renunciation is better than turning away from the world and its objects after drinking the Divine Nectar of Nam. In this age of Kal Yug, listening to the Shabd Dhun, is the most rewarding.   This Audible Life Stream is the sweetest, softest, and purest, and is always resounding within us.   It comes straight from the Highest Deity, the True Lord.   It is the heritage of all mankind.   It is present in sinners and Saints alike, save that the former are unaware of it.   Even when we are asleep at night the Audible Life Stream does not stop.   So why not become conscious of it and enjoy it, and go to our Heavenly Father, to whom it will lead us?

"Has not Socrates said, 'Know thyself'? Self-realization is essential before God-realization. So long as we do not know ourselves, we cannot know Him.

Our soul is covered with the wrappings of lust, anger, greed, attachment and pride or egotism; and so long as they are not removed, it cannot know its true nature and its kinship to God.   Just as a lamp gives no light when covered with a number of black cloths, so also the radiance of the soul remains hidden so long as its wrappings remain.   We can get rid of these coverings by listening to the Shabd.

"When, gradually, the light of the soul becomes visible and it begins to see itself, it is only then that it is aware of its identity with the Lord. So it is by Simran (initial practice of meditation given by the Master) that we are connected to Shabd Dhun which, in turn, leads us to self-realization and God-realization.

"We have to find Him within us and not outside. If we are to knock at the doors of any church or temple, we should knock on our own door within.   That door is the Gateway to Sach Khand* and is located in the Eye Center.   If we concentrate the attention there with faith, love and devotion, as instructed, by the Master, we transcend the cycle of births and deaths and attain God-realization."

---

*Literally "True Home". The stage from which the soul originally descended.

CHAPTER ELLEVEN

THE MASTER SPEAKS

A general discussion period with the Master would follow the reading of the Satsang. During these discussions, we were encouraged to ask Him any questions we wished, to bring up points of doubt or uncertainty that might trouble us, or to just sit quietly and absorb the peace one feels in His presence.

For many of these talks, I would bring along my shorthand notebook and record the conversations verbatim. The talks reproduced in this book are largely the resulting transcriptions from these notes. In a few instances, in order to contribute to the understanding of a subject, I have borrowed lines from the many other discussions held with the Master both in India and during His world tour in 1964. I have also tried to include the Master's replies to those questions which have repeatedly been asked of Him in such discussions— questions which apparently arise in the minds of a great number of seekers and disciples on the Pathway to God-realization. It is hoped the reader will keep in mind that the truth of the Master's words on these questions does not vary no matter where or when He speaks them.

Though there is a wealth of spiritual wisdom contained within these talks, they are not related here for the purpose of covering the entire scope of the Radha Soami Path, nor do they begin to present all the topics which we discussed with Him during those months. Rather their object is to present the Living Master to the reader through His own spoken words, as they represent His endless patience, His deep-rooted humility, and His keen sense of humor. He never "preached" or gravely lectured to us, but always spoke in an easy, conversational manner, keeping a general feeling of "rapport" throughout the group.

The first discussion selected for this book occurred on a morning in late November. The busy few days which had followed the Master's return from the November tour now had ended, and He was able to give more time to the small group of foreigners during the daily English Satsang hour.

The sun's rays were generously warm when we gathered on the patio in the Master's rose garden that morning. And as if by prearrangement, they cast our shadows behind us as we sat facing the Master. After Khanna Sahib had finished reading the translation of the Satsang Maharaj Ji had delivered the day before, there was an expectant moment of silence. It seemed that every one of us had harbored a question or two, saved only for this moment, yet no one wanted to initiate the discussion.

It was Maharaj Ji Himself who spoke first, saying, "Please don't feel shy to ask me any questions." He smiled. "I'm quite used to these press conferences."

At this a ripple of easy laughter passed through the little group, in the midst of which an Indian doctor, who had known the Master for many years but who was just beginning to study Sant Mat seriously, sat forward in his chair and addressed the Master. "Maharaj Ji, why do we in this world want salvation?" he asked. "Why do we want to go back to the Lord?"

Maharaj Ji listened attentively to the doctor's question. Then he began, "If we could find true and everlasting happiness in the pleasures of the world, we

would never even think about the Lord.   But we know
we cannot find that happiness here.   We look to the
richest man in the world, to the healthiest man in the
world, to the politicians who command the whole world
—are they happy? Perhaps they are more miserable
than we are.   Since we cannot find peace while being
in this body, then why do we want to cling to this body?
Why do we want to remain here only to suffer from the
pleasures we run after?   Being tied to this world, we are
separated from Him—and this separation is the root of
all our misery.   Naturally we cannot find peace by
running more into the world.

"Often Saints tell us that our soul is a bride, the
Lord is the bridegroom," He went on.   "A devoted
wife can find peace and happiness only when she is in
the company of her husband.   If she is separated from
him, she will be miserable.   No matter what treasures
of the world may be given her, she will have no peace
in her unless she goes back to her husband.   Similarly,
by means of this parable, Saints point out that unless the
soul returns to the Lord, it can never attain peace.

The Master paused for a moment, then added, "But
our desire for the Lord should be based on *love*, not
fear.   We want to go back to Him not merely to escape
from the world, but because we *love* Him, we want to
meet Him, we want to merge back into Him."

The young doctor nodded his head.   "But here in
this world there are so many religions and paths which
lead to Him that one who seeks Him becomes confused,"
he commented.

"When we seek the Lord within, there is only one
Path which leads to Him," the Master pointed out
deliberately.   "You see, it is very simple logic.   If the
Lord is one and dwells within this human body, then we

must seek Him there within us. And since our human structure is the same for all, it is not even conceivable to think that for a Christian there can be a different Path to God-realization than for a Hindu or a Sikh or a Muslim. There may be differences in our interpretation; there may be differences in our understanding— but there cannot be two Paths leading to the Lord. When we seek Him within, we will find one Path— the Path which was, which is, which will remain. It is as old as we humans are; it is the Pathway of the Sound and of the Light. But when we try to search for Him in the churches and mosques and temples, in organizations and groups, there may be one hundred thousand different paths for us.

"It is just for mental satisfaction that we say, 'I have become a Christian,' or 'I have become a Sikh.' These are just ways of living in the world—we are what we are. It hardly makes any difference what dress we wear, or whether we convert to one religion or to another. Our body is the same, and it is not within our power to change it. These outward religions are just coverings, regardless of what label we may give them —Christian or Muslim or Sikh or any faith. As long as we are doing the real meditation—searching for Him within—these coverings make absolutely no difference."

The Master paused again, allowing us to absorb this concept. Then He went on, "And every Saint, no matter from what country or age or clime, who has travelled on the Path to God-realization has this same message to give us. No Saint comes into this world to establish a different Path of meditation, to lay the foundations of a new religion, to set one nation against another, to set one religion against another. They just come to give us the real mystic teachings, and to show us the Way and the Truth which is one. If, with an unbiased mind, we try to make a research in the teachings of those Saints, we will definitely come to the conclusion that the spirituality at the base of every religion is the same. With the advance of time, that spirituality is lost—what is left with us is nothing but shells, rituals and ceremonies, nothing but organizations. The essence is lost; Truth is lost. We become the slave of those organizations. We are even exploited, many times, for selfish reasons. But if we go to the depths of any religion with an unbiased mind, we will find the same spirituality contained in the teachings of its scriptures— whether it be the Bible, or the Quran, or the Granth Sahib, or any other scripture. Religions are man-made; Saints only tell us about the Path which leads us to the Lord. And if we follow that Path, every religion is ours."

Maharaj Ji looked at His hands folded in His lap. Then He looked up and said, "Saints don't bind themselves to any particular religion. They only believe in the religion of love which comes from within. Their concern is the real love and devotion of the Lord in our heart, our sincerity and earnestness in our desire to meet the Lord. They are open to everybody, always."

"Is it necessary to have a Master in order to travel on that Path?" the doctor's face still seemed puzzled.

"Yes," Maharaj Ji told him, nodding His head. "For since we cannot see nor comprehend the formless God while in this human-consciousness, and since we want to reach that stage of consciousness where we can meet Him and merge into Him, we search for His men —God-men. They are God-realized souls and are in constant tune with Him. It is through our association with them that we automatically come in touch with the

Lord. Mystics often explain the relationship of Saints to the Lord as that of a wave to the ocean. A wave arises from the ocean, and again blends itself back into the ocean. If one were to throw an object into the wave, the wave would carry it into the ocean's depths. Similarly, if we merge back into the Saints by practicing the method of meditation they teach us, they will carry us back to the Ocean of God. Our real Master is not the body, but the Shabd, the Word, the Light that is within every one of us. Christ said, 'No man cometh unto the Father, but by me.* I am in the Father, and the Father in me.'† So when we become Him—the Saint who has already become the Father—we become the Father. Through that channel we transcend the domain of mind and maya (illusion). Only real love and devotion for the Lord through the Saints can take us back to Him."

"Maharaj Ji, of what value to us are the ascended Masters, such as Christ?" asked an American seeker, Mr. Thomas§ who had recently arrived at the Colony.

The Master turned to him and smiled. "I am nobody to comment, but speaking from my limited knowledge of the Bible, I find Christ's teachings to be exactly the same as those of the Eastern Masters. So I give Him the same status as other Masters."

"Then the Christ does describe the inward path— the path of the Shabd," another in the group spoke up.

The Master nodded His head. "It is very clear that Christ explains to us that we must seek the Lord. He emphasizes that the Lord is within us, and that the

---

*John 14 : 6.

†John 14 : 11.

§For the purpose of these pages, Mr. Thomas is an assumed name.

search for Him should be continued within the body. He said, 'The kingdom of God is within you.'* He refers to the Shabd as the Word or Logos, the Holy Spirit, the Living Water. He indicated that we have to pass through many stages of consciousness before we reach God-consciousness, when He said, 'In my Father's house are many mansions.'† The Master raised His hands slightly. Like a classic dancer He used His hands to complement His speech—but never too frequently to be distracting. As He spoke, His hands moved with a grace and fluency of expressiveness which so harmonized with His words that one rarely even noticed them.

Then continuing, He said, "You see, the seat of the soul and the mind knotted together is just behind the eyes. Christ referred to this center as the 'single eye,' as the 'straight gate....which leadeth unto life,§ and as the 'door'. From this point," Maharaj Ji said as He touched the space between His eyebrows, "all our consciousness is pulled down by the senses and scattered in the outward world through the nine apertures of the body—two eyes, two ears, two nostrils, the mouth and the two lower apertures. Our first step is to withdraw that consciousness from the body back to this single eye from where we start on our real spiritual journey.

"Christ said, 'Knock, and it shall be opened unto you.'** That one phrase alone is sufficient indication that there is something which He wants us to see, to understand. Always we knock from outside; doors are opened from the inside. The Lord is within us,

---

*Luke 17 : 21
†John 14 : 2
§Matt. 7 : 14
**Matt. 7 :7

but our consciousness is now outside. When we bring back our consciousness to the eye center which is the door to the kingdom of heaven, and 'knock' or concentrate our attention there, that single eye opens and we begin our real search for the Lord. Here Christ also said, 'Seek and ye shall find.'* Here the Path to the Lord is revealed to the disciple, for it is here that the Word—that power which will eventually take us back to our original home— is fully contacted. The Word is so attractive and compelling, so far superior to the pleasures of the senses that we at once become attached to it and are automatically detached from the senses."

"This is very interesting, indeed," commented Mr. Thomas.

"Of this point Christ said further, 'The light of the body is the eye. Therefore, if thine eye be single, thy whole body shall be full of light.'† Now we close our eyes and see nothing but darkness inside, but when we will open that single eye, all darkness will vanish and we will behold that Light. We will merge in that Light; we will become that Light. There we drink that Living Water, that nectar of the Word which will lead us to everlasting life.

"Christ referred to the Word or Logos," the Master went on, "when He said, 'the wind bloweth where it listeth, and thou hearest the sound thereof, but canst not tell whence it cometh, and whither it goeth; so is every one that is born of the Spirit.'§ He refers to the Holy Ghost as the Word, the Spirit which is within

---

*Matt. 7 : 7
†Matt. 6 : 22
§John 3 : 8

every one of us and with which we can only be in touch
when we 'knock' at the gateway here at the eye center.

"Then He says that when the Word of God is
heard, the dead shall pass from death unto life; they shall
rise. We are all dead, but as far as the world is concerned
we are living. As far as the Lord is concerned we are
dead, for we have forgotten Him and have given ourself wholly to this world. But with that Living Water
which we taste from inside, Light comes in us; life
comes in us. Then we are dead as far as the world is
concerned, but we are living as far as the Lord is concerned."

A silence followed the Master's words—a silence
which held our thoughts as we contemplated the wisdom
He gave us. Never before had I heard this interpretation of those Biblical phrases.

Another disciple broke the silence, saying, "In
some forms of Christianity today, it is taught that dead
people are all sleeping in their graves and that on the
Day of Judgment they will rise out of their graves and
be counted."

The Master's eyes twinkled and He smiled. "Well,
that would be quite a mess!" He exclaimed.

The whole group burst into laughter at this. The
interpretation of scripture which had been brought up
was a prime example of the extreme to which misinterpretation and dogma can go, and the Master had
easily directed our minds to see how comically far we
could take such extremes.

"You see," Maharaj Ji continued after the laughter
had died down, "it is *we* who are sleeping, having forgotten the Lord. We are in a deep slumber in the snare
of maya and illusion and attachments. But we will
rise out of sleep, out of death, into life everlasting when

we become aware of the Shabd.   Then we will awaken to God-consciousness."

Again the group became reverently serious and stilled by the Master's words.   It was incredible how easily He could evoke new reactions in us, and as closely together as the waves of the sea.

"Then the 'resurrection of souls' which is so often mentioned in the Bible is an individual affair," a voice from the back row concluded.

"Yes," the Master affirmed.   "Everyone faces his own day of resurrection—it is not a day of universal resurrection."

"If He taught this Path," Mr. Thomas interpreted after some time, shielding his eyes from the insistent light of the noonday sun, "then Christ would be adequate to serve for those who choose Him rather than choosing a living Master?"

"No," the Master spoke emphatically.   "He was only good for those souls who came into his contact while he was *living*.   He said, 'As long as I am *in* the world, I am the light of the world.'*   He was the light of his disciples, of His own initiates.

"You and I cannot apply the teachings in the Bible to the person of Jesus Christ himself," the Master said further.   "All his teachings were directed to His personal disciples who were there in His presence, but we cannot make use of that personality now.   Very beautifully he told them, 'Yet a little while, and the world seeth me no more ; but ye see me : because I live, ye shall live also.'**   He also said, 'At that day ye shall know that I am in my Father, and ye in me,

---

*John 9 :5
**John 14 :19

and I in you.'* These are all mystic expressions to be understood. In essence, He said, 'I will leave you as far as the physical form is concerned and as far as this world is concerned, but as far as you are concerned I will be with you forever in my inner Radiant Form. Now you doubt me because I am in this flesh. When I will manifest myself to you, you will never doubt me, for you will see me there inside, in my Radiant Form.' But this message was meant for those people to whom He was speaking, those people whom He initiated. We cannot apply those words of His to Him now. We have become so involved in Him and His personality that we give no attention to the teachings He gave. If we are really following His teachings, we would search for a living Master, from whom we would learn how to follow Christ's teachings. Then we can be led to Christ too, if we are interested to meet Him."

"The Bible says that Christ was the only begotten Son of God," Mr. Thomas persisted. "Is this not true then?"

"You see," Maharaj Ji began, "we must not forget those souls who were born before the Christ, to better understand this question. Christ served as Master for the people of His time, but as we know, this earth was created many millions of years ago. Christ came only about 2,000 years ago. What about the souls of those who came before the Christ? Did they never need a Master? Did they not have a Christ to save them? Were they condemned forever? The Lord could not have been so unjust to them. For the Lord has only one means for us to reach Him, and as His love embraces everyone and is within everyone, all may have a chance

---

*John 14 :20

to seek Him. We cannot say that just those who lived in Christ's day and onward will be saved. Christ Himself never said, 'I also take the sins of those people who were born before you.' Nowhere will this statement be found in the Bible."

"But it is said that He was crucified to save us from our sins," Mr. Thomas said. "Did the crucifixion have any significance?"

"Perhaps He may have given an example to the people that having everything within Him He didn't want to use His power to save himself, His real kingdom being not of this world. Perhaps He was taking the karmas of His disciples on Himself and giving it on His own body. But He knows best what was behind His crucifixion. I cannot say; I am nobody to comment on such a high personality."

"Yet Christ was the only Master who was crucified, wasn't He? Or am I wrong in this assumption. I'm not too well up on my history," Mr. Thomas admitted with a smile.

"Well," the Master told him, "it seems that the fate of practically all the Saints has been the same. Saints are never recognized in their own time by the world. While they are here, the world doesn't tolerate them. We are all so much ensnared here, so much attached to each other, so much the slave of our dogmas and rituals and religions that we cannot *hear* them." The Master's eyes flashed as He spoke. "Three or four saints were crucified in the same way as Christ—on the cross. And Muslim mystics have been burned alive. Their skin has been peeled. They were made to sit on hot iron plates and in boiling water, to give their lives. If we read the history of the Saints throughout the ages, we find what they had to face from us was really terrible!

Yet now we say we worship them. But I think we are *not* really worshipping them or following their teachings, for our lot and condition is still the same in this world." Then in a softened voice He added, "If Jesus would come today to us and proclaim Himself perhaps we would give Him the same fate as that of 2000 years ago."

Again there was silence in the garden as we recognized the truth of the Master's words. Then Mr. Thomas spoke up again. "Back to the question of Christ's prevailing divinity—a question which has always been an enigma to me—why did the teaching come down to us that we can adopt Him as our Master if there is not some truth in it?" The American seeker seemed determined to get the question clear in his mind.

Maharaj Ji answered, "Generally the disciples of every Master are so much in love with Him that they think that besides him there can be no other Master—whether past, present or future. Out of *love* for him they feel that He is the *only* true Savior who has come into the world. In their zeal they absolutely forget the essence of the teachings of that Master, and wrongly interpret them. Then we become the victim of the resulting dogmas and rituals and ceremonies."

Silently Mr. Thomas pondered the Master's words. Then he commented, "And most of the Masters worshipped today lived so long ago that we cannot even be sure of the scriptures we read!"

"That is right," Maharaj Ji nodded His acknowledgement. "From whatever little I have analyzed the Bible, I feel that Christ's teachings were not written down while He lived. They were probably carried from mouth to mouth. Now for example, you have just listened to Khanna Sahib read a discourse. Yet if you were to go to another room and try to write the discourse down, how much of it would be left? Perhaps 30 percent will be what you actually heard, and 70 percent will be what you *thought* you heard and tried to recall. If you explain what you heard to another person, and he in turn tries to record it on paper, hardly 20 percent will be recovered. Then if the written words of that third person were put into different translations, into different languages, much of what little he understood of the original discourse would be lost. Perhaps, in the course of all the translations and revisions, some people may also suppress certain teachings which they feel interfere with their thinking. How much is left ultimately?"

The Master then turned to all of us and continued, saying, "And that is, I think, the state of the Bible. From what I have been able to understand, nobody wrote down verbally Christ's words when He spoke them. His words were passed on from one to another, then brought to a book and finally translated into different languages. Perhaps if the New Testament had been dictated or written by Christ Himself and exactly preserved through the centuries, we would have an unbroken, continuous sequence of the mystic teachings. Here and there we do find these teachings, but we have to dig deep into the Bible for them; we have to find certain passages and link them together before we can know their essence.

"Moreover, He purposefully did not explain openly the esoteric mystic teachings, but rather gave them in parables. He said, 'Unto you it is given to know the mysteries of the kingdom of God; but to others in parables; that seeing they might not see, and hearing they

might not understand.'* For He and his disciples
were hunted; they were not liked. If people in those
days could not understand him and crucified Him, how
will we understand him now, after so many centuries
have passed, when His real teachings are not given to
us in their original form? So many things have been
suppressed; so many things have been misinterpreted,
forgotten and lost. We need a key; we need someone
to explain to us what the inner teachings mean, to show
us the way to the Lord today.

"And this problem of misinterpretation applies
not only to the Bible," Maharaj Ji added. "I know of
teachings of other Saints who have written with their
own hands—teachings which have not been altered or
translated or revised. Not a word has been changed—
yet their teachings are not being rightly understood
today. The basic concept of their teachings has been
twisted out and lost. And we have to look back only
a few centuries to the day when those saints lived.
What to say of Christ's teachings?"

"Would you explain to us where ritual has its
origin in religions, and why it cannot be valuable to
us if we are truly moved by it?" asked a South African
lady in the group.

The Master turned to her and replied, "These
rituals and ceremonies don't lead us anywhere inside.
They may promote a certain type of emotion in us;
they may build a certain type of atmosphere around us
for meditation—to that extent they may be helpful.
But there is always danger of our becoming slaves of the
rituals—then it is harmful to us. All rituals and
ceremonies had a purpose and meaning behind them,

---

*Luke 8:10

originally. It is when we lose that meaning that we become the slave of them.

"For example," He went on to explain, "in most of our churches and holy temples, we light candles. Originally the purpose behind this was to remind us that we have a light within our consciousness. For our *real* temple, the temple of the living God, is our body. In this temple there is a 'flame,' a light. That ritual served only to remind us of that light so that we may try to achieve that light and see it within ourself. Now if we start lighting the candle punctually every day as a habit, before long we forget altogether why it is lit. Then we become a slave to the ritual, and it is absolutely of no use to us."

"I think," began Mr. Thomas, his face breaking into a wide smile, "that what You are telling us is finally getting through to me. In other words, it all boils down to the fact that we get off the track through our own misinterpretation, so we always need a living Master to keep us *on* the track—to really put us on the inward Path !"

"That is the essence of the Sant Mat teachings," the Master said to him, nodding His head in affirmation. "You see, if one could work for himself to the point of God-realization, definitely he wouldn't need a teacher. But it is very difficult to work for oneself, because then we are more or less, just working for our mind—self-deception I would say. For we definitely need a Master to find our *real* Master inside. Otherwise the mind can deceive us, can even make us believe that we have met a Master inside. We need somebody to put us on the inward Path, to enlighten us as to what God is and how to worship Him, to reveal to us where He is and to be our guide on that Path.

"We can take a very simple example from this world," He continued. "We go to schools; we go to colleges; we get degrees; we get practical training before we can say that we have some knowledge in our line of study.   I don't think we come across anybody who has just by his own efforts become a doctor, a professor, or an engineer. We always need teachers at every step. When we cannot achieve worldly ambitions by our own efforts, how can we achieve God-realization by our own efforts?   We are so much under the sway of mind and sense that unless there is somebody to shake us free from these roots, we can never reach Him.   We always need a guide, an elder brother, an adviser—give Him any name.   Names are just confusing to us.   Call Him anything, but we definitely need a teacher to learn the science of spirituality. And," He finished by adding, "it is impossible to progress inside without a teacher.

"Why is that, Master?" asked another disciple.

"There are so many temptations; there are so many different obstacles which will come in our way.   Unless someone is there to show us how to cross them and to keep us away from the pitfalls that will confront us, we will make very little progress," He answered.

Then I asked, "Maharaj Ji, if a person were initiated by a Master in one life and then had to come back again for another birth, would he have to be initiated all over again by another living Master?"

"Yes," the Master said firmly. "Every time we have to be initiated by a living Master. All Masters are one, and when once the seed of initiation is within us, then the Masters don't leave us at all. If we don't improve in one birth, we are given a chance to improve in another birth—but we can only improve if we are again brought into contact with a living Master. We need initiation, but there is a difference between those initiations. For example, some land has to be plowed, prepared and fertilized before it is fit for cultivation. Other land may be so fertile that one has only to throw a seed onto it and the seed will sprout. Similarly, Satsangis who come for the second or third time are much more receptive to the teachings than those persons who come for the first time on the Path, though they still need to come in contact with a living Master."

"We read in the books that the Master meets us at death, whether we make progress in our meditation or not," I said. "This *is* true, isn't it?"

Maharaj Ji smiled. "The Master doesn't just initiate us and then forget about us; He is responsible to take us back to our Father. If we are remaining within His commandments and are doing our best to improve ourself in our meditation, He is *bound* to meet us and take us back. The Master will definitely come, for if we are honest in our duty, He will be honest in His duty."

Then Mrs. Neilsen, an American initiate who had just arrived the week before, spoke for the first time. "Maharaj Ji," she began, "Is each succeeding Master responsible only for His own disciples?"

"He is responsible for His own disciples, and for His Master's disciples as well," Maharaj Ji replied, turning to her.

"You mean on earth?" she queried.

"As far as the Master is concerned, for their inner needs also."

But, her face wore a puzzled expression, "I thought each one took care of his own followers?"

"There is no difference in Masters," he told her quietly.

The Master paused briefly, allowing us to think over His words. Then He went on, "You see, Masters are all rays of the same Ocean of Divinity. The body is not the real Master. He is that Power, that Shabd, that Nam. This body Saints take on just to contact us and explain the Path to us, to collect their allotted souls who are ready for initiation at that time— their 'marked sheep'. We think we see them as any other body outside, but actually they are made of pure Shabd itself. It is immaterial which body comes; because we are not to merge in a body. Through our Master we are to merge back into the Shabd, the Word. Every soul which has the seed of initiation ultimately merges back into the Lord through the Master. And all Masters are one; there is no difference among them," He finished simply.

The Master's words reached to the very core of the Sant Mat teachings, and answered the unspoken question of many a disciple. It was as if the Lord Himself had spoken to us. And indeed, He had. I remembered the Biblical phrase describing Christ in the gospel according to St. John: "And the Word was made flesh, and dwelt among us."* But time is illusion in the presence of eternity— the Word *is* made flesh, and dwells among us...

After a long moment had passed, the Indian doctor spoke up again. "Maharaj Ji," he began thoughtfully, "is it possible to get a *wrong* teacher? How do we know for sure who a real Master is—one who can really put us on the Path within?"

"I generally advise seekers that even if they spend their whole life in their search, it is not time lost, it is time *gained*," the Master's tone was emphatic. "We

*John 1:17

should never plunge blindly into anything. You see, we must satisfy our intellect so that it may not be a barrier in our way, so that we can progress on the Path. We must make a thorough research and investigation before starting on the Path.

"For example, a simple man and an intellectual man both want to drive from here to New Delhi. The simple man asks the first person he sees to direct him to the road leading to New Delhi, and as soon as it has been pointed out to him, he starts driving without confirming those directions from anyone else. But if he were to meet another man on the way who tells him that a different direction leads to New Delhi, the simple man turns and changes his route at once. And if yet another person meets him on his new route, he can be put off the track again––he is so simple that he can easily be misled; whomsoever he meets on his way, he believes.

"On the other hand, the intellectual man going to New Delhi from Bombay will not act on the first advice he hears. Even if one were to tell him that a particular route definitely leads to New Delhi, he wouldn't believe him unless he obtained corroborating evidence from nine or ten other sources. He may also study a map to further verify the directions. Then hesitatingly, he will start. In the beginning he will observe the signs and milestones along the way and study the road along which he passes. But once he is convinced, he drives straight on to his goal with confidence. Then he wouldn't be swayed even if a thousand people were to come in his way to mislead him. From then onwards, his intellect will not take him to New Delhi, but his practice of driving and his confidence that he is on the right road will lead him to New Delhi.

"Similarly on the spiritual path, we should never just close our eyes and jump into anything; we should never make our decision with emotions or just to please our friends. Then we may be deceived and misled; we may be easily disillusioned and discouraged; we may become frustrated at once. For with a wavering mind and doubts in our heart, we will never progress at all. One thousand and one questions, one thousand and one doubts will come in our way. So we must take as much time as we need to understand what Sant Mat is. Even if we spend a whole lifetime in research and investigation, it is not time lost, it is time gained. We are just boring down deep our foundation, deep our roots. We are building on pure rock. And the deeper the foundation, the stronger and higher will be the construction we can build up."

"But once we are convinced that this is the right Path for us to follow," Maharaj Ji went on to say, "that this is the right guide for us, then we have not to worry with our intellect. We don't require books then. We don't have questions. We don't require involved discussions—we just require devotion and practice— nothing else. The intellet itself will never lead us back to Him. But the intellect is a friend for the intellectual if he knows how to use it."

"Master, one enigma which has always bothered my intellect is the existence of Kal, or the devil, as it is called in English," the South African lady put in. "Is it a being with a soul or is it the mind?"

The Master smiled at her. "You mean, you want to have a conception of him—what he looks like?"

"We have tried to imagine him."

"I think it is better not to analyze what he looks

like. Kal is a power, it is universal mind.* As the
Lord is actually the Shabd or Word, the same type of
parallel applies to Kal, as Kal is universal mind. All the
souls we find in this universe are under his domain, and
thus cannot get release from birth and death. The
only way to go beyond it is by attaching ourself to
somebody who is beyond that domain—that is the Lord
Himself. That is why we search for a Master who
has gone beyond the reach of the negative power and
has merged in the Lord."

Then Mrs. Nielsen asked, "Is Kal a lower manifestation of the Supreme Father? Or is he something
else?"

The Master replied, "Nothing has come without
the Father; nothing *existed* before the creation besides
the Father. Our universe is the projection of the
Supreme Being, the Father. Therefore Kal has also
come from Him. He has an allotted task which he is
carrying out."

"Does the negative power, then, derive power from
the Supreme Father and act under His orders?" she
asked further.

"Whatever he is doing, he is doing by the order of
the Supreme Being. If we were to say that the negative
power does everything independently, irrespective of
the Lord we would mean that he is more powerful than
the Lord. But everything is under the Supreme
Father, projected by Him—nothing is beyond Him.
For example, in a city or state there is a mayor, an
inspector general of police, a warden of the jails. Each

---

*The technical name for universal mind in Hindi is Brahm,
belonging to the second stage of progress of the initiate of a Master
of the Shabd.

has his allotted duty to perform, yet they cannot act independently of the mayor of the city. We cannot abuse the mayor because the police are directed to catch us when we disobey the law, or because the warden is commissioned to jail us or execute us when we have to pay for our misdeeds. They are doing their duty. Similarly, Kal is doing his duty."

After a short pause, Maharaj Ji continued, "But we should not try to formulate a conception of the negative aspect or dwell on those thoughts. For if in your city you are a good citizen, you are never bothered by the police. Only criminals are frightened of the police, and ponder over what they do, how they punish, what the jails look like. They are always worried because they know they are bound to do something for which they will have to pay. But when we have come on the Path and are attending to our meditation, what fear do we have of a negative power at all? Why even think about it? We are good citizens. We have a guide to lead us inside."

The Master's words rang true, for it is well known that whatever one dwells upon, that he is. "As a man thinketh in his heart, so is he."

"Before we come to the Path, do we worship Kal or do we worship the Lord?"

"Kal is the administrator of the universe, but that does not mean that God is not in every one of us, regardless of whether we are on the Path or not. Our heart yearns for God; we love Him, we worship Him whether we know the way of worshipping Him or not. When we feel that those people who are not on the Path are not loving God, we are wrong. They are loving God, but they don't know how to love Him. They are under the sway of mind and negativity. Actually, in whatever way you love Him, it is He whom you love, for He *is* love.

"The inclination of the soul for the Lord is always there," the Master went on. "The negative power only forces us to seek Him; otherwise we would never try to reach Him. We are in tune with the Lord, and with His grace we are put on the inward Path to worship Him and to transcend the negative power and this illusion. Nothing exists without the will of the Lord ultimately."

"Maharaj Ji," the Indian doctor began again, smiling self-consciously. "As an Indian guest, I don't want to monopolize this discussion, but the subject of Kal has raised another question in my mind."

"Oh no, it's quite all right," the Master smiled at him. "You may ask all the questions you like."

"Thank you Maharaj Ji," the doctor's smile widened from one of self-consciousness to one of relief. Then his face became serious as he said, "I have read in the Radha Soami books that the five instincts of the mind are kam or lust, krodh or anger, lobh or greed, moh or attachment, and ahankar or ego; and that these are instincts resulting from the mind's attachment to the senses. Since these are the barriers of our mind which shield us from God-realization, could we also say that Kal is our physical mind?"

"No," Maharaj Ji replied. "Our mind is the *agent* of the negative power or universal mind or Kal— whatever name you want to call it. As the soul has its connection with the Lord, so the mind has its relationship with universal mind; its power is derived from there.

"You see," He explained, "as we discussed previously, the seat of the soul and the mind knotted together is just behind the eyes. From here the mind is pulled down by the senses and is subject to the five instincts you spoke of, kam, krodh, lobh, moh, and ahankar. Therefore the mind has become the slave of the senses. Our soul is the slave of the mind, and consequently is slave of the senses also. When the mind is running to the senses, we cannot have a more severe enemy, but when we attach it to the Shabd it withdraws from attachment to the senses and becomes our friend. Then the mind is no longer subject to those five instincts. With the help of the Shabd, it then returns to its origin at the second stage of the Path, and merges in universal mind. Then the soul is no longer dominated by the mind; at this stage it is released from the mind and rises above it. The whole process becomes reversed, because then the soul is controlling the mind and the mind is controlling the senses. But unless the mind returns to and merges in its origin, the soul cannot be released from the negative power and cannot begin its real spiritual evolvement to God-realization."

"But there is no proof of so many of these theories," Mr. Thomas observed thoughtfully, his face again serious. "The scientific western mind always wants to demand proof before accepting anything. I seem to get one doubt cleared up and another one comes along to take its place.'"

"To really know the teachings of the Saints is to experience them for ourself," the Master told him. "Until then we have to accept all these theories with our intellect, as a sort of working hypothesis. Intellect is a great barrier in our way. We have to pierce the intellect with the intellect by weighing every question and searching for logical explanations which will satisfy it. Then we will be sure as far as the intellect is concerned; but beyond that we cannot be sure until we experience these theories.

"For not by intellect can we understand God, in any way. When we will *leave* the intellect, the mind, then we will know what God is." The Master paused and smiled. "But then we won't be in the sphere of mind to know Him by our intellect. For to know Him is to go back to Him, to merge back into that Ocean. That is the only way to know the Lord—not intellectually."

The smile on Mr. Thomas's face had returned, as he said, "And I suppose that as we progress in meditation we will find that our questions are being answered automatically."

The look of kindness visibly deepened in the Master's eyes. "When the real love for meditation comes within us, the real devotion comes within us, hardly any question is left. We think now that we have lots of questions, but when that realization of love and devotion comes, we find that we have no questions. The further away we are from that devotion and real love, the more abundant are our questions. The nearer we come to that point of love and devotion, our questions are automatically resolved. We think, 'this is not necessary; that is not necessary; it hardly matters to me.'

"For the answers come from within. They don't come from anywhere outside. They are not spoken. These questions are essentially only doubts within every one of us, but the stage comes when nobody has to explain things to us, the answers just come."

Words would rather minimize the expression on Mr. Thomas's face—an expression which mirrored a new understanding. And it seemed that the understanding had very little to do with only the words the Master spoke.

Then Mrs. Bea Hemming, a gentle, soft-spoken English woman from Rhodesia, entered the discussion for the first time. "Maharaj Ji, would it be possible for all of us to experience a sample of light or sound right now, while sitting in this room?"

He smiled in His familiar teasing way, and said, "You mean you want a high school diploma before you get through elementary school?"

The group joined Mrs. Hemming in laughter at His words. What children we were at times! But Mrs. Hemming had not given up hope of a more favorable response to her question, and spoke to the Master again, saying, "Just to encourage...?"

The Master remained silent for a moment. His eyes were lowered and He looked at no one. All of us gathered there became very attentive at this question and waited for His response with bated breath. Perhaps this question had entered the minds of others in the group, but no one had yet had the courage to voice it.

As if speaking to us all, the Master raised His eyes and said, "It is more than encouragement if we know the secret of meditation and are devoting our time to it. Is this not any encouragement? You see," He went on in a reverent tone, "the Lord has given us the facilities by which to remember Him. Is this less Grace? At least He has created that *desire* in us for Him. This is the biggest Grace the Lord can shower. It is His Grace that He is making us impatient to meet Him... *that* is His Grace," He finished quietly.

CHAPTER TWELVE

ON TOUR WITH THE MASTER

On an evening early in December several of the foreigners visiting the Dera stood on the platform of the railway station at Beas. Except for the six of us who stood there, the servants who helped us with our baggage, and Khanna Sahib who had accompanied us, the station appeared as deserted and quiet as a ghost town. For it was only by prearranged, special request that the Frontier Mail, which daily passed through the station, would stop there.

We were all eagerly discussing the places to which we would go during the next two or three weeks. For the long-awaited tour with the Master was underway. Those of us who had planned to go would now have the opportunity to see India's rural and city life first-hand, to be the guests of Indian Satsangi families at every stop during the tour, and most of all, to witness the Master at work outside the Colony gates.

We heard the high wail of the train's whistle long before the black shape of its engine came into sight, pulling an endless snake-like train of cars behind. With a shriek of steam and clamor of wheels against rails, the train stopped just barely long enough for us to scramble on board and find our separate, reserved compartments.

Mrs. Ross and I shared a first class "ladies' compartment" during the all-night journey from Beas to New Delhi. The compartment was small and somewhat dusty, with barred windows and a lock on the door for protection during the many station stops throughout the

night. But we each had a berth, an accommodation
which is assured in first-class travel since the number
of passengers per compartment is limited and prearranged. The most inconvenient aspect of first-class
travel (which really isn't "first-class" at all—there is an
even better class above it, the "air-conditioned class")
is that one must carry his own bedding and enjoy a
steady accumulation of dust over everything including
himself, no matter how tightly the windows are shut.
Oftentimes it becomes necessary to cover one's nose
and mouth with a damp cloth in order to keep out the
dust when it is particularly thick. There are still two
more classes of travel below first, both having no
restrictions on the number of passengers in a single
compartment, with no cushions on the hard wooden
benches of third class.

During the journey we visited the others of the
group who had reserved compartments in the air-
conditioned coach, and were surprised to see the luxury
and comfort they were enjoying. There was wall-to
wall carpeting, wood panelling, wide-foam-rubber
seats and berths, a table and closet, and a "steward"
included in the accommodations. Being twice the
cost of first-class travel, this class appeared to be twice
as comfortable as well.

And then, New Delhi—said to be one of India's
most westernized cities with its carefully-planned construction, its broad, tree-lined streets, its predominant-
ly modern, pseudo-classical architecture. We arrived
hungry, tired and looking forward to seeing the Master
who had arrived in the capital city the previous day.
Mr. Leeming and I were met by Mrs. Sheela Bharat
Ram's chauffeur and driven directly to her home. Mrs.
Bharat Ram had welcomed us to New Delhi when we

had first arrived in India, and invited us to stay with her for the few days we were to spend in Delhi during the tour. Her house was as beautiful as I had remembered it from our first visit. The architectural design alone could not be surpassed anywhere; a structure pleasing to the eye with many curving terraces, spacious verandas, and rows of slim columns. The surrounding gardens were profuse with color; a picturesque fountain of water bubbled and splashed into an island-shaped pool. Though quite modern in design, the house and its surroundings presented a picture of dignity and traditional stateliness to the eye.

The day that followed was crammed with activity, as we toured New Delhi's shopping center—Connaught Circus, and visited many of the hundreds of bazaars in the busy market-places. For the most part, India's shops are open bazaars with no walls facing the street. Each bazaar consists of a long bench for the customers to sit on, facing an equally long but wider platform upon which the merchants sit cross-legged and display their wares. And such a variety of wares one can buy! Endless yards of colorful silks and weaves and hand-loomed saries, all kinds of bright jewellery and trinkets; Oriental sandals; hand-carved elephants and gods of cherry-wood and ivory; brass vases and urns of all shapes and sizes.

But the high point of that first day in New Delhi was the Satsang in late afternoon. Once again we beheld the beloved Satguru's face; once again we sat among thousands upon thousands in hushed, pin-drop silence for two hours, drinking in the outflowing peace and love which come from His presence. I heard it said that there were fifty to sixty thousand people attending this Satsang, a number which actually exceeded the number of those who had attended the October Bhandara.

It differed little from the Satsangs at the Colony, except that the platform seemed higher, rising up a good twenty feet in front of us. There was still the familiar shabd singing while awaiting the Master, and as at the Dera, we were told that hours before Satsang time the people had begun to swarm into the area, sitting close together on the ground and spontaneously chanting the shabds. Again we heard that mounting wave of "Radha Soami" pass through the crowd when the Master came. And when He spoke, it seemed even quieter than ever before in the congregation. His every word was absorbed, as for many of the people it had been a long time since they had heard their Satguru speak. When it was over, we somehow found a pathway through the crowd and were whisked away in a waiting car to Mrs. Bharat Ram's home.

And the next day, Sunday, began with Satsang at which there were even greater numbers than the night before. A tea and dinner followed at the home of a devoted disciple and his family, the Mehtas, then one or two quiet mid-afternoon hours were spent in the company of the Master—and suddenly another day was gone almost as soon, it seemed, as it had begun. Shortly after five we drove to the airport to see the Master off and bid Him good-bye for another few days— until the next lap of the tour. He was flying to a small town outside of Bombay for a few days while we were to travel straight to Bombay by train and were to meet Him there. All too soon our Beloved Lord said "Radha Soami", to us and boarded the plane. We stood there without speaking a word until the tiny, blinking lights on the wing-tips had vanished and we could no longer hear the hum of the engines. Strange that the tears should spring to one's eyes at such a brief parting.

The train journey from New Delhi to Bombay lasted for a day and a night—a full twenty-four hours. But we found the day a good time to see India's passing and varied scenery as the train snaked its way through the land. From the barred window of our compartment, we looked out on numerous little "mud villages" and thousands of acres of wheat and sugar cane fields. Often we would see a dark brown back leaning over a scythe in the tall wheat or walking behind a wooden plow pulled by a solitary white bullock. And once in a while we would see a lone, bearded sadhu clothed in saffron-colored robes with his matted hair and wooden staff, walking slowly along a rough and dusty roadway.

When the train passed close by the villages, I noticed that they were clean swept, right down to the courtyard walls and the mud houses. Most structures were of the same light earthen color; all were smooth and clean. The streets were surprisingly free of garbage and litter. Often I could see the village laundryman, the dhobi, beating the dirt out of clothes by the side of a stream or village pond or well; the banks surrounding him covered with brightly-colored clothing carefully stretched out upon the ground and drying in the warm sun. Here and there I noticed neatly arranged rows of dark pancake-shaped objects, which I learned were cow dung. Once the Master had referred to cow dung as the "wealth of India," since it is used for everything from fertilizer and fuel to a mixture of clay and water to give sturdiness and strength to the walls of the mud houses. Gandhi Ji very aptly spoke of India's mud villages as "six hundred thousand dung heaps."

And always, standing lazily or lying in curious heaps, were cows. India's "sacred" cows. They ranged in color from dusty black to cream white; some were round and well-fed and decorated with bright colors, but more plentiful were those skeletal thin ones—their hides draped in loose folds on their bodies or stretched over protruding, angular bones. Invariably they dotted the landscape, gathering by village ponds and fields or sleeping in village streets. It seemed that the cow was the one constant factor in the ever-changing Indian landscape. I soon learned that the sanctification of the cow in India is derived more from its symbol of fertility and usefulness to the Indian people than from Hindu orthodoxy.

But the cities through which we passed were a striking and sharp contrast to the appearance of rural India. The cleanliness of village lands disappeared under the rubble and refuse of narrow, crowded streets—streets lined with open sewer trenches and wooden lean-to bazaars, streets flanked by cows, chickens and children.

Bombay only intensified this contrast. On the one hand there were clean modern structures and many handsome buildings with massive and ornate Victorian architecture, fashionable thoroughfares, and a trend towards westernization that was reminiscent of New Delhi. On the other hand there were the tiny, twisting streets, littered gutters and poorly-clothed Indians sleeping on the ground.

All throughout India, but particularly here in the great port city of Bombay, often termed the "gateway to India," the centuries crowd together and seem to wrestle with each other for predominance. Directly in front of him, one may see a thatched hut with a thin dark stream of smoke rising from a heap of stones by its side, where a sari-clad woman is cooking chapatis; while perhaps only a hundred yards away, one may see the ultra-modern towering lines of a luxury hotel outlined against the sky. And then too, one can see on India's streets and roads the entire evolution of transportation—bullock carts, buggies, and horse-driven tongas; bicycles, rickshaws, and scooters; buses, automobiles, and pedestrians. One may even see an occasional camel.

If the reader has studied any of the current books which tell of India, he has no doubt found that reports of both her appearance and of her spirituality differ sharply. For a critical western tourist may spend a few weeks or months sightseeing through the subcontinent, taking in all the big cities and particularly the slum areas, perhaps even finding the opportunity to spend a few hours in a "primitive" native village. A thorough tourist may also visit the bathing ghats at the River Ganges to get a closer look at the "strange habits" of the Hindus, where he would be assailed by scores of beggars thrusting their hollowed begging bowls under his nose or extending a warped, crippled limb. Of course, his report will not in any way resemble that of one who seeks to find the truth beneath the surface, or of a native-born Indian who writes of India's abundant beauty. To be most objective in reconciling these conflicting angles of vision is to recognize that India changes her dress at almost every turn. The visitor's opinion of India depends on his own preconceived ideas of her culture and religion, and on the purpose of his visit to her shores. In other

words, what he is looking for he will most likely find—
for India is possibly the most varied and contradictory
country in the world.

A Westerner often tends to blame India's diversity,
particularly her poverty and backward ways, on the
religion of the people. For reincarnation and the
theory of karma, as viewed by the West, usually denote
fatalism. And such a viewpoint does indeed have much
truth in it. Fatalistic beliefs are exactly those which
have for so many ages left the East complacent in its
poverty and backwardness, though reincarnation dates
back to an age when India was a wealthy nation.
Among many Indians, the predominating attitude
seems to be, "Why should I try to do anything to
improve my condition? It is my lot to be born this
way and there is nothing I can do about it. I must
submit to it, since it is a necessary step on the long road
to Jivanmukti (release from birth and death)." And
so the Westerner will most often discard the theory of
reincarnation and karma as mere fantasy when he sees
the effect of a people's belief in it. He reasons that it
cannot be a sound philosophy if its cumulative result
is that India is, as it may appear to him, the most
poverty-stricken and disease-ridden nation of the world
with its rural people reluctant, often unwilling, to be
helped by western attempts to update and improve
their conditions.

According to a more thorough interpretation of
karma and reincarnation, however, today's conditions in
India have not arisen from the existence of those cosmic
laws themselves, but from the *approach* to them by the
people. A man's birth and circumstances are predeter-
mined, it is true; but he himself molded his own destiny
in a former birth. For it is one's *efforts* and *attitudes*

and *motives* concerning his actions and his world which create his next world. While knowingly accepting and facing one's circumstances is a right attitude to have, complacency belongs on the other side of the fence and may be called justification for the mind— or even a form of escapism. The Master teaches that one should strive to carry out one's duty to the best of his ability and understanding, not looking for the fruits of his actions and leaving the results to the wisdom of the Lord. And this in no way invites or condones complacency and inactivity.

Then the question arises, why do the Masters not erase the deplorable conditions which exist in the world, if it is within Their power to do so?

To begin with, the primary mission of a perfect Master is that of *redemption* from this worldly consciousness. It is a mission of mercy in the most profound sense of the word, for rather than improving our world for us so that we may find contentment in our surroundings, He bestows upon us the gift of deliverance to far higher and purer realms of consciousness. This is His principal function.

But this question allows us to examine even more deeply into the Master's relationship with the cosmos. Though we in the material planes may not be aware of the overall effect of His presence, "It is also an important function of a perfect Master *to bring light and love into the world*," writes Dr. Johnson, "that all men may profit thereby. Not simply His disciples alone, but the whole world. This is a part of the Master's secret work. No one may follow Him into the secret chambers of His retreat and there see all features of the Great Work which He is doing. His special work is for individual disciples, but He works also for all mankind,

"Let us state this point in the most concise language, so that it will be understood. *There is not a living being in all the world that does not receive benefit from the Master.* This statement may not be easy to understand, at first, but it is literally so.

"The Masters are sometimes criticized for 'not coming out and doing something for the world.' But how little do such critics know about what the Masters are doing. The Master is the "Light of the world'... The Master increases the sum total of the light and the love of the whole world, and every sentient individual gets some benefit. We need not worry over the method. The fact of greatest importance to us all is that the Supreme Father illumines and blesses the whole world through and by the agency of the Masters...."

During the few days spent in Bombay, we were nearly overwhelmed by the hospitality and love for the Master shown by the Satsangis living there. Mrs. Ross and I stayed at the apartment home of Mr. and Mrs. Gopi Chand, both disciples of Sardar Bahadur Maharaj. And each day was filled with tours, meetings and visiting with countless disciples, and most important of all, Satsangs. As in New Delhi, already the large Satsang Hall, which had been erected for the use of approximately 3500 disciples, was not big enough to accommodate the steadily increasing numbers of seekers from Bombay. More than 20,000 initiates and seekers attended the Satsangs during the Master's visit, and the Satsangs had to be held outside the Satsang Hall in a huge tent or under canvas coverings to shield the people from the sun.

We didn't see the Master very often during those days, for He was continuously busy. It seemed that there simply would not be enough hours or minutes

in the day for Him to give everything its needed attention. But the Master managed it all very smoothly,
spending long hours seeing to every detail of the work
that needed to be done, and giving time to those disciples and seekers who longed to see Him privately.
Every morning He appeared before the whole Sangat
for half an hour while the pathi chanted shabds.
Following this He gave private interviews until lunch
time. After lunch the business affairs and problems
of the Bombay Sangat which had been waiting for His
special attention were taken care of. During the rest
of the afternoon, He read and answered the unending
volume of correspondence which followed Him wherever He moved. And every day at six o'clock He again
appeared before the entire Bombay Sangat and delivered a nearly two-hour long discourse. But even then
His work-day was not finished, for after Satsang He
spent another hour or two graciously giving more private
interviews to the continuous stream of seekers and
devotees. During the last two days in Bombay, He
gave initiation to great numbers of seekers throughout
the morning hours and on into the afternoon of each
day. But in spite of His strenuous routine every day,
Maharaj ji always remained relaxed and in cheerful
humor.

For a small handful of us, the high point of the
entire tour was contained within the next four days.
It was as though all the events of the days before had
only been leading up to this time. This part of the tour
was to cover two days in Sangli at the palace of the Raja
of Sangli State, and a day in Poona, arriving back in
Bombay on the 13th of December, and leaving for home
in Beas the same day. These were the last days of the
tour for us, as the Master was to leave us at Bombay

and continue touring alone for another week. And I
have relived every minute of those days, countless times.

We all shared a large, single compartment on the
first lap of the journey to Sangli—from Bombay to
Poona. There were seven of us including the Master.
Also in the group was Mr. Ahluwalia, who had joined
us at New Delhi. Though a very unassuming person,
he was often lovingly referred to as the "big wheel of
the Dera," since he was responsible for keeping the
business affairs and general operations of the Colony
well oiled and running smoothly, under the Master's
guiding direction.

Needless to say, we spent little time gazing out of
the window while in the Master's company. The
atmosphere was light, and the conversation often flowed
freely. The three-hour journey passed far too quickly
and it seemed as if only minutes had gone by before we
reached Poona where we were to change trains. When
we were leaving our compartment, the Master looked
around and asked, "what can I carry?" Then His
eyes rested on my suitcase lying halfway under the seat
and He promptly picked it up and carried it out of the
compartment.

On the railway platform, the Master was greeted
by a small group of disciples, and for twenty minutes
or so, He stood there, God-like and serene giving them
His long-awaited darshan while they eagerly but quietly
gathered around Him. For now their blessed Lord
had come, and they could not take their eyes away from
His face.

Mr. Ahluwalia told us that whenever the Master
traveled by train, groups of disciples would gather at
each station where the train was scheduled to stop in
order to have a possible glimpse of the Satguru. One

might see a very curious assembly of people gathered together at such times—representing all the varied classes and cultures of Indian society. Perhaps the only way that one could ever see a group such as this standing together in an Indian railroad station would be in the Master's name, which completely breaks down the walls of caste and creed which have predominated for so long in Hindu India. "Many times," Mr. Ahluwalia said smiling, "I have seen the Master leave His train compartment every forty-five minutes or so all throughout a night, when traveling on an all-night journey. For if He didn't, somehow they would manage to get into His compartment," he laughed, remembering. Then he said, "For the most part, though, an attempt is made by us to keep His schedule and mode of travel a secret to avoid this. But yet, perhaps by His will, it always seems to be found out by at least a few."

The all-night trip to Sangli was not quite as comfortable as our previous train-traveling had been, to say the least. In fact, it was somewhat like a ride in a cattle-car. As Maharaj Ji laughingly put it, "It will digest your food for you." And I would not like to have a moving picture of our appearance when we were greeted at the station in Sangli the next morning. Yet out of all of us, the Master looked quite unaffected by the night's journey, and was as always immaculate in dress and appearance.

The Raja himself was there to receive us, though it was so early in the morning that the sun had not yet begun to rise above the horizon. And then began a day so full of activity and new experiences that it nearly equalled my first day at the Dera. From the station we were driven directly to the Raja's palace guest house, a magnificent structure where he and some of those in his family now live. The two South African ladies and I shared one large room, a dressing room, and a large, well-accommodated bath. Friendly servants seemed to be everywhere to tend to all our needs. It was a strange feeling to be treated so grandly and hospitably by so royal a family.

"Officially" the day started with the most formal breakfast I had ever attended—a pattern for all the meals that followed at the guest house. Formally dressed waiters in red turbans and golden cummerbunds served us on silver dishes; we drank from silver goblets; we ate with silver flatware. The Master saw to it that we were all at ease in these unusual new surroundings, as course after course was placed on the table. Any dish which He recommended, we would consume without hesitation for automatically it became parshad (blessed food) at the Master's table. For many of us, it was the first meal in His company, and what could have been more ideal or symbolic for this occasion than the first meal of the day!

Immediately after breakfast we went to the Raja's palace gardens and enjoyed the atmosphere of the deep tropics. The arrangement of the gardens was not in accordance with a strict, orderly design, but rather gave the appearance of natural growth and spontaneous beauty. Tall triumphant palm trees interlaced and crisscrossed their arms high above our heads, forming curious patterns with the blue sky. The air, moved by gentle breezes, was sweet with the fragrance of tropical fruits and flowers.

"Watch over there," said the Master, and our eyes followed his gesture to the base of one of the garden's stateliest trees. An Indian was there beginning ascent of a coconut palm. We watched as he quickly worked his way up the limbless trunk, his muscles clearly defined under smooth, brown skin. Patches of sunlight through the palm fronds seemed to dance and glint on his back as he climbed. Finally reaching the top, he plucked a ripe coconut and then began his descent. We then looked around us and saw that the neighboring palms were giving their fruit to others who had climbed their trunks as well, and soon we were savoring the fresh taste of fruits I had never seen before, much less tasted, such as papayas, mangos, guavas, and maltas.

But the best part of the morning was yet to come—in fact the most meaningful and memorable experience of the entire tour—when we visited another part of the Raja's estate where others in his family reside. There we were led through more gardens to a small building, erected in remembrance of the Great Master, Baba Sawan Singh, and used for the sole purpose of meditation.

Just outside the entrance, we removed our shoes, and in stocking feet silently entered the little meditation hall. The single room was bare of furniture and the walls were clean and white, free from needless decoration. At one end of the room there was a low platform and upon the wall above there hung a life-size color painting of the Great Master with a fresh garland of flowers placed beneath it in his memory. The floor was of smooth marble and spread on its surface were rugs and mats upon which to sit in meditation.

Without speaking a word, we all sat down for meditation together, the women on one side and the men on the other. I could not really say how long we were there; it could have been a few minutes or it could have been more than an hour. In the peace and tranquility experienced then, there was no room for a sense of time. We were all effortlessly swept up in the sea of His love—no doubt there sat among us those who were joyfully meeting and communing with the Master's Radiant Form within, and reaching untold heights of blissful consciousness and glory.

The rest of the day continued in the constant company of the Master, excluding only two hours in the early afternoon. It was about 3:30 when we began to collect in the drawing room for tea, and I said to the Master, "You are spoiling us, Maharaj Ji, giving us so much time with you. Just in the last two hours we have missed you very much."

He laughed and in a seemingly off-handed way said, "What, then, will you do when you leave India?"

"I don't know," I replied with an involuntary shudder. "I don't even want to think about that."

Suddenly a silence fell upon us at the Master's words. For it was as if He had spoken to each one of us. What *would* I do when it came time to leave, crossing oceans and being separated from Him by a distance of more than ten thousand miles? The very thought of it brought tears to my eyes. But He answered our thoughts when, after a few moments had passed, He said, "when you miss someone you are never alone; but when you don't miss anyone you are always alone."

At dusk, Satsang was held in the temple of the Raja's palace. When we arrived, the small temple was overflowing with enthusiastic devotees and seekers. Lit by silver chandeliers, the balcony-lined room was fully panelled with richly-hued, cherry-brown wood. All the Indian women present were wearing red saris which were brilliant and colorful.

At first it seemed strange to walk into a Satsang gethering and not hear the familiar chanting of shabds to welcome the Master. But while many of the people were unaccustomed to Satsang and had never seen the Master before; though their dress, their language, and their surroundings differed from the Indians of the North—their faces mirrored that same quality of love and wonder and joy when the Master entered the temple and sat before them. Some whispered and talked of Him among themselves; some involuntarily stood up as if to see Him more clearly; some just remained silent and motionless in a world of their own. And the Master, always the King, delivered the discourse in His usual serene yet dynamic manner. At one point the lights failed and the microphone went dead. Maharaj Ji, quite unruffled and undisturbed, just sat and waited for it to be repaired, while His pathi, sitting next to Him on the platform, chanted a shabd. But, as one soon learns in the company of a Master, nothing ever happens without a reason. The incident helped to make the gathering more quiet, and Mr. Leeming mentioned that this electricity "failure" had happened many times before at various Satsangs he had attended on tour. A smile spread across his face. "And it usually happens when the audience is not as quiet as it should be."

At the closing, a Satsangi who lived in Sangli translated that Punjabi discourse into the Marathi language spoken by the people of Sangli State. Though we could not understand him, we could see that the translator was quite fluent, particularly since we knew that he had had no time for preparation. There is a popular expression in India that the subcontinent has almost as many languages as cities.

When it came time to leave the palace temple, a path had to be literally forced open through the crowd by the attendants in order to allow the Master to walk to the waiting car.   Many of the people, unused to the presence of a Master, were most demonstrative in expressing their new-found happiness.   I followed directly behind Maharaj Ji, and saw that great numbers of the people were attempting to fall at His feet and touch His clothes.   But never does the Master allow people to touch His feet, one of the many indications of His profound humility.   And that night in Sangli was no exception to this rule.   No mere man could possibly have managed so gracefully.

Just as He was getting into the car, I caught His glance and gave Him a tentative smile.   And in return He smiled so sweetly, completely unaffected by all the excitement, as if we were the only two people for miles around.   I became oblivious to the warm, starry night, oblivious to the milling swarms of people pressing around me.   I felt caught and swept up into that sea of joy again.

But the excitement in Sangli that evening was mild when compared to the many other incidents which have occurred when the Master is on tour.   The most extreme example of the unrelenting devotion and unfailing attendance to the Master's Satsang was related to me by a disciple from California, Mrs. Jaqueline Volk, who toured with the Master a few months later.   The scene was Calcutta, during a time of heavy local communal fighting, a time when the sharp blasts of gunfire constantly echoed through many of Calcutta's streets.   The dates scheduled for the Master's visit, which occurred every other year in that city, happened to fall within the worst of the fighting days.   But it made no difference to the Master and caused very little concern among those who were in the touring party. One always feels extraordinarily secure in the presence of the Master—so much so that a cause for the greatest alarm is hardly given a thought.

This feeling prevailed during His entire stay of three days in Calcutta. Every evening Satsang was held with the sound of gunfire and fighting in the background, yet the numbers of those who attended, their faces calm and radiant in the joy of seeing their Beloved Satguru, reached high into the thousands. Daily warnings from city authorities were radioed to the people to stay off the streets, yet they still came. On the day set aside for initiation, bullets even flew dangerously close to the Master's car as He neared the Satsang area—yet the number of those He initiated that day exceeded and nearly doubled the number who had been initiated in Calcutta two years beore. For no barrier, no matter how overwhelming or frightening, can stand against the force of the Master's call.

Returning to our stay in Sangli, each day was filled with the company of the Master at banquets and Satsangs and during quiet talks. The second day was somewhat of an afterglow in the wake of the experiences we had already enjoyed. In the morning Maharaj Ji gave initiation to about two hundred people. He used no microphone, as the group was small; and He encouraged them to gather closely around Him, much as a father lovingly talks to his children. And so indeed it was.

At lunch I mentioned off-handedly that I would like to ride an elephant and Maharaj Ji heard me. So he asked Mr. Ahluwalia to arrange a ride for all of us, if it were possible. He then looked at me, His eyes twinkling with humor, and said, "If you can't ride the elephant, you can take a tree ride."

At this I was puzzled. Tree ride? Then I told Him how I used to climb trees in Boston and had even spent one or two evenings meditating in a tree, smack in the middle of a cemetery, in order to find a quiet and solitary spot away from the city's crowds.

He chuckled at the story, but didn't seem surprised. "I know", He said, "that's what I mean."

But I got my wish about the elephant. As a matter of fact, the Raja's elephant was "rogue," or in a state of temporary elephant madness, and was chained to a large platform which happened to be in view of the area outside the temple where Satsang was to be held that evening. We went to Satsang about fifteen minutes early to see him. The poor creature seemed very restless, and would have been dangerous if he had been let loose. The "ride" came when the attendant coaxed him to lie down on his side and I went over and leaned against his massive head, being very careful to stay clear of the strong trunk which could throw a man fifty yards. And later, during the outdoor Satsang, we were distracted from time to time as the elephant occasionally rattled his chains.

The next day we left the palace in Sangli to travel to the Raja's estate in Poona. And it was a unique day for us in the Master's company, for it was His birthday. The day began at 5:00 a.m. with tea and packing, since we were to leave at 7:00 o'clock. At 6:45 Mr. Ahluwalia came into our room bringing each of us a lovely bouquet of flowers to give to the Master: He Himself carried a large garland of multi-colored flowers. When we entered the Master's room a few moments later, Mrs. Hemming acted as our spokesman, and handing Him her bouquet, she said quite spontaneously, "Maharaj Ji, you who are always the Giver, please take all our love." There were tears in her eyes as she spoke to Him. The Master took the bouquet and thanked us all. How kind He is, we thought at that moment, for He even gives us our devotion to Him.

Our being together with Him lasted only a short five minutes, but I cannot remember ever having more thoroughly enjoyed a birthday party. In the few remaining minutes before we left for Poona, I had to excuse myself and go off to weep unrestrainedly and with great joy. It did me good, for the tears were of gladness, and it seemed as though I were washing out my soul and my mind and my heart, and cleansing away the barriers and obstacles that separate one from the Lord. I felt strong and fresh when it was over, ready to face anything, and happy to be alive.

We separated into two cars for the four-hour drive to Poona. Just what I had hoped for came true—Mrs. Hemming, Mrs. Ross and myself were told to ride in the same car, the Raja's personal car, with Maharaj Ji. Once on the road, I took out my diary, thinking that it was a good time to do some writing. But before I had a chance to get started, Maharaj Ji turned around and asked to see it. As I was sitting directly in back of Him, I passed it over His shoulder and sat there holding my breath while He leafed through the pages. He stopped about half-way through, when He came upon some loose, typewritten pages and inquired about them. I told Him that they were accounts typed from the shorthand notes I had taken during the daily discussions in His rose garden. He smiled and nodded His head. He leafed through the rest and then read the last entry I had made. When He closed the book and handed it back to me, He very quietly said, "Thank you."

Immediately I opened the diary to the page He had read and quickly scanned it, finding that in one passage I had written at length of His nobility and beauty, and how amazing it is that He can be so humble and yet is the embodiment of God in reality. Involuntarily I looked up at the Master. He was looking out of his window, though disinterestedly, and His face wore its familiar expression of serenity and calm. Quietly and modestly He sat there, as would any ordinary man, yet the deliverance of hundreds of thousands of souls rested on His shoulders. Only three feet away from me sat the Living Lord. Ah, it was incomprehensible, this mystery of mysteries.

The silence was broken by Mrs. Hemming who could contain herself no longer. "Maharaj Ji", she began, and the Master turned to her. "Though it's your birthday, we want to ask *you* to give *us* something!" She laughed self-consciously at her own words.

The Master, with a hint of mock incredulity in His voice, smiled teasingly and asked, "Now what or how can I give on my birthday?"

The South African lady, now serious, requested that He explain a statement He had made to us a few days ago at tea, namely, "When you miss someone you are never alone; but when you don't miss anyone, you are always alone."

"Oh, yes," He replied. "When you are missing somebody, you are always in the memory of somebody; you are always in love with him, you are always in tune with him—you merge in him. You may be surrounded by a hundred people but yet be alone."

If only we could fully realize the essence of that phrase—a realization which we knew would come only with spiritual progress.

It was not long before Mrs. Hemming spoke up again and suggested that we stop at some rest station. In a matter of minutes the driver turned the big red limousine into a tree-lined drive and we came upon a lovely bungalow hidden from the main road. Maharaj Ji very kindly helped us to find our way about and after ten minutes or so the station wagon from the palace— the one that had been used as transport for us during our stay—drove in to stop beside the limousine. To our surprise it was not only filled with those people from the palace who were following Maharaj Ji to Poona, but sitting there in the back seat was the Raja himself. We had had no idea that he was coming so soon, as he had told Maharaj Ji he would follow on much later. Humble as he was, he had not wanted to deprive us of any comfort by coming with us in his own car. Maharaj Ji soon convinced the Raja that there was plenty of room in the car and that we would be most distressed if he did not continue the remaining portion of the journey with us. The Master pretended that He had not known that the Raja was only a short distance behind us, but we all knew that He had, in fact, arranged this "accidental" meeting.

On our drive to Poona we wound through magnificently scenic mountain areas, the road twisting and climbing up steep grades and down through valley passes. Round and round the lofty mountain slopes we drove, from where we were able to see whole villages built on the terraced mountain landscapes.

The journey was not over before we had a small Satsang, instigated by Mrs. Hemming. She asked Maharaj Ji if Saints were ever reincarnated.

He replied, "Saints are all one in essence and

emerge from the same source, as waves rise from the ocean and merge back into the ocean."

"I mean," she interjected, "do individual Saints reincarnate, having had past lives?"

"You see, there are different kinds of Saints who come into this world," He explained, "that difference depending on the stage of spiritual development they had reached in a former life.   One type of Saint is He who has made definite inner progress in His past life, and finishes the spiritual journey in His present life, thereby becoming a Saint.   Another may be a born Saint, one who descends directly from the Supreme Father.   He is known as a Param Sant, the first one I mentioned is a Sant.   Generally, when a Param Sant comes, He has been sent by the Lord for a particular purpose.   The line of Masters which follow Him may go on for some time, but slowly it disappears.   Any particular line of Masters can never go on indefinitely."

"Is it necessary, then, for those Saints to have a living Guru?" asked Mrs. Hemming.

"Even a born Saint, a Param Sant, must have a Guru.   That is the necessary and unbreakable law. It would be a contradiction to Sant Mat if it were possible for a true Saint not to have a Guru.   For example, we have a pair of candles, one lit and one unlit.   The flame of the lighted candle need only touch the wick of the other to instantly set it ablaze.   But if there is only the one lighted candle, then the wax, wick, and all the materials necessary for making the other candle have to be collected and assembled before the second flame can burn.   In the same way, a Param Sant needs only a 'technical Guru' to become a Master Himself—no other preparation is necessary.   But," He added, "the spark must be given."

"Then a Sant is one who has to work up through the different stages to become a Master?" Mrs. Hemming spoke thoughtfully.

"You see," Maharaj Ji told us, "Saints who just come straight from the Lord prepare their disciples and develop them to the extent that they reach the same stage of God-realization. Some disciples are given the gift of reaching that stage from their Master without having to put forth any effort on their part at all. Others, also through discipleship, have to work their way through all those stages of the spiritual journey and merge into the Lord. It is just as some men are born rich, while others have to work for years to become rich, and still others may be picked up from a roadside by a rich man who then shares with them all his riches— some Masters are born Saints, others work up to it, while others are given all the wealth of spirituality by their Masters."

After a pause He added, "But that stage itself is the same, unchanging Ocean of spirituality. Once it is reached, all Masters are the same."

"Does every Saint become a Master to initiate disciples?" I asked.

"No," He answered. "There may be many disciples who reach that stage, but only one or two are appointed to carry on the work of bringing others to the Path."

His words confirmed the fact that there may be more than one living Master on the earth at a given time whose mission it is to call others to the Path—a fact which He confirmed Himself when asked. "Rather," He told us, "there may be many Masters living in different parts of the world. They are not restricted by number or by country."

"Do Masters have karma?" I asked.

"Even a born Saint, a Param Sant, has to have karma in a sense, for without karma nobody can exist in this world. It is the karmic law which keeps the universe in creation—every step here is a karma. But Saints are masters of the karma; they are not slaves of the karma; they are not bound by the karma. They can even take our karmas and make us free in an instant —what to say of their own karma. Generally, though, they don't like to break the law of nature, so they live in it. But yet they are above karma."

"In a meeting last month, you told us about the violent way in which most of the Saints and Masters have died and have been crucified, and I have heard of how many of them have suffered through serious illnesses. Is this the karma of their disciples which they are working out on themselves?"

"Though some is their own," He answered, "mostly they take the karma of their disciples. They help them in many ways—ways of which the disciples may not be aware—physically, mentally and spiritually. We may think they are suffering, but they do not suffer; they are helping us, sharing with us. Yet they are not controlled by karma. Karma is rather under their control."

"You see," He went on, "the body is not the Master. When they leave the body every day at will, it doesn't make any difference what you do with their body. They are suffering only as far as the world is concerned, as far as our outside eyes are concerned... but He cannot be crucified."

The Master's words were spoken quietly, but they carried with them a power of meaning which cannot be described. With them, we were silenced for the rest of the journey to Poona, our eyes staring out unseeing on the vista of passing scenery, our thoughts steeped in the wonder and significance of the Master's words—of His very presence.

We spent only one night in Poona. For some reason I hadn't expected Poona to be impressive as a place of beauty, and was surprised to discover that it was the most attractive town I had yet seen in India. Called a hill station due to its elevation and cool, dry climate, many Indians spend summer months there to escape the heat of the cities and villages of the plains. We lodged in the Raja's Poona residence, and again were nearly overwhelmed by the Raja's generous hospitality. Our every comfort was graciously attended to. Again, as I had found everywhere we traveled in the Master's company, that desire to serve others in His Name was paramount and foremost in the hearts of His disciples. The Raja of Sangli presented the best demonstration of this humility that I had yet seen, his kindness seemed to know no bounds and extended equally to all his servants.

The following day found us back in Bombay, where we were greeted by throngs of enthusiastic Satsangis, so glad to see us again and delighted to have the Master's darshan. I felt a sadness in spite of all the gaiety, however, because that day we were saying good-bye to Maharaj Ji for a week, and the tour for us had come to an end. Maharaj Ji had yet to visit one or two more remote areas, and we could not accompany Him because of lack of transport. So, after a busy day in the great Gate City, Mr. Ahluwalia, Mr. Leeming and I constituted a tired threesome when boarding the train that was bound for Beas, while the others in our touring party took a plane. We had, however, a peaceful and quiet thirty-six hour journey in the air-conditioned coach, each one of us having a private compartment.

Finally, early on Saturday morning, we again saw the familiar and so friendly domed towers of the Satsanghar silhouetted against the sky as we entered the gates of the Dera. And no place on earth but the Dera could have looked so good and so welcome to us then.

CHAPTER THIRTEEN

BACK IN THE ROSE GARDEN

The discussions which we had enjoyed in the Master's rose garden before the Bombay tour were only preludes to the talks with Him which came during the holiday season in late December. Though Mr. Thomas, our principal source of questions, had left for the United States shortly before the tour had begun, there were now a few more Satsangis from the West, with more questions to ask. And the first feelings of awe and restraint had disappeared, so that all our questions seemed to take on a more direct and thought-provoking flavor.

As time went on, it became increasingly apparent how clearly the Master knew one's heart; often He answered one's most hidden thoughts. In fact, it seemed that He not only knew one's thoughts, but veritably directed them. For example, one of us would often find himself asking a question which he had not even thought of previously, only to discover later on that someone else in the group had been bothered by the same question for weeks, but had not had the courage to ask it himself. On the other hand, there were instances when one of us would ask a question yet feel that he had not at all expressed his thought clearly. The Master would handle such a situation either by asking, "What was that? I didn't quite understand your question." And the disciple would stop for a moment, think about it, and speak again—surprisingly enough using words which exactly stated his problem—whereupon the Master would give him the answer he was looking for. Or the Master would simply ignore the question and answer the thought. At such times one of us might come forward brazenly trying to say, "Oh no, that is not what He means at all". The Master would patiently listen and perhaps give another answer as well. But later on we would discover that the answer which the disciple really wanted had been given by the Master the first time.

It was Norman Krause, an American businessman who had accompanied us on the tour, who initiated the discussion on this particular December morning. When Khanna Sahib had finished reading the English translation of the Satsang, he began, "Maharaj Ji, would you explain to us the reasons which lie behind the necessity for a vegetarian diet?"

"If we are practicing meditation," Maharaj Ji answered, "but are not on a vegetarian diet, what we are gaining we are losing at the same time. The explanation is karmic. We can divide this whole universe into five categories, according to the number of the five elements or essences in each category. These elements are water, earth, air, fire, and ether or akash. The entire plant kingdom comprises the first category, since it contains only one of the elements—that of water. The insect world, snakes and poisonous creatures underground make up the second category, where the two elements of earth and fire are active. In the third category are the egg-born creatures such as the bird kingdom, containing the three active elements of water, fire and air. The fourth category is comprised of all the animals, the category in which all the elements are active with the exception of ether or akash, the reasoning element. The human being, having all five elements within him, is at the top of creation."

Mr. Krause nodded his head and sat back in his chair.

"In this world," the Master continued, "killing is in every sphere, for without killing no creature can possibly exist here. When we breathe, we take in life; when we drink a glass of water, we take in life; when we walk, we crush so many insects under our feet. The living must subsist on the living here, but Saints always advise us that we should collect the *least* burden of killing during our life span. Since we have such a heavy load and store of karmas with us already, we should try to reduce that load—not rather add to it. For instance, if we are given eighty pounds of weight we can barely walk; it is difficult to even stand under it. But if we are merely wearing a shirt on our back, we can run. In the same way, the karmic burden we create for ourselves by killing birds and animals for our food is much heavier than that of killing vegetables. It is not that we do not take in life, it is a question of the degree of life which we consume."

"That easily explains the question that people sometimes raise by saying that vegetarians still take in life, whether they eat meat or not," Mr. Krause commented.

"Yes," the Master acknowledged. "And we can clearly see this law of degree at work even in this world. For if we pluck a flower from another's garden, at the most we can be reprimanded. But if we slay another man, we are imprisoned for life or executed. Similarly, the karma we collect from eating vegetables during an entire year can be cleared from our path by a day's meditation. But if, on the other hand, we are carrying on a wholesale killing of creatures in higher categories for our stomach, and yet we are meditating at the same time, we are losing whatever we are gaining. The balance remains the same, and there is no use of our meditation at all. And if we don't do our meditation and go on increasing our load of karmic debts, it then becomes impossible for us to carry on, to bear up under that weight. Then we are pulled back to this world again and again."

Maharaj Ji paused for a moment, then added, "Saints always point out to us that we should try to leave this world, for a place where one soul kills another soul for its living is not worth our existence at all. And when our purpose of existence becomes God-realization, naturally our course is to remain vegetarian during our life span."

Mr. Krause nodded his head. "But how can we explain vegetarianism to those who say, 'Why should I give up eating meat when someone else does the killing, if I don't kill the animal myself?' "

"Then it becomes a question of supply and demand," Maharaj Ji told him. "If all of the local inhabitants of a city one day decide not to buy any meat from the shops, the next day we won't find any meat for sale. When we demand, the supply comes. Animals are killed because we encourage that they be killed. Actually, we are as much a part of the killing as if we had done the killing ourself. We are prompting others to kill for us; we are provoking them; we are part of the conspiracy of that killing."

Continuing, He smiled and said, "I once met a Buddhist and we discussed this subject. I put forth the argument of how can one justify eating meat, since it is a known fact throughout the world that Buddha was non-violent, a vegetarian. Buddha would not even kill an insect. The Buddhist said to me, 'Oh no, no. I never kill either. My servant just brings meat for me and I never even so much as tell him what I want. He just goes to the market, places the food on my table, and I eat.''

"I asked, 'Who pays for it?''

"He replied, 'Oh, that is only a little bill I pay every month'.''

Laughter filled the air at the Master's anecdote. Then He continued in a more serious vein, "You see, these explanations are just justifications for our weaknesses. We don't really try to analyze the basis of why we are not to eat meat, why we are not to kill. If we understand the reasons behind it, naturally we don't share in it.''

"Master," began another in the group, "could you explain how we can intellectually satisfy ourselves on the subject of reincarnation?''

"Yes," said the Master. "When we find so many ups and downs in this world, when we find so many disparities—rich and poor, healthy and diseased, idiots and geniuses—when we see those who are born blind, born freaks, born beautiful, then we begin to search for an answer. Why is everyone not equal in this world? Why does everyone have a different destiny, different fate, from another? We recollect and wonder about these questions, and remember the law of cause and effect. Then we have no other explanation but reincarnation, but karma, which is essentially the law of cause and effect itself. Those who suffer with no apparent reason during this life, must have done something in their past life or lives for which they are paying now; otherwise the Lord would not seem to be so unjust to them, while good to others.''

"Is it ever necessary for a Satsangi to reincarnate

into an animal after initiation?" asked another.

"What do you mean by necessary?" the Master asked with a curious smile.

"Could it happen?"

"No," the Master shook His head, still keeping His smile. We all laughed then—it was good to hear this verification of what we had read in the books from the Master Himself.

"Even if his karmas are bad," He continued, 'he will not be sent back from the human birth into an animal form. We don't come down, we go up. We may get another human form to improve ourself, but we will not go back."

"Don't some people do wrong things and come back as animals?" asked a South African lady.

"Yes, but not initiates."

"Many people find this difficult to accept," she commented.

"If we don't behave like a man and act like a beast while we are human, aren't we entitled to go back into those forms? Our desires pull us back to those births where we can fully satisfy our instincts and desires. But the Lord doesn't find excuses to send us back down from the human form. We only go back when we want to go back; when we don't want to make the best use of this human form and we have strong desires which cannot be satisfied in the human form."

"Then does the soul who has those desires and goes back to the animal form have to go through the whole evolutionary round of birth and death again?" asked Mr. Florentine Perez, an elderly South American disciple who had arrived at the Dera that week.

"No," the Master turned in his chair to speak directly to him. "A soul does not lose all its human evolution by going back. It does not go through the same round again. If we once have to take a step lower, we can come back to the human form directly, and then make our way up."

Then I asked, "One point which has always interested me is whether or not one is conscious of the fact that one has taken a lower form for a birth?"

The Master replied, "If one were to take a lower birth, say as a dog, he would not be conscious at all that he had taken that birth. If he were conscious that he was once a human, then if we were to try to kill him, he would be happy that he was being relieved of his animal body. But he is contented; he wants to live as he is born. He would be happy as a pig even. For no soul, no matter in what form, wants death. This is, you see, a quality of the mind, of Kal—that we have to be contented where we are born and not conscious of the karmas and desires we created to bring us to that form. If we were to know the sins we committed and the desires we entertained to bring us to a physical form, yet at the same time were aware of the undesirability of the form in which we were imprisoned, then we would at once cease creating any new karma to draw us back again. Then the world would cease to exist; the universe could not go on. And when we, the top of the material creation, are not conscious of what forms we have come from and what brought us here, how can one in a lower species be conscious of his origin?"

"Another question, Maharaj Ji", another in the group began. "If it is so beautiful in the astral heavens, how can we ever be pulled back here at all?"

"Even now we don't want to go away from here," the Master's eyes sparkled with humor."

A round of spontaneous laughter rose at His

remark. Then He continued, "We see so much suffering around us, yet if anyone were to say, 'All right,
prepare yourself, you are going to die.' Are we prepared to die? No we say we have so many things to
do yet.

"We think we are prepared, though. The Great
Master used to tell us a very humorous story which I
have repeated many times," Maharaj Ji smiled in
remembrance. "An old lady had a very ill daughter.
She prayed to the Lord to save her, saying, 'Oh Lord,
take away my life; I cannot see the suffering of this
girl. Let her live; I want to die in her place.' Then,
as it happened, a black waterbuffalo came into the
woman's yard. But the buffalo looked quite strange—
its head was covered with a black container which
held its fodder. While trying to eat the fodder, its
horns had pierced the container and it stuck to the
buffalo's head. Now when this buffalo approached
the grieving mother, she immediately thought that the
Angel of Death had come for her. At once she said,
pointing to a corner of her house, 'My daughter is in
that room ! Please take her !'

The Master's words evoked a torrent of laughter
in the group. We could clearly identify ourselves in
that story.

When the last of the laughter had died down, I
spoke up again. "Maharaj Ji, you mentioned before
that an initiate cannot go back into an animal form.
We have also read that we will never take more than
four human births after our first initiation. Is that
right?"

"Yes," He nodded. "Even one life is enough if we
don't have any strong attachments with the world."

"But what if one doesn't make any progress inside?

Does that make any difference?"

"Our coming back to this world depends upon many things, but mostly on the strength of our desires, our cravings, our longings, our karmas, and attachments. Even if we haven't made much progress during our life span, yet we have few desires and little attachment with people—nothing can bring us back. We are taken to certain stages inside from where we can work and make our way up. On the other hand, sometimes we do make progress inside to some extent, but if we still have very strong attachments with the world we are brought back to clear those attachments and make further progress.

"It depends upon the individual situation," the Master went on. "But there are no failures in Sant Mat. We are always ahead, ahead, and ahead. If we do take another birth to make progress, we will be born under much better circumstances as far as meditation is concerned, as far as devotion for the Lord is concerned—not from a material point of view. Ultimately we have got to go forward, and every step, every birth is a step forward—not backward."

Then Daryai Lal, who rarely missed joining our daily discussions, added, "And most important, it is the Grace of the Master which makes it possible for us to clear our attachments and go back to the Lord."

Somehow the meaning of Daryai Lal's statement silenced us all. For we did not have to look very far to find the Master to whom he referred. He sat right there before us.

Then Mrs. Neilsen spoke up for the first time that morning. "Master," she began, "You were explaining earlier about the suffering which some of us go through for no apparent reason, and that its origin lies in karma and reincarnation.''

The Master nodded acknowledgement.

"Then there is no such thing as injustice?" her voice ended in a question mark.

"No," He said. "There is no injustice. From a worldly point of view, we some times say an event is unjust as it may appear to us. But from the Lord's point of view, we cannot say that there is injustice of any kind. For instance, an innocent man is hanged, and we discover later that he was innocent of the accused crime. From a worldly point of view this is a great injustice, but from the Lord's point of view, it is no injustice at all. The man only received what he had earned from some other act in a previous life."

Seeing that we wanted Him to continue, the Master went on to explain, "You see, there are three kinds of karma: pralabdh, kriyaman, and sinchit. Pralabdh karmas, or the so-called fate karmas, are due to actions and desires in previous lives and determine our present birth and circumstances. Kriyaman karmas are those which we are creating right now, or the new seeds we sow in our present lifetime. In other words, while we reap the results of whatever we have done in the past, good or bad, we are at the same time creating more karma for the future. The third type of karma is sinchit, or reserve karma. In a single birth one cannot pay for all that he has sown in his past lives. Supposing a man kills a thousand chickens in one lifetime, naturally he cannot pay for all those lives in one human form. So these karmas have been stored and have accumulated through lifetime after lifetime. Though we don't deal with sinchit karma in our present life it nevertheless has to be accounted for in subsequent lives.

Then a question which had entered the minds of all of us at one time or another was voiced by Peter Mitchell, a young man from Northern Rhodesia. He was among those who had recently arrived at the Dera and was to be initiated the following week. "Master," he began, "how can one tell whether one is going through a fate karma or one is creating new karma ?"

Maharaj Ji turned to him. "In the initial stages it is very difficult to tell," He replied. "One cannot differentiate until he progresses in his meditation up to the second stage on the Path, the stage of universal mind, and the mind merges in its source. Then the mind is clear, clean and free from the influence of karma. But what little karma we accumulate here is automatically taken care of by our daily meditation."

"Could astrology be called a karmic outline of a life ?"

"Perhaps astrology could be called a map of how our life will go," Daryai Lal put in, looking at the Master for confirmation.

"Yes," Maharaj Ji affirmed. "But astrology is just a science—reading about your future destiny— nothing more. And only one in one thousand astrologers are right in their predictions, generally they are imposters or they do not know how to interpret what they see. At best, they will only give us a scant outline of our future with few details. And, He added with emphasis, "astrology definitely cannot help us to achieve spiritual liberation."

"But would you object if we went to an astrologer?" asked a young man from America.

The Master smiled. "Our destiny is not to be changed by visiting one. Why worry about knowing what it is? If, for example, you are told that you are going to meet with an accident in a car, and believe it, then every time you are in a car the fear of an accident will be on your mind. It is better *not* to know our destiny, for only that will happen which has to happen."

"What is palmistry?" I asked then. I had always wondered about the validity of hand-reading.

"Palmistry is also just a science, a branch of the same science as astrology. Hand-reading, forehead reading, astrology, and so on—all these methods just give the bare facts of one's life. But I wouldn't advise going to an astrologer or palmist at all," the Master said again. "He may or may not be right. And if your future is not to be changed, why worry about knowing it?"

"How much free will do we have, actually?" Peter spoke up again.

"Actually we have hardly any free will at all," the Master answered. "Since it was not within our power to choose to be born in a particular country or a particular family, in a particular atmosphere, our mind has been molded to think in the direction which these circumstances have shaped. We say 'This is my decision, it is my free will.' But we forget what has led us to think in that direction and to form that conclusion. A person who isn't born into an atmosphere of a good family and has not the advantage of good family teachings, his way of thinking will be absolutely different from that of another person who has come from different circumstances. Both will say they have free will, but it is obvious that their circumstances and environment have molded the direction of their thinking. Everything is channeled, planned, you see. And in that channel we look and think and move about. Even within that sphere, though, we still have some free will—but very limited."

"Where does effort come in, then?" asked Mrs. Nielsen.

"We should perform all acts as if we were 'sowing new seeds' with honest intentions not to do anything wrong as we understand it, because we don't yet know whether we are reaping the result of the past or sowing a new seed. If with all honest intentions, however, a bad act does occur, it would probably be past karma. But the good intention *must be* honest," He gestured for emphasis.

"Is there any 'rule of thumb', so to speak, which one can apply *after* performing an action to discern whether or not he has sown a new seed?" asked Peter.

"Again, we cannot make a hard and fast distinction," the Master replied. "Generally speaking, when we carry a strong sense of guilt about an action, we have definitely created new karma. But those actions which we forget at once—they are predestined, and are old karma. But we still cannot draw a hard and fast rule."

He waited for a moment and then said, turning to all of us. "We should not worry about making these karmic distinctions. For if we are daily attending to our meditation and are trying to remain firmly on the principles of Sant Mat, always keeping our destination in mind, naturally we will hardly be sowing any new seeds for the future at all; and if any, they would be very insignificant and would be dissolved through our meditation. But if we are not faithful to our meditation and to the teachings, of course the temptations will be with us also."

Then Mrs. Hemming entered the discussion by asking, "when we become disciples, are our fate karmas changed from their original plan?"

"We still have to go through those karmas, though some of them become ineffective through meditation," the Master said to her. "For instance, a brutal stab may be reduced to the pain of a pinprick. Some karmas we may even go through in dreams, but we still have to undergo all of our allotted karmas."

The South African lady nodded her head.

"Doesn't the Master take over a disciple's life destiny and change his karmas at initiation?" she asked.

"The Masters always give you support, and help you to go through your karmas," He assured her, smiling. "Generally, they help a disciple a great deal. If at any time a disciple really can't go through a particular karmic experience, the Masters postpone it for some time. Many times they reduce our load of karma so that we do not have to pay full account—sometimes they even take our karma on their own bodies," He said quietly. "But in some measure the disciple has to go through his karma, definitely. The Lord decides *when* and *how* we are to pay off our karmic debts for our best spiritual benefit.

"For example," He continued, "say that you were destined to undergo a serious car accident. The accident must happen, but it will happen in such a way that you will be protected; you will not feel much pain as a result of it. You may even become aware while driving that, 'I am going to meet with an accident.'"

Then He turned to all of us, saying, "Saints always advise us that whether we are reaping the fruit of good karma or bad karma, we should always keep our attention in the Lord, unconditionally resigning to His will. By His Grace our own outlook towards those events and how they are going to take place changes. We adjust to them and face them without being affected. You see, the real purpose of the Saints, their real service to us, is to pull us out of this world of good and bad, of illusion, and take us back to the Lord. And every experience we have is meant to further that mission."

"Another question, Master," Mrs. Nielsen said. "Would you tell us the value of prayer according to the Radha Soami Path ?"

"Prayer is usually placing the desires and wishes of our mind before the Lord to be fulfilled. We are all beggars at the door of the Lord. And the Lord is a very good giver, but we are very poor beggars. We don't ask Him for the Jewels which He wants to give us; rather we ask for those things from which He wants to detach us. And most of the time we don't know what we are praying for when we pray," the Master smiled. "We may spend four or five years in praying for a favor, and perhaps we will then pray for another ten years to get rid of that favor!"

Everyone broke into laughter at this, for we could easily see the truth of His words in our own lives.

"When we pray to the Lord to have our worldly desires and wishes granted, no matter what they may be, we are devotees of the mind," the Master continued after a moment. "Our mind creates desires, and we pray to the Lord that those desires be fulfilled. That is, we are trying to ask the Lord to submit to the will of our mind rather than to ask the mind to submit to the will of the Lord. This makes us slaves of the mind, as we are asking the Lord to grant the mind's demands. We should instead try to become the slave of the Lord, by being happy with what He gives us. We don't know what His purpose for us may be, nor do we know what is best for us.

"For example, a mother is nursing a child, and the child becomes ill," He went on to illustrate. "Though the child cries for sweets, the mother knows that they will only aggravate his fever and will not give him any. She only gives him bitter medicine whether he likes it or not. Not because she doesn't love him; rather she loves him more than the child realizes. Similarly, sometimes we feel we are not heard; that the Lord doesn't help us. But that is absolutely a wrong conception, for we don't know what may be best for us."

The Master was silent for a moment, allowing us to absorb this concept. Then He went on to say, "The Great Master used to tell us about a lady who approached Him once and begged Him to give her a son. 'I have been married for twenty years,' she complained to Him, 'and have not had a child so far.' The woman was greatly distressed, for an Indian woman without a child considers herself to be a failure in marriage.

"The Great Master nodded His head in understanding. 'All right', He told her. 'I will give you a child if you will do what I say.'

" 'I will do anything !' she assured Him.

"For six months, regularly and daily do your meditation for three hours a day. Then you may come to me and I will give you as many children as you wish!"

"At the end of six months the lady returned to the Master as she had been told. The Great Master smiled at her when she came to Him. 'How many children do you want?' He asked her.

" 'Please, none!" she cried. 'Oh, please—don't take away what you have given me now. I ask for nothing else—no children. Just don't take away what you have given me!' "

Again laughter filled the air when we had heard the Master's story.

"So you see," He said after a while, "until we get something better, we don't know what is best for us. And when we are His devotee, He is not unmindful of all our daily needs. For example, when a maid works at your house very dutifully and does not ask for anything, you always feel like giving her something—you want to please her because you are so appreciative of what she does. But if another maid is always grumbling and asking for things, you don't feel like giving at all. So if we work in the name of the Lord, if we are meditating on His Name and have submitted ourself to Him, if we are humble at His door and are resigned to whatever ever He may give us—He will definitely give us much more than we could ever dream of."

"Can we pray to the Master for spiritual progress?" I asked.

The Master opened His folded hands. "If a beggar is not going to knock at the door, how is the owner of the house to give? If a child doesn't weep, his mother cannot know he is in need. For instance, here in India we have maid servants who watch after the children. The housewife, in order to attend to her work, has the maid servant take the child out to play. But the child cries for the mother. Though the maid tries to humor the child and absorb his attention in every way she can think of, still he continues weeping for his mother. The mother cannot tolerate this and runs from the house and embraces the child. In the same way, we are all children playing with material objects and worldly faces in this world, but remaining away from the Lord. When we will withdraw ourself from the desire for all things of this world and have real longing for the Lord,

He cannot bear it. He comes to us and embraces us."

When the Master had spoken these words, I could not but remember the same concept as given by Christ, "Seek ye first the kingdom of God, and His righteousness; and all these things shall be added unto you."*

"I don't suppose there is much value in the repetition of mechanical prayers," said another disciple in the group.

"If our prayers are mechanical without meaning, they are useless," the Master said emphatically. "Heart, *heart* should speak. We should always pray to Him for His mercy and guidance, and for that prayer, whether we speak words or not is immaterial. For in the language of love no words are required, no particular time is required. When the heart speaks at any time, in any way, He hears."

"I can never forget the time we asked the Great Master to give us an example of the kind of prayer which comes so easily from the heart, many many years ago," Daryai Lal said. "The prayer He gave us was so beautiful that I wrote it down and it has remained with me all through the years." He pulled from his pocket a small worn notebook—the one I had seen him refer to many times for quotations and incidents concerning the life of the Great Master—and thumbed through its yellowing, handwritten pages. "Here it is," he said smiling, and began to read :

" 'My Lord! I am ignorant, I do not know what to ask from you. Give me that which you think best for me. And give me that strength and wisdom to be happy about what you deem fit to give me, and about how and where you keep me. I have no virtues, no

---

*Matt. 6:33.

devotion. My actions are all dark and sinful; I possess no merits and the mind has thoroughly crushed me. For a sinner like myself, O Lord, there is no refuge but Thy Blessed Feet. Please take me under Thy shelter. I want nothing more. Make me Thy slave, that I may become Thine, and Thou mayst become mine!' "

The Master nodded His head appreciatively. "Beautiful," He said, "it is a beautiful prayer." As it so beautifully tells us, we must submit to the Divine Will of the Lord in our daily life; and in our meditation there should be no worldly thoughts and desires—only resignation to Him. It may help us, however, to pray to the Lord just before meditation in order to generate a spirit of love and faith, and to keep our mind still and free fom extraneous thoughts. But we should never substitute prayer for meditation, for prayer itself cannot take us back to Him.

"But whenever we pray, we should ask only for His Grace and His mercy, and strength to face cheerfully and gracefully whatever He has in store for us, enabling us to keep our attention towards Him. We should earnestly pray to Him within, and remain calm and happy in the faith that the Master will help and guide us when we turn to Him. Pray for His forgiveness for our sins, and beg Him to give us His love, that we may merge in Him. That is real prayer, the Jewel, to ask the Lord for Himself," the Master finished quietly.

A long silence followed. Then an American lady changed the direction of the discussion by asking, "Maharaj Ji, does a doctor take on the karma of his patients?"

"No," He replied. "A doctor just does his duty." "Then those of us who want to help each other who are ill or in trouble of some kind may do so?" she asked.

"Practical help we may always give to others," He replied. "But never with the intention that they should help us sometime now or in the future. We are meant to help people. Why not? We are not isolated from society and the world. We should always help others."

The American lady seemed puzzled. "But there are those in the West who feel that if they help another person a great deal, they are going to participate in taking their karma upon themselves," she told him.

"No, no," the Master smiled and shook His head. "We should be very happy to do so. We shouldn't be self-centered or ego-centered, you see. It is a very rare opportunity and a privilege to help another—as human beings we should be useful and helpful to each other. But with a *detached* mind.

"You see," He went on to explain, "when we serve, we take our ego a little out of ourself, for it is our ego which does not like us to serve anyone at all. And the object of the Path is to rid ourselves of the ego so that we may merge in the Lord. We should help with our best intentions and best ability, but we should not be involved in their problems so much that we make ourselves miserable. We have to share our happiness with others; we have not to share our misery with them."

"I see," she said smiling. "It is good to have this question cleared up at last."

Then Khanna Sahib put in, "Maharaj Ji often says in Satsang that the cementing force is love, and those who love the Lord will love his creation too. So whenever you see that creation in distress, naturally your love will outflow to that creation and be of use to that creation. Otherwise, how would that love radiate itself?"

"And kindness to humanity is the root of all religious mindedness," Daryai Lal added.

"This is all very true," the Master said, "but we are in a real position to help others only when we have helped ourselves; when we have something *within* us to share with them. For when that happiness, peace and bliss, when that love and devotion for the Lord develops within us, then we *radiate* that happiness and love everywhere.

"And," He went on, "when we help ourself we automatically help others in many ways of which we perhaps don't even know."

"How is that Master?" asked the American lady.

"If a Satsangi is attached to the Shabd, to the Master, that force is so strong that those who are attached to him will automatically be benefited. For example, if we are tied to a bulldozer and a dog is tied to us by a chain in our hand, which way will the dog be pulled? He is not strong enough to pull us back; rather the force of the bulldozer will pull us, and the dog will be drawn along too. Similarly, when a Satsangi is attached to the Shabd, it will one day pull him up to the Lord. Because of *this* attachment, those relatives and friends who are attached to him will be drawn in that direction as well."

"But there are people in the West who accuse us of being selfish by meditating and following this Path," Mrs. Hemming put in. "What may we tell them?"

"The question of selfishness is something which has been greatly misunderstood," the Master said. "Everybody is selfish who is not in this world." In fact, without being selfish, we could not live a day here.

We say, 'I want this car for myself, I want this house.' When we are so selfish in the material world why not be selfish in saying, 'I want salvation for myself.'?"

A ripple of laughter passed through the group at this new light which the Master had shed on the often heard criticism against the inward Path. Then we quickly became silent, hoping He would continue.

Just then Daryai Lal smiled and said, "It is often said that if through devotion to a living Master one attains God-realization, he can do more for humanity in one day than he could otherwise do in twenty years as an ordinary man."

We looked at Maharaj Ji for his confirmation of Daryai Lal's remark.

The Master nodded his head. "By seeking salvation we are not really selfish at all. When we reach our Goal, and through love we merge in the Lord, then we are not selfish. For the Lord is everywhere, and when we become part of Him, how can we be selfish? We are part of everybody."

Again we fell into thoughtful silence at the Master's words. The ease with which he dissolved the major objections and criticisms raised against mysticism, always giving us new angles of vision, never failed to amaze and intrigue us.

"Maharaj Ji," Mrs. Day, another South African lady, entered the discussion, breaking into our thoughts, "We often read in the books that it is of prime benefit for our meditation to always stay in the company of Saints, but those of us who live so far away from the Dera can't have this company. What can we do to combat the bad atmosphere around us?"

"Atmosphere is our own creation," the Master replied. "For we are all alike essentially."

"Here at the Dera, though, it is so much easier for one to 'create a good atmosphere' than at home in the West," she said in a subdued voice.

Maharaj Ji nodded in understanding. "If we are living in good surroundings, that will naturally affect us. And here at the Dera we are living in the company of Saints. But just by thinking of them we can divert our attention to the spiritual Path and devotion to the Shabd. You have your own atmosphere—you *create* your own atmosphere.

"As explained at the time of initiation, our sole object of coming on the Path is realization of the Lord; the only purpose of our meditation is just to merge in Him. And we are supposed to devote time to our practice every day. But the mechanical meditation alone is not sufficient. We have to *live* constantly in that atmosphere of meditation, to keep us away from the vices and temptations which may pull us down. For if we let our mind loose just a little, it takes us far, far away from our destination and makes us dance to its tune. So we have to keep reminding our mind that the object of this human birth is God-realization. And to create that atmosphere, we read books, we try to keep good company, we attend Satsang."

Mrs. Day nodded her head and sat back in her chair. "What is the importance of Satsang and the benefit of group meetings when the Master is not there in physical form?" she then asked Him.

"The object of meeting together, wherever we are, is just to help create a healthy atmosphere for our meditation, to build that atmosphere of love in which we have to meditate, in which we have to *live*. That atmosphere should become a fort for us to live in this world. And in group meetings our doubts can be cleared and questions resolved; we can derive strength and inspiration from each other; we can derive from each other that *urge* for meditation. We should feel in every group meeting that our love for the Master has been strengthened, that there is more love and devotion and faith in us now for meditation, that there is more peace within us."

The Master paused meaningfully for a moment, then continued, saying, "You see, our meditation is the positive approach to our destination—all others are the means. The company of good, devoted souls, group meetings, discussions, reading Sant Mat literature, singing devotional songs, prayer—to us they serve just as means to an end, but are not the end itself. They will not give you God-realization; but they will help build that atmosphere of love around you in which you can meditate much better. So sometimes we need the means, if they create in us a real longing for the Lord and will benefit our meditation. Then they may be called the essential means."

Then Peter asked, "Master, if our company, because of our daily job or where we live, is not good, will that atmosphere of meditation we create *change* the company? In other words, can our meditation change our environment?"

"By meditation we strengthen *ourselves*," the master spoke with emphasis. "We have to move and live in the world as normal human beings, but by meditation our will power becomes so strong that we can smilingly face whatever environment our destiny may place us in. We won't feel much of the ups and downs of the world around us. Whether by meditation we are able to change it or not is very difficult to say, but we will definitely be able to face it gracefully

—a fact which may have an effect on our surroundings, too," He added.

"If we try to pick out all the thorns and thistles of this world, we can never succeed," the Master went on to illustrate. "But we can wear strong shoes on our feet and then the thorns will never affect us, never hurt us. Saints come to give us that armour, that spiritual handle by which we can rise above the ups and downs of the world. We will only find genuine happiness when we merge back into the Lord, and when *that* happiness comes in us, the whole world seems happy to us."

After a long moment of silence the Master spoke again, saying, "I can well understand how difficult it is for a Westerner to be a Satsangi. The life and surroundings—everything is very different there from here at the Dera. Yet we cannot compromise with the Sant Mat teachings."

There was a sympathetic note in his voice, and it seemed that He addressed each one of us in that group personally. Always His voice reached our ears like an instrument of music, enriching and complementing the words He spoke. Softly then strongly, sweetly then firmly—these qualities came in His speech as the rise and fall of music. At times His tone was intimate when directed to a particular disciple, at other times His tone encompassed all of us, as now.

"What a misfortune that we could not have been born here," someone in the group said ruefully, as if to himself.

The Master's eyes deepened with kindness. "Each man's destiny is different from that of another man," He said. "Our karmic desires and attachments bring us back to that part of the world where we can best fulfill those desires."

From the expression on our faces, it was obvious that we were all thinking the same thing. What an unfortunate desire it had been that had placed us so far away from the living Master.

But no one needed to express the thought aloud. As if in answer, the Master said quietly, "It really makes no difference. The distance creates a problem only in our mind. The Lord will come to us anywhere. For Him, the universe is one...."

As I walked slowly back to the Guest House that morning, those words stayed in my mind like a sweet, unbroken melody... *The Lord will come to us anywhere; for Him, the universe is one...*

CHAPTER FOURTEEN
DECEMBER DAYS AT THE DERA

A cold, dreary, misty morning greeted us on the 21st of December. Winter seemed to be finally announcing itself and we were all suffering from colds. Unfortunately, it was the coldest morning yet and this date had been chosen for a wedding ceremony.

We were all looking forward to seeing how Maharaj Ji would conduct this service. As is common to wedding ceremonies of religions all over the world, I expected that there would be an exchange of vows and some form of ritual. But we were all in for a surprise, because the Lord was performing this marriage service and He doesn't find that ritual and ceremony are necessary.

At 9:45 a.m. we sat down somewhat farther from the front than usual. The clouds spread over the dais were in colors of red and gold instead of the customary white—this change being the only noticeable difference from any other morning. Soon the bride and groom, accompanied by their respective families, took the seats of honor at the foot of the dais. The bride was lovely in a way that brides are everywhere, and was dressed in a striking red sari, the color customarily worn by brides of all faiths in India.

When we had been seated for some minutes, Maharaj Ji arrived, and with folded hands said the familiar "Radha Soami" greeting to us. He knelt and touched his forehead to the dais in remembrance of His own Master, while everyone in the audience bowed their heads. Then, sitting down in the cross-legged posture, He wrapped a large Kashmir shawl around

Himself, the color of which exactly matched the pale gold turban on His head.

This is the way every Satsang begins, but this morning there seemed to be something different—something more. Immediately there was a reverent hush and we sat in pindrop silence as the chief pathi, dressed in black, chanted an Indian shabd to a strange, moving melody we had not heard before.

Maharaj Ji was like a king—this morning He appeared as no ordinary mortal ever could. The morning mist gently swirled around His form and seemed to add an even more ethereal quality to His darshan. His gaze rested upon each of us for long moments and attention was at its peak throughout the entire Sangat congregation. And the spell cast on us was not broken when He began to speak—oh so softly, into the microphone. No one moved, no one made a sound. There were just His gentle voice and His captivating eyes that held us suspended, transported, during the whole hour-long Satsang.

When the Master finished speaking, the bride and groom rose and went forward to stand at His feet. With hands folded, one after the other, they knelt as He placed upon each of them a garland of colorful flowers. Afterwards, when the bride and groom again sat down, we saw a dozen men carrying large, flat plates above their heads step to the foot of the dais. They stood quietly for a moment while the Master closed His eyes. Then, after a nod from Him, the contents of the plates were passed around among the people. We were handed little cups shaped from leaves and twigs and filled with the food. All began to eat this very special preparation, called parshad in India, into which the Master had poured spiritual power with His glance.

Shabds were sung as we ate, and yet none took their eyes
from His face. For a brief moment, I looked around
me. The currents of love which flowed between the
Master and His disciples before Him then were as
visible as the sun. One girl sat very still, poised with
her fingers halfway to her face. As she looked up at the
Master, the tears streamed silently down her cheeks.
I saw no more just then, for I quickly turned my eyes
back to the Master and kept them there until He left.

That very day during our discussion, the Master
was asked if there were times when more grace and love
flowed from Him than at other times. At first He
smiled and said it was too personal a question. But with
our further insistence, He told us, "Our receptiveness
may be different, but the Lord's love and grace never
change. When a mother finds special occasions as
excuses to give gifts to her child, it does not mean that
she then loves him more than at other times—though
the child may think so. Her love for him never changes.
And His love for us never changes."

The day which followed and the few remaining
days before Christmas showed a gradual increase in
the crowds. The Satsang location was moved from the
small area in front of the Dera library to the large
grounds surrounding the Satsang Ghar. Already the
crowds exceeded those present at the October Bhandara,
and we looked forward to seeing the expected one
hundred thousand or more on December 29th. Every
day during those holidays was an inspiration, and all
worth writing about in detail for these pages. But to
do so would require a volume in itself, so I will mention
the highlights only.

The best way, probably, to give an adequate description of our feelings so far away from our native land

at Christmas is to quote an entry from my daily journal. The sentiments expressed there reflect the thoughts which were veritably "in the very air we breathed," and were common to all of us.

"It's Christmas Morning, 7:00 a.m. I have just returned from the balcony of the Guest House facing northwest. For the first time I watched as the lofty peaks of the Himalaya Mountains emerged from their cloak of misty dust, and sunglints of ice and snow blended to give an ethereal brightness in the distance. Yet they seemed startlingly close, as if replacing the northern vista of sky completely. A long wisp of cloud hung upon the mountain sides and extended its arms to surrounding peaks, linking them together, as if it were a soft white ribbon. A Christmas morning gift from India, it seems.

"Right now it's Christmas Eve back home and my family is sitting around a fir tree, exchanging gifts and celebrating the birthday of the gentle Nazarene. It is a strange feeling to be so far away from that celebration this year, but there is no remorse or longing from the traditional activities this Christmas morning. For this coming day will be enjoyed in a far different but far more realistic way than ever before. While most of the world is remembering a Master who lived two thousand years ago, we are here at the feet of the *living* Christ, the *living* Lord, the One who, in the flesh, has come to reunite us with the Supreme Father and give us those truths and that great love which Jesus bestowed upon the disciples in his fold.

"For this is the great Plan—to become initiated by the *living* Master, one who can answer our questions; one whom we can see and touch and love in this world; one who removes our doubts and conflicts and who becomes an everlasting friend, as our beloved Maharaj Ji has become. Throughout all time and all eternity, until time becomes non-existent, He will remain with us. In fact, we will become one with His Inner Form, the Shabd, and will be transported to the Ocean of Light and Love which is God—never again to suffer the agonies of separation from Him. But in our limited world, before the veils have fallen from our eyes, we are all as crippled children stumbling and falling in the darkness, trying to pick ourselves up without strength and help. So we need someone we can trust to take our outstretched hand; someone to whom we can give all our love with all our being. Then there is no need for blind hope and constant struggling for that which we cannot see; there is only deep-rooted joy and peace that come from the certain knowledge of the Lord's ever-present and never-failing love."

And so, with these thoughts and our good fortune always conscious in our minds, we passed the Christmas season at the Dera. On the morning of Christmas day itself, there was an extra long Satsang held in the large field behind the Satsang Ghar. It is said that two hundred thousand people can fit in that field, and in fact, it was accomplished in April of 1962.

The number of people attending the daily garden visit after Satsang was larger than usual. We chatted for a while and then took pictures. The Master's manner was jovial and humorous—He seemed so much like one of us.

In the afternoon, we entertained the Master at the Guest House. Chairs were placed around the spacious lawn, with long tables in the center filled with sweet dishes and many other kinds of delicious Indian foods. About fifty people were present—Maharaj Ji, the Dera staff and other Indian Satsangi guests, in addition to the ten of us present from abroad.

When tea was over, we settled down in the chairs for the "entertainment program." For a while there was quiet, but no tension was in the quietness; it was full with His love and peace. The Master's eyes were lowered, His hands quietly resting in his lap. We knew He was not really with us at that moment. And then, as if spontaneously, Miss Louise Hilger near His side quietly started singing a Shabd in Punjabi. Her voice rang with sweet tones of devotion and sincerity, and the Master, with His eyes closed and head slightly bowed, never moved. The Shabd was one which told of love and taking refuge in the Master, completely surrendering oneself to Him; it told of His mercy and benevolence in coming to redeem us, in taking us out of this blind well of illusion, and reuniting us with the Lord. When she was finished there was an appreciative moment of silence. Then Maharaj Ji said, "Beautiful," and we all broke into applause.

But then, suddenly, I found myself being ushered up to the chair next to Him to sing a shabd too. I really balked at this because in the last weeks before Christmas my teacher, Mrs. Khanna, had been ill and I had only learned one line of the shabd. But despite all my flustered protests, I didn't have much choice, and soon heard myself starting to sing. Having had so much time to practice that one line, I sang it through quickly, but then abruptly stopped. Again there was a moment of silence, only this time the silence was of expectancy, waiting for the rest. Maharaj Ji turned and looked at me with a questioning smile on His face. "That's all?" He asked, "One line?" With a suppressed laugh I spread my hands helplessly and the silence was broken—

this time with more laughter than applause. When this died down, much to the gratitude and enjoyment of all of us, Mrs. Khanna came to the rescue and sang the shabd beautifully in its entirety.

When she finished, the group again became silent and introspective. A poem was read by a very dear man, Trilok Chand, an elderly Satsangi of many years and a permanent resident of the Dera. But the real highlight of the program came when Miss Hilger read a few extracts on love, translated by Mr. Ahluwalia into English from a Punjabi book written by the Great Master.* Everyone gathered closer together around the Master—some sitting on the rug at His feet. The luminescence of dusk was quietly setting upon us and the birds were murmuring their songs in the trees as she read the words. There was a strange intimacy and a sharing among us all at this time. A tangible, peaceful joy pervaded the atmosphere, and our hearts were full with gratitude.

The dusk was fading into darkness when she finished reading, so the group moved into the Guest House hall where films were shown of Maharaj Ji's recent Bombay tour, together with slides of the Dera and previous trips and activities. But I was too busy thinking about the last few days to be very attentive. And not only that, my chair was directly across from the Master's.

But there came moments of pain, too; the pain of recognizing and being shown the many faults and shortcomings that are present in the ego-self, the faults that relentlessly batter at the mind in its struggle to rise above

---

* *Gurmat Sidhant*, a two-volume, 2200-page work which has been translated into English; often referred to as the encyclopedia of Sant Mat. The English title of the work is *The Philosophy of the Masters*, and consists of Five Volumes.

them. Many and many a time it is the power of the Master's love alone which is strong enough to pull one through these "dark nights of the soul." No other thought, no other consolation is acceptable.

I remember one night in particular—another evening during which slides and movies were shown. This time those of us from the Guest House who had taken pictures earlier in the fall and had had them developed were to show them to the Master. We gathered there in the old Guest House and waited for Him to come. I made it a point that night to be one of the first ones in the room where the pictures were to be shown, so that I would be sure to get the chair right next to the Master's—even better than being seated across from Him. I had it all arranged, knowing exactly where He usually sat, and waited confidently while the others filed in and took their seats. Finally, when anticipation had seemed to reach its peak, the Master came. Joyfully everyone stood to receive Him—I feeling most joyful of all, knowing that He was going to sit down next to me. But then, something very unexpected happened when I motioned to the empty chair next to me with my hand.

He just smiled happily and turned away, saying, "For ladies—not for me." Whereupon He sat in the row behind—next to another lady!

It was all I could do to keep from bursting into sobs right there at that moment. They seemed to choke me, but instead I smiled and looked away, tears inadvertently stinging my eyes, as someone else took the chair which had been so carefully reserved for Him and Him alone. There was no watching of pictures for me that night—it required all the concentration I could muster to keep myself under control.

When, finally reaching my room at the end of the evening, I let the tears flow unchecked. But slowly the awareness dawned on me that the Master had been teaching a lesson—the lesson that we are not to plan how He is to do His work. Perhaps the lesson also carried with it the hidden truth that the Master is within us, that He loves each disciple with the same immeasurable love, and that we cannot, dare not, lower that love to our own small terms. Slowly the tears changed from those of anger and hurt pride to those of shame and repentance. How little do we know, really, of the nature of that Love? How little do we realize that the "bitter medicine" which we may receive at times is the greatest sweetness?

The next morning, when the Master mounted the dais to give Satsang, His direct and meaningful glance told me of His forgiveness, and of that love. The tears which came from my eyes then were those of gratitude.

During the December Bhandara, life at the Dera underwent a complete transformation. Wherever one walked there were small crowds of people holding private Satsang, performing seva of some kind, or talking among themselves of the Master. Satsang was held every morning and the numbers kept multiplying each day as the actual celebration day, the 29th, drew near. This December 29th date is in remembrance of the death anniversary of Baba Jaimal Singh. The crowds numbered more than expected—slightly over one hundred thousand. Even though Maharaj Ji had done extensive touring throughout the previous months, the people could not be satisfied, for they still came, intent upon seeing Him again. On foot they came, sleeping on the cold ground at night, and sometimes travelling for days just to have His darshan. During those days there must have been more cases of the common cold in one place than anywhere else in the world!

Our garden talks were continuing every morning after Satsang and following that I would start to do the typing work that had been given to me. I had made a "bargain" with Maharaj Ji that I would type at least twenty pages a day in order to finish a certain book manuscript by December 31st. We had made this agreement on the 22nd, and every day I would type at breakneck speed to try to make the deadline and see Him when the regular seva period was over at 5:30 p.m. By His grace, I made it every day—sometimes just barely, and usually running to meet Him at the last minute.

When I would reach Him, He would always ask right away, "How many pages?"

And I would reply, "Twenty, Maharaj Ji." And we would laugh.

One day I had typed only nineteen and a half pages because I had reached the end of a chapter. But when He asked the usual question and I said, "Twenty, Maharaj Ji", a knowing and amused smile crossed His face.

"Complete?" He asked, with raised eyebrows.

"Well, not exactly—only nineteen and a half," I confessed, and explained why.

"Oh, I see," He said and the matter was dropped.

The next day I announced that "twenty and a half" pages had been completed. He nodded approval and said, chuckling, "We're making progress." I'm sure that He was not only referring to the extra half-page, but to the new truthfulness as well. Not the smallest item can be hidden from His gaze. What folly to try, for not only can He read one's heart, He too dwells therein.

Seva time for the entire Sangat started at 3 :00 p.m. each day, continuing until the sun began to set. The work itself was "moving the earth". The high ground next to the Beas River, furrowed with deep winding ravines and gullies, was entirely unsuitable for building upon. Therefore, the earth closest to the river was dug up, placed in endless thousands of baskets, and carried closer to the Dera proper. A large, serviceable area was, thereby, being levelled off for building on in the future. An operation like this, if done with bulldozers and a crew of men, would run into a large fortune in cost. But at the Dera, serving the Lord is the sole object and it costs not a penny.

One day I finished working early and joined the thousands who were carrying the heavy baskets on their heads. The experience this time was somewhat different than the grass-carrying seva had been in October. The crowd numbered six times as many and they walked more closely together. Dust raised from the ground under our bare feet mingled with the earth on our heads, and was thick in the air. But it made no difference, and did nothing to quell the great crowds' enthusiasm and happiness. The Master sat in a chair on a rise close by the gully where the earth was being deposited, and His darshan spurred us on as we made trip after trip. Some were actually running with eagerness to see His face, and when coming close to Him, would linger as they dumped the earth into the ravine, not taking their eyes away until they turned away with their empty baskets to fetch another load. All the while shabds were being sung and occasionally a group would chorus a number of "Radha Soamis" to the Master as they emptied their baskets. Again I was reminded of how it must have been in Christ's day.

When the sun began to grow red and approach the edge of the sky, I relinquished my basket and gratefully sat down a few yards from Maharaj Ji's chair. He was clad in white with a light, tan-colored shawl around His shoulders. The pale gold of His turban captured the last bright rays of the sun, and appeared to cast an aura of light around Him. His form was so attractive that He was like a giant magnet drawing myriads of tiny iron filings towards Himself. There were, at this time, thousands of people lining up and crowding together on the sides of the gully—just looking at Him. The number kept increasing as the sun lowered further in the sky, and gradually they began to move closer and closer.

Then, somehow, a woman and her child managed to break from the crowd and quickly approached His chair. With folded hands, she and the child knelt at His feet. He motioned for her to stand and said something in a low, sweet tone to the child. A smile spread across the boy's face and happily he turned to go. But the woman remained immobile gazing into His face, until one of Maharaj Ji's attendants took her arm and gently moved her away.

Suddenly the stillness that had been cast on the crowd was broken and they moved in one body, rushing towards the Master as if to express all their love for Him in a single moment. Then things started to move very quickly. Immediately Maharaj Ji rose from His chair, and those attendants closest to Him rapidly made a way for Him to walk to a gate near the area. Ropes seemed to appear from nowhere in their hands,

and were held up to restrain the crowd. Quickly
we walked through the gate; it was promptly closed
and locked behind us. Now there was a wall of thorny
bush, wire and trees separating us from the thousands.
Their feet sounded like thunder on the other side of
that impenetrable wall. But a few brave ones came
crashing through it—the desire and longing to see the
Master every possible moment so great that their whole
beings were temporarily converted into superhuman
machines.

Finally, after quickly walking along a path through
an uncultivated field, and then through a narrow lane,
we entered a door in the back wall of the Master's
compound, slipped through a short passageway in the
servants' quarters, walked down a few steps, and lo
and behold, we were safe and sound in the Master's
rose garden! Maharaj Ji turned, quite unruffled and
serene, and excused Himself until our regular meeting
that evening in His drawing room.

We were all excited as a result of our experience
during the past few moments and thought that it had
been a unique and rare event. But we soon found out
that this kind of expression on the part of the crowd
was not unusual during the big annual Bhandaras,
when more than one hundred thousand people are
gathered together. That was why ropes were always
carried by those accompanying the Master, and it
explained the precision and skill they displayed when
making a path for Him. When the intensity of spiritual devotion and desire to see the Master simultaneously
moves through so great a crowd, such incidents do
happen.

Yet there is never any cause for alarm, as I saw a
few months later when a similar incident occurred. At

that time the number of people at the colony was greater than one hundred and fifty thousand, and it didn't seem possible that there could be ropes enough or men strong enough to restrain the crowd. The attendants were desperately trying to keep things under control, but they were not succeeding. It was then that I saw just how powerful and wondrous is that devotion. For the Master, seeing that the situation was now entirely in His hands, simply turned, faced the people, and raised His right hand. Instantly a hush swept through the crowd nearby. They became still; they smiled; many folded their hands. Softly spoken words of "Radha Soami" could be heard in the quietness of the hush. And as we walked back to the Master's compound, it seemed that the hush had spread throughout the entire colony. Such is the power of that love. After all, He is God in human form, the Word made flesh. And everything, every heart, is in His hands always. How can there ever be cause for any alarm?

An example of the disciples' deep faith in the Master and of their longing to serve Him presented itself the following morning. It was a clear demonstration of how eager Satsangis are to give help to those in need at His smallest suggestion.

At Satsang, Maharaj Ji announced that the library had been converted into a temporary medical building, set up for the purpose of donating blood. The Punjab State Blood Bank had come at Maharaj Ji's invitation, with trucks of equipment and five teams of doctors and assistants. There was a crying need for blood plasma for the thousands of wounded soldiers and hospitalized victims caused by the Chinese aggression against India. In very few words, Maharaj Ji

explained this need to the people before Him, and
mentioned that it would be a form of seva if members
of the Sangat would offer their blood in the love and
Name of the Lord.

Those few words from Him were all that was
needed. During the following four days, the medical
staff was kept busy hour after hour; always there were
large groups of donors standing in closely packed lines
outside the library door. On the small porch just
before entering the building, a doctor and a team of
assistants checked the donors for physical fitness and
designated how much blood each donor could safely
give. As there were so many who waited, only those in
absolutely perfect physical condition were accepted. I
saw many turned away in disappointment. On the first
day, I joined a shift of ladies who were ministering to
those who had just given blood. It was my job to
pour coffee or tea and give out cookies to the donors.
And I shall never forget the expression of surprise and
amazement on the faces of the doctors and the staff as
they tended to people so eager to give their blood that
hundreds upon hundreds of them patiently stood on
their feet for hours just hoping for the opportunity. In
fact, the rush of donors was so great and unexpected
that the staff simply could not cope with it, and Maharaj Ji had to make an appeal the next day in Satsang
that ladies should refrain from giving their blood.

When the wagons of blood reached the central
laboratories for conversion of the blood to plasma, the
authorities in charge were completely amazed at the
quantity, and flashed back to enquire: "Are you sure
it is human blood?" At the end of the four days more
than one thousand people had donated a total of five
hundred and sixty four pints of blood—a fact which

is paramount to a miracle in India.

The 29th of December was a day to remember.
After Satsang Maharaj Ji took us on a walk. Satsang
had lasted over two hours, and the garden visit necessarily had to be cut short, postponed until late afternoon. But when the Master left the garden and walked
out of the compound, we followed directly behind Him.
And what an exciting walk He led us on! We
went right through the big community kitchen and the
huge dining area at its busiest time of the day. Food
was being prepared in enormous quantities to accommodate the entire one hundred thousand people then
present at the Dera. It was Maharaj Ji's job to walk
through, a task He performed every day, giving
His blessings and approval. The visit from the Master
was so necessary to the preparation, distribution and
eating of the daily meals, that the people would refuse
to work or eat unless they were sure He would come.
Rows and rows of great cauldrons, set over fires
glowing in great holes dug in the ground, were bubbl-
ing and boiling, filled with vegetables. Large quantities
of grass, collected from the river bed in October, were
fed to the fires. At another place were dozens of large
circular iron plates, also placed over fires burning in
holes dug in the ground, on which many hundreds of
chapatis were being made every two or three minutes.
From there we entered the room where the chapatis
are stacked, hot from the ovens and ready and waiting
to be eaten by the hungry multitudes. The chapatis
resembled thousands of small plates piled from the
floor to as high as one's head and nearly filling the
room. And here Maharaj Ji took off His shoes and
walked close to the steaming chapatis. For a single

moment all activity stood still while He bowed His
head and folded His hands. It was like a moving
picture film, racing along at rapid speed and then stopp-
ing suddenly, picturing everything suspended for a
moment before continuing the reel.

We walked through the dining area itself where
some ten thousand or more people had already gathered,
waiting to be given food. This number would com-
prise the first shift—in fifteen minutes another shift
would be waiting and so on until all the people had
eaten their fill, one meal for everyone taking close to
three hours to complete. But the whole operation worked
with astounding precision. There were thousands of
capable cooks, servers, organizers, waiters, and runners
to keep the machinery running smoothly and quickly.

As the Master moved through the crowd, happy
murmurings of "Radha Soami" greeted Him and
followed us like a tidal wave. There is a particular
uniqueness about the way His disciples spontaneously
pour out that phrase to the Master. As if all the
gratitude in their hearts were trying to express itself
in those two words. Their eyes are brilliant, reflecting
His light, and folded hands are extended towards Him.
Those closest to His path search His face, hoping for a
glance, so happy to be that near their Lord.

After what seemed a very short time, we passed
through a small doorway in the lungar (kitchen) wall
leading to the area just outside the Dera office. Maharaj Ji ascended the stairs of a platform and sat down to
face thousands more waiting to give donations and
gifts to the Dera.

Here there were two lines of people filing by the
platform, women on one side and men on the other.
As each one passed offering his money or blankets or

pillows or whatever he wished, he eagerly looked into the Master's eyes. Many would even touch their foreheads to the platform at His feet, though Maharaj Ji would always try to prevent this with a gesture of His hand. Some He would even turn away if He knew they couldn't afford to give. Some He would give special attention to, to others He would give no heed. For it is in the Master's power to look into one's heart and see if one's motives are sincere and loving, or if one seeks a reward of some kind. Behind each word He spoke and each gesture He made, there was a reason and a purpose—always in the best interest of the disciple and motivated by love.

Only initiated Satsangis are allowed to give, and all others are refused. All money and goods collected from the Satsangis are turned over to the society at the Dera, a body of twenty-seven men who share the ownership of all Dera property. Under the Master's guiding hand, they designate how funds can be best used for the benefit of all the Sangat, *i.e.*, for the construction and maintenance of buildings for the publication and distribution of books, for providing for and maintaining the free kitchen, for maintaining a free hospital and giving medical aid to all Satsangis and to members of nearby villages, and for giving aid and support to elderly or disabled Satsangis.

The Master Himself never takes a penny for His own personal use, nor does He accept gifts under any circumstances for Himself. He is entirely self-supporting and takes enough time from His busy yearly schedule to supervise the running of a family-owned farm at Sirsa, Sikanderpur—two hundred miles away from the Dera. This trait of self-sustenance is common to all true Masters.

During the months that had gone by, I had seen seva take on many forms—this giving of one's wealth comprising another form of service to the cause of Sant Mat. All Satsangis seemed to place such a high value on every kind of seva for the Master—from carrying dirt on their heads to cooking chapatis or giving grain. Continuously they looked for any work they could find and would, with glad hearts and zeal, plunge into the work no matter what it might be. From personal experience I knew what great joy it gave to participate in these activities.

One day I asked a white-bearded disciple who lived at the Dera to tell me more about seva. He said, "Seva or service to the Master is a unique privilege. It is as good as hard cash towards spiritual progress. All the people come together—the high and the low, moving together and working together shoulder to shoulder. It may be called 'immediate credit' to your spiritual uplift." But somehow his words didn't really answer my question, so I then approached the Master, notebook in hand, and this is what He told me :

"There are four types of seva—with body, wealth mind and soul. The first three sevas are all means to the fourth, the *real* seva which is connecting the soul with the Shabd.

"Service with the body will help remove the ego from us by serving the masses and the Lord's creation. There is great humility in such service as we come to feel that we are all alike with the other people of the world, and that this world is to be shared. We work shoulder to shoulder with every man as our brother. By physical seva we lose the idea that our body is something superior to that of another. And if the whole day we bother about our body and ourself, naturally our thoughts won't center on meditation when it comes time for sitting.

"Service with wealth means that we are to detach ourselves from worldly objects by using our wealth in the cause of Sant Mat. For surplus wealth often becomes a source of evil for us and pulls us down. It drugs us to the senses and foolish indulgences. By spending it and using it in the cause of Sant Mat, we are keeping ourselves detached from it. As Christ has said, "It is easier for a camel to go through the eye of a needle, than for a rich man to enter into the kingdom of God.'* That teaching doesn't refer to people having wealth, but rather to people who are *attached* to wealth and material possessions. If we are conscious of wealth, our mind will always be taken out to the sensual pleasures and the worldly desires which wealth can fulfill. Naturally our mind will not then be drawn to meditation.

"Service with the mind means that we are to train our mind to follow the principles of the spiritual path. As you know, these are adhering to a strict vegetarian diet, not partaking of alcoholic beverages, leading a clean moral life, and sitting for meditation regularly and punctually every day.

"But the real, the best and the highest service is uniting the soul with the Word. The other three are the means which help us to achieve that end."

"How may we make our daily routine into seva when we are away from the Dera?" I then asked.

He replied, "If we use our body and our wealth and our mind as if they belong to the Master, then we are serving, no matter where we are. In the daily,

---

*Matt. 19:24,

official routine of life, we should always keep in our mind that we are doing the Master's duty. Our *self*, our *ego* should not come into it. Then it is always seva."

The Christmas season didn't pass without a special gift being bestowed upon us by the Master. And as it came from Him, the gift was spiritual. On Christmas eve, we were invited to attend the initiation of Peter Mitchell and Manfred Sack, both of whom had come to the Master from South Africa. The initiation was held in the now unused parlor of the Great Master's house. There were ten of us in that small upper story room, seated on the floor facing the Master. And for two hours there was no other world, no other people, nothing except our small group.

It is true that the greatest things happen in the simplest ways, for here was the Light of the world bestowing upon two thirsty souls the nectar of truth, wisdom and love, and giving them the Key—the knowledge of the Audible Life Stream by and through which they would travel through stage after stage of higher consciousness eventually to reach the Absolute Source, the Ocean of Love and the core of all wisdom and light from which all existence has sprung. By all outward appearances, a man was giving instructions to a small group of people, but in reality He was taking upon Himself the administration of the karmas that these two young men had been collecting for millions of lives. In fact, the entire responsibility of releasing them from the material world and guiding them back to that Ocean was now His. This is what He guarantees His disciples at the time of initiation, and from that moment on there is absolutely no chance of failure.

So there we sat before the King of kings on that Christmas Eve, and tried to comprehend the immensity of everything. The Master very softly and gently spoke and we were more than ever conscious of His love for us. The room was dim, but a magical, secret sunbeam from a shaft near the ceiling rested on Maharaj Ji's form. His eyes were deep and intense, and they never left the two boys. Most of us had been initiated in another country by proxy so we too were hearing the Master Himself speak those secret words for the first time.

There is no more I can write—a description of this, the greatest moment can only be remembered and relived, not captured by the written word.

When it was over, I felt as though I had been initiated for the first time. . . .

And thus the December days passed, each one bringing with it a new experience, a greater understanding of the Path, and more precious hours and minutes with the Master. It wasn't very often that He revealed Himself to us, in fact He would go in the opposite direction to conceal His dominion over us. But one day, something very interesting happened to us all.

The day itself presented a dreary picture. Clouds were scattered in the sky, and a raw wind whipped at our clothes. There was some talk of rain expected that afternoon. We were told that the garden talk after Satsang that morning had to be postponed until 5:30 in the evening, as Maharaj Ji was to be busy with interviews. We were resigned to the fact that we wouldn't see Him at the customary time, and had no other thoughts about it.

But when Satsang was over, we followed Him as usual, though thoroughly intending to turn off at His gate and continue to the Guest House. I was walking in his footsteps, and when He came to the gate, I tried to turn and go the other way. But it was not possible. My legs simply could not move in any direction other than right behind Maharaj Ji. An indescribable force was pulling me forward. The others must have been captured by that same force, their footsteps behind me continued without hesitation, yet their faces seemed questioning. Without knowing why, we followed Him through His garden and on to the veranda of His house. He sat down there and we too sat down. A helpless silence followed. We were all feeling ashamed for not obeying orders, yet not understanding why we could not.

Then I said, "Master, we want to apologize for coming in here with You, today."

There was a short pause, and the Master's face softened. Then He replied quietly, "It was inevitable that you did. We cannot help but follow the Master."

Before His words were all spoken, a streak of lightning shot across the sky, and a loud clap of thunder made us start on our seats. Then the clouds, which had quickly gathered into a thick, heavy darkness, opened up and poured down a heavy torrent of rain. All around us the big drops pounded the earth and bent the trees. The Master told us to pull our chairs closer to Him, away from the sides of the veranda and further under the roof.

"Ask Him if He will always protect us as He protects us now from the rain," whispered the woman sitting next to me. But there was no need to ask. We all knew the answer. There was no need for words at all while the rain spent its fury upon the ground.

CHAPTER FIFTEEN

ON LOVE AND DEVOTION

Our discussions continued every day and my note-book was rapidly being filled with page after page of the Master's spoken words. It seemed that each discussion bettered the last one in interest. The group had grown larger; a few more disciples from America and South Africa had arrived. But our number still did not exceed a dozen people, and the intimacy we shared during those discussion with the Master became increased.

The most inspiring talk of all during those busy weeks came one evening in early January. The questions raised and discussed then were those which deeply affect every disciple of the perfect Master, for this Path is based upon love for God and devotion to the Master—in fact, to realize that Love is the only reality, and to merge in the Ocean of Love which is God Himself, is the Goal for which every disciple strives.

It was 5:30 p.m. and the colony's seva activities were over for that afternoon. As every day, we followed the Master from the seva area to His house and assembled there in the drawing room for a priceless one to two hours with Him. This particular evening there was a touch of despondency in the air, for our beloved Maharaj Ji was to leave the Dera in another three days. Perhaps that is why the talk centered on devotion and love. He knew our despondency and was giving us His grace.

The silence was heavy; no one in the group wanted to start talking. Maharaj Ji Himself was the first one to speak. "It's a good thing I don't have any questions." He said with laughter in His voice. We followed His lead; our laughter seemed to clear the air of its heaviness, and the questions began to flow.

"Master, how can we love those around us, those we live with, and not be attached to them?" Peter opened the discussion by asking.

The Master smiled gently. "When you love everybody you are attached to none," he told Peter.

Peter thought over the Master's answer, but the puzzled expression still did not leave his face.

The Master opened His folded hands. "And loving everybody means loving only that Power which is in everybody," he went on. "We may only be trying to justify certain weaknesses when we say, 'I am loving His creation.'"

He paused for a moment and smiled. "I will tell you a small example in the life of a Persian mystic. Once he was walking along a road, followed by some of his disciples. As always, he was remaining in the devotion and love of the Lord. Then a dancing girl came very happily down the road, and when he met her, he just kissed her, exclaiming, 'Oh! how beautiful the Lord is !'

"His disciples, because their Master had kissed her, also kissed her, they too saying, 'How beautiful the Lord is !'

"Well, the Persian Master took note of this, and when he had walked a little further down the road, he saw a blacksmith hammering a red hot piece of iron. Promptly he went and kissed the iron, saying, 'How beautiful the Lord is !'

"But his disciples hesitated and didn't seem to want to kiss that hot iron at all. The guru then asked of them, 'where is your love for the Lord now ?'

The Master raised his hands at the conclusion of the story, and we all broke into unrestrained laughter. How well we could see ourselves in the moral of that story.

"So you see," He said when the laughter had quieted, "sometimes we try to justify our weaknesses in this way. We say we are not loving the person, we are just loving the Lord in him. But love for everybody is attachment to none—attachment then is only to the Lord."

Then another voice in the group ventured, "But what should our relationship be then with our family and our friends? Don't we have to be attached to them to a certain extent in order to live with them? This has always been a difficult problem for me to understand, Master."

"There is a difference between attachment and duty," he replied. "A wife has a certain duty towards the husband, and a husband has a certain duty towards his wife. These are karmic relations of give and take, actually, and are certain responsibilities to be fulfilled. We have to play certain roles as a husband, as a wife, as a son or daughter or parent. When that role is finished, we have no more relationship with each other. We have to live in this world as a matter of duty, taking full responsibility as a wife and a husband as a citizen, and yet not be attached to them nor affected by them.

"A married daughter visits her parents," he went on to illustrate. "Affectionate and very loving to them, she works in their house and plays with her brothers and sisters. Yet she is attached to her husband living a thousand miles away from her. Her mind is not there in her parent's home, but with her husband. We have to live in this world like that, performing all our duties, yet keeping our heart in devotion to the Lord, where it should be.

"A bee flies to a bowl of honey," He continued. "If she sits on the side of the bowl, she will take some of the honey, taste it, and fly away again with her wings dry. But if the bee were to jump into the honey, she could not taste the honey then, her wings would become heavy, and she would die. If we will keep our attention, our mind and our heart in the Lord, we will enjoy this whole world. But if we will forget Him, this same world will become a source of misery to us. Now we are in love with the things He gives us, and have forgotten the Giver. We are not grateful to the Giver; we are grateful for what He is giving us. We can only enjoy His gifts if we love the Giver and are grateful to Him."

After a brief moment, He gave another example, saying, "If a child holds the hand of his father and goes to a fair, everything pleases the child. Boys and girls are playing in the moonlight; colored electric lights are everywhere; shops and bazaars are full of sweets and things to do. The child is dancing with happiness, thinking probably that he is deriving happiness from all he sees in the fair. But the moment he leaves his father's hand and gets lost, even though everything in the fair is still the same, the child weeps and cries— nothing appeals to him. Why? Then he realizes that all the happiness and joy he had been deriving from the fair lasted only as long as he was holding his father's hand. The real happiness he was deriving from his father's presence, not from the fair. Similarly our Father is only One, in Heaven. As long as we are in tune with Him, we are in love with Him, we are attached to Him—this whole world will be full of pleasure and joy for us, because we are happy within. But if we lose His hand, if we forget Him—this world will become a miserable place for us and it will become impossible for us to live here.

"When we are forgetting the Giver and falling in love with what He is giving us," the Master concluded, we are *attaching* ourself to what He gives us and *detaching* ourself from Him. But if on the other hand, we attach ourself to the *Giver*, we will enjoy this world and our worldly relationships much better—yet we will go back to Him. So our attachment should be only to Him, and to nothing, no one, else."

Then Mrs. Nielsen entered the discussion by asking, "Master, what is the nature of hate? Isn't hate just another form of attachment ?"

"Hatred is a negative attachment, but it is still an attachment," He affirmed. "Otherwise, how would that person whom we hate affect us at all if we never were to think about him? Actually, we cannot drive him out of our mind when we hate him, so we are very much attached to him.

"When there is real love for the Lord within us, there can be no hatred; the question of hating anyone doesn't ever arise. We may dislike someone's bad habits, but we never dislike the person. Guru Nanak says, 'Oh Lord, the whole of this creation is Thyself; Thou hast created the universe and beyond. Thou art there within all. How can I call "evil" those people wherein Thou art dwelling?'

"The Masters take us above all rivalries and jealousies, color bars, caste systems, racial prejudices and so on. And I would say," He added meaningfully, "that when we are hating anybody we are only hating ourself."

The Master's words rang true; we all understood His meaning.

"Is it, then, the God within the soul that the person loves?" Mrs. Neilsen asked, "We can only really love others when we go inside?"

"You see," the Master said, "The purpose of being on the Path is to merge back into the Lord. When do we love each other? When we have purity in our heart, when we have devotion in our heart. The more we are nearer to our destination, the Lord, the more we are nearer to each other. The more devotion and love for the Lord is within us, the more we find we are close to each other. On the other hand, the more we are away from Him, the more we drive away from each other. When Christ said, 'Love one another,' we forget the real essence behind it. For we can only love one another when we see the *Lord* in one another. Then we don't love persons, we love the Lord within each one of us. We are not lost with individualities and personalities then. We are lost in our love for the Lord. When we are in tune with Him and find Him within every one of us, the question of our individual ego doesn't arise.

"Everybody wants to find peace in the world, but our approach is political, is economical, is social," He went on to say. "As long as we are looking towards these things we can never achieve that peace. We can never convert countries and nations to one ideology. If on the other hand, our approach were to become spiritual, we would come much closer to each other. Nations would come closer, countries would draw nearer to each other—if our object were one, if our love were one. But if we forget Him, we ignore Him, we don't know who He is and yet we want to try to create peace in this world, we can never succeed.

"Now we want to create peace with the help of arms, with the help of superiority, with the help of social reform, by changing the political structure of the world, by converting people to the political ideology of our own way of thinking. But the politician may try the whole of his life, and he will never succeed howsoever he may try. It is just self-deception. We are talking about peace, and preparing for war. If we want real peace, we must first search for it within ourself. And we can only have peace within ourself when we are in tune with the Lord. The more we are drawing near to our destination, the more we will find peace. Generally, when you meet Satsangis or fellow travelers on the Path, you don't need any introduction. You at once feel so close to each other that you feel you have known one another for ages. Why? Our object is the same; our love is the same; our destination is the same.

"So," the Master concluded softly, "when we are nearer to our destination, when we are nearer to Him, then we will find love in every one of us. There will be no hatred amongst us, no malice against each other. There will be no ego. We will be on the same spiritual platform; we will be *much* closer to each other. The love will flow from within us; we will radiate love. For then we will see only the Lord everywhere and not individualities."

A silence fell upon us all. By His words, the Master had just given an answer which has been sought since the beginning of history.

Then Mrs. Mutter, an American disciple who had recently arrived with her husband, asked, "Will Maharaj Ji please speak to us about that love of the Lord?"

"The love of the Lord is the *only* love," He began, turning to her. "Unless we long for something, or miss something, our mind is never prepared to make any sacrifice to attain it. Love for the Lord is the basis of our spiritual Path. Without it we would never try to seek Him. The real yearning, the real longing for Him, always pulls us towards Him automatically."

Mrs. Mutter was silent for a moment. Then she asked, "What can a beginner Satsangi sacrifice?"

"When we long for the Lord, when we are in love with Him, when we miss Him, the mind is then prepared to sacrifice anything to achieve Him," he said. "And the sacrifices are to detach the mind from the world and its relationships, and to bring it inward rather than let it go outward to the sensual pleasures.

Then Otto, a young man from Germany, asked, "Then can we make the mind pure by first detaching it from the world and sensual pleasures.?" Otto, we had learned, was a scholar of the Bhagavad Gita and other Indian and Hindu scriptures. A disciple of our present Master, he had been at the Dera before, and had spent a few intervening years visiting various ashrams and shrines in India. He, in fact, looked entirely at home in Indian attire, and wore the turban and uncut beard of a Sikh.

The Master turned to him and said, "Unless the mind is attached to something superior, it cannot become detached from the worldly pleasures and attachments. It cannot be done intellectually, by merely commanding oneself; it cannot be done by running away to forests and deserts, nor by austerities and self-punishments. Rather, these extremes attach too *much* importance to the world."

The German youth shifted his position. "Then it

is not at all possible to achieve liberation just by giving up the worldly life?" he asked.

"You see, we not only have to clean the utensil, we have to fill it also. We must fill our heart with the nectar of the Shabd or Nam before we can be released from birth and death in any way, and go back and merge in Him," the Master explained.

"So the Shabd is the only way?"

"Yes, it is the only factor. Only the Word, the Shabd, the Audible Life Stream can take us out of this world of mind and maya with its temptations. The Shabd comes from the Lord Himself, from our destination. When the mind is attached to that nectar, it is *automatically* detached from the senses. For that nectar is so sweet, so melodious, so attractive and compelling, that longing for the Lord comes in us and our mind is effortlessly detached from the worldly objects. But without the help of the Shabd, we may try to live the purest life, yet we can never succeed in escaping from birth and death in any way. We will definitely get certain advantages—we may go to heaven for thousands of years, we may come again as a ruler or king, we may be born a millionaire—but to say that we will escape from birth and death is absolutely a wrong conception. Naturally, only a pure heart can meet the Lord, but to become pure to that extent we must first attach ourself to the Shabd."

"But I have read in the Bhagavad Gita that by renunciation one may achieve salvation," Otto pointed out.

"The teachings of Krishna, as explained in the Gita, say that one should become neh-karma, that is, become free of one's karmic liability. But again, the mind cannot become free unless it is first attached to something superior to the sense pleasures. In the Gita, and in some other scriptures, it is said that detachment from the world can be achieved by thinking processes and by running to the forests and deserts. But this is not true, for it will only bring temporary relief. It is only self-deceptive. You may cover burning coals with ashes, but the moment the ashes are removed, the fire just smolders and burns again. You may imprison a black snake in a basket, but the moment you remove the cover, it again leaps out to strike at us."

"Suppose one had this relief for a long period of time. Could he then eventually reach his goal?" the German youth pressed the question further.

"The desires will always remain, for there has been a suppression in the mind rather than a conquering of the mind, no matter how much time has passed. When we are attached to the Shabd, the question of suppression will never arise, for desire for worldly pleasures will not even enter the mind at all. If one is living in the forest and the idea of living in a comfortable house is in his mind, he still cannot call himself free from desire. But if he were attached to the Lord, the Shabd, he wouldn't think of owning a house at all."

The German smiled and nodded his head.

"Suppose a river is flowing," the Master continued, "and we put a temporary dam across that river. How long will we be able to hold the water ? Perhaps a week, perhaps a month—but when too much water will be backed up behind the dam, the water will burst through it, and rush out and overflow the river banks. But if we build a dam so that the river is channeled in another direction, the dam will be permanent and the river will start to flow in the new direction.

"So we cannot give *vacuum* to our mind. We

cannot control it by austerities, by analysis, by suppression, by withdrawing it from worldly situations. Only attachment can create detachment in us. Detachment never creates attachment within us. For the moment the mind gets a better hold, we again dance to its tune. Now our tendency is downward, but with the help of the Master and with the help of our spiritual practice we have to make our tendency upward. Our real spiritual journey starts at the Eye Center, so we have to withdraw our consciousness to this place and attach ourself to the Shabd in order to follow that Path, in order to get back to our home, our destination, our Lord."

"Master, getting back to the subject of our family, many of us have often wondered about the marriage relationship itself. Does it hinder spiritual progress to be married?" an American gentleman asked.

"Marriage doesn't make any difference at all; it is the attachment and where our attention lies which pull us down. As we discussed before, marriage is a duty and a responsibility, not an attachment. As long as we are aware of this fact, marriage cannot pull us down. Actually, we can do our duty much better as a husband or a wife if we are not attached to them and are aware of our duty. When we are attached to the Shabd, to the Master, and living in the atmosphere of Sant Mat the whole twenty-four hours of the day, these duties will not bother us or make any difference to us. It is the mind, not the body which matters to us then. We have to do our duty, but we have to keep our mind in His love."

"You will find that nearly all Saints and Masters have been married, have had families, and have lived as house-holders," said Daryai Lal.

Maharaj Ji nodded His head. "You see," He said, "there are certain advantages in marriage. There is not too much suppression of certain desires of the mind, nor dwelling on them. Otherwise, there may be an unconscious pulling downward of which we are not even aware. We cannot conquer the situation by ignoring it. Even if we run to the forests and take shelter in temples and churches—what do we leave behind? We need clothes to cover our body, we need food for our stomach, we need shelter to give the body rest. Though we think we have withdrawn from the world, and we do not leave anything behind, we still take *ourself* with us. Being in this world, being a part of this world, we should not become a slave of these human instincts, though they may take their own course. We have to live *in* the world, and yet not be *of* the world.

"Eventually," He went on to say, "as we progress on the Path we will find that these desires will automatically leave us. For example, if a beggar is asking for alms and we try to snatch some pennies from his hand, he is prepared to defend his money—to die for it. But if we were to offer him a dollar or a pound, he would just drop his pennies to take the dollar in his hand. The pennies to which he had attached so much importance are forgotten when he gets something better. The mind reacts in the same way. Meditation automatically withdraws us from all these things, and we don't feel interested in them anymore. But while our duty is there, we should attend to it, and at the same time attend to our main duty. We should never forget *that* duty for which we have received this human birth. If we keep that destination in view and walk in that Light, these things won't bother us at all."

"Thank you, Master," the American spoke again.

"You are so patient to keep going over and over these questions with us."

"Maharaj Ji," I began then, "why did we ever come down here in the first place? What is the reason for creation?"

"To know the answer to *that* question," the Master said smiling, "we have got to know the Lord. The limited intelligence of our mind is not sufficient to understand why this universe has been created. If a child asks his mother, 'Mother, how was I born?', the mother just smiles and keeps quiet. Perhaps she may tell him a humorous story such as "I found you in a basket,' or 'I found you by the roadside.' Not that she doesn't know how he was born. But the child must grow and develop to understand it himself. So I think we have to spiritually grow and develop to understand why this universe was created and why we are a part of it. Even if Saints were to explain it to us, we wouldn't understand them. We would just have to take their words on faith—there is nothing in this world by which to prove that their words are true.

"Instead of analyzing why we are here, let us try to make our way up to reach Him and merge back into Him," the Master gestured for emphasis. "That will be a more objective and practical view to take. And then we will know why He has created the universe and why we are a part of it." He smiled again. "But perhaps when we reach that stage, we won't even care to know."

"When the soul merges back into that Ocean, does it ever come back down again?"

"Would the drop *like* to come out?" Would a drop like to remain a drop, and not become an ocean? Would the soul like to remain a soul and not become

God? A thing which was but a barrier is removed at that stage. You see, if that desire to be individualized remains, the soul would never go to that stage at all. For these desires are with the mind, and the mind is left far behind in order to reach that higher stage of bliss. Where is desire itself left?"

After a long pause, Peter, seeming to be unusually thoughtful and introspective that evening, asked, "Master, what is meant by the phrase which we often hear, 'Guru is greater than God?'"

"This is just a form of thanking the Master," Maharaj Ji told him, "of expressing love and devotion for Him. Generally, all Saints have said that God and the Master are one but without the Living Master we can never meet the Lord. Only He can connect us with the Audible Life Stream, the Shabd; only He can guide us on that Path within. He comes from the Lord; He will go back to the Lord. Therefore, it has been said that 'Guru is greater than God,' for through His contact we too may go back and merge in the Lord.

"And automatically," He continued, "if we see that everything must go back and merge in Him—if we are looking from the top—there is no question of anything 'greater' than the Lord. But we are now looking from the bottom. This expression is just a disciple's way of thanking the Master."

"I see," Peter said, nodding his head. He rested his chin on the palm of his hand and started at the Persian design of the rug. After a moment he looked up at the Master and asked, "Master, when we are in Your presence, should we close our eyes and try to go within, or should we look into Your eyes?"

The Master smiled tenderly upon his disciple. "When you are in love, and are facing the object of your love, what do you do?"

"Look at it."

"Well?"

Peter seemed quite pleased with the answer and again fell into silence.

"Maharaj Ji," began Mrs. Nielsen when she saw that Peter had finished, "I read in one of the books that when the Great Master was a disciple He wanted very much to be with His Master in the physical form. But I've also read that beholding the Radiant Form of the Master is a far more superior experience. Why would the physical form be desired at all?"

"Love for the physical form leads one to the Radiant Form," He said.

"What about the people who are in America and will never see the physical form?"

"Meditation is the main thing. Through meditation they will come to it. Nothing can exceed the experience of inner darshan of the Master."

"But," she persisted, "would that not be adequate? If one could have inner darshan whenever he desired it, why would he want outer darshan at all after that?"

"It is very hard to say 'why,' for there is no question of comparison at all," He replied. "Every lover is always with his beloved, that is true; but still he wants the beloved's physical presence....why? There is no 'why' in love."

"When having inner darshan, does one's desire for physical darshan lessen?" asked an Indian lady.

"No, it doesn't lessen," He said. "it sharpens. You see, the more love one gives, the more it grows."

"I would think that it would be just the opposite—when one doesn't have something the attempt to get it is fascinating, but once the desire is fulfilled it loses its savour," Mrs. Nielsen remarked.

"I am not talking about the physical now," He said. "In devotional love, there is no possession at all. Love is giving, not expecting. There is always giving."

"Maharaj Ji also often says," put in Khanna Sahib, "that so far as this love for the Master is concerned, it constantly grows. There is no waning—constantly loving, with greater love, more love, intense love— there is no end to it. It is never satiated."

The Master nodded agreement. "It hardly makes any difference. The intensity of our desire for outer darshan also grows as we become more and more advanced inside. Though the Master never leaves us right from the very beginning to the end, the intensity of our desire to be with Him, to love Him, to be devoted to Him, goes on growing the more we advance inside."

When the Master finished speaking, another disciple asked a question which many of us had longed to know more about from the Master : "Could you tell us something about what the Radiant Form of the Master looks like?"

The Master answered, "it is very difficult to say what you *see*. Actually, it is what you know, what you feel, what you *realize*. When you come back you may not be aware whether you have seen the eyes or head or whatever, but yet you know that you have seen the Master. There is nothing physical about it—though we feel, we know, we have recognized Him, still it is not physical. We cannot describe what we have seen, but yet we see Him. So that Mater will be the Master— there is no question of changing form—but if you say that He will be in the same clothes or in the same form as you see Him now, this is a question of your individual way of thinking.   Because we cannot describe what we have seen, actually."

"Is there just one form for all the initiates?" the disciple asked further.

"It is just one Power," the Master said, "If you bring a thousand pitchers full of water into the sunlight, you will see the same sun reflected in every one of them. But each pitcher doesn't contain a separate sun.   The sun is one, and is giving light to all the pitchers.   What you see is its reflection.   Now the Lord is within each one of us, but that doesn't mean that we have so many Lords.   He is one.   So for us the Master is just One— for all His disciples he is One—and yet He is within every one of us.   And yet He is separate from every one of us."

"What happens to a disciple when his Master passes on?   Should he find another living Master?"

"As far as that *disciple* is concerned, his Master is always living.   The Master is responsible not only to initiate us, but to take us back to the Lord Himself. Once we have accepted a Master in our life, we should never look to anybody else to serve as our Master; we can get help from each other; we can derive strength from His disciples or His successor; we can resolve our doubts and find help—but we should only look to *our* Master, as a Master.   For us He is forever, and He will remain for us, forever.   The body is not the Master, our Master is within us and He remains within us. He watches us, He guides us, and He takes us back to the Lord.   So an initiate should never feel that his Master has left the physical form.   He never leaves a disciple."

A moment passed while we thought about His words.   Then Peter began in a thoughtful tone, "Master, before a person can achieve successful medita-

tion, he must be able to love You, and before he can
love You, he must be humble enough to realize who
You are. How can we be humble and how can we love
You more?"

"They are all connected," Maharaj Ji told him.
"If there is love there will be meditation, and if there is
meditation there will be love. Only meditation and
attaching ourself to the Shabd can lead us to the real
awareness of love. Meditation brings an understanding
of love, I would say ... an understanding and a conviction of the Path which leads to more meditation.
And meditation in turn leads to a greater abundance of
love. The real love you can only feel when you see the
Radiant Form of the Master inside. Then nobody can
shake you. The whole world's opinion will not be able
to shake you. The outside love—sometimes we feel,
sometimes we don't feel. Sometimes we have faith,
sometimes we doubt. The real love begins to come
when we actually see the Radiant Form of the Master
inside."

Then Peter asked, "Is it possible to love the Lord
at this stage at all, or is it just self-deception or emotion?"

"Love is always the same," the Master answered
him. "It is only our awareness of love which changes as
we progress in meditation. When our mind is attached
to the senses, our awareness of love is different than it
becomes when we start detaching it from the senses and
attaching it to the Shabd at the third eye. At both
places the mind is there, but at one stage it is a lower
mind, and at the other stage it is a finer, purer
mind-consciousness. So there is a difference in our
mind's approach to love and understanding of love;
but the mind at both these stages is still mind. When
the mind merges in its source in Trikuti, the second stage,

then the soul is released from mind-consciousness altogether, and the awareness of Love is then the awareness of the soul. That awareness is much finer, much more sublime and pure than that of the higher mind or universal mind. For the nearer the soul is to its own origin, the more intense and powerful and refulgent is the love. When it leaves the mind and rises above the mind, then only does it realize its own beauty, its own radiance, its own love and affection for the Lord. And it is only that pure love and affection that takes the soul back to the Lord.

"But love itself," He added, looking directly at Peter, "right from the lowest stage to the highest, is the same. The intensity we feel will be changed; our awareness of love will be increased; the aspects will be different to us at different stages of the spiritual journey."

The room was filled with silence for a long moment. But we wanted to hear more of those words, so beautifully, as though divine music, did they reach our ears. As He spoke, the love He was describing flowed from Him with such sweetness and abundance that it was as if we could reach out and touch it.

Then quietly, humbly, almost as if afraid to disturb that sweetness, Peter asked, "If one tries very hard to be humble at this stage, will that help him in progressing on the Path?"

"Being humble will come when you have that real love. Without love we cannot be humble. For to be humble is just to lose ourself, to merge ourself in the other one, to lose our own identity. To be humble is to surrender ourself unconditionally to the Master and to subdue our ego. When we read the literature and writings of past Saints and Masters, we find that they were very humble. 'The lowest of the low,' they call themselves. 'The slave of the slaves.' That humility comes only when there is no 'I'. As long as the ego is there, the mind will continue to assert itself."

When He finished speaking, Mrs. Mutter asked, "Will Maharaj Ji tell us how to unconditionally surrender to the Master?"

"Well, what *is* surrender ?" the Master returned the question. "Surrender is when we take our ego out of us, when we take that 'I' ness out of us. As long as the mind dominates the soul, there will be no real surrender" He said. "When the soul dominates the mind, then we can say that we are in position to surrender to the Lord. Then we are not always I and I and I. Then we just become 'Thy'. Even in this outside love, to a limited extent we merge our will in the will of another person; we try to merge our happiness in the happiness of another person. Never do we try to exert ourself or force the other to adjust to us. We always try to cooperate, to submit ourself to the will of the other."

"In the same way, when we merge into the Shabd, when we fall in love with our meditation and the devotion to the Lord. to the Master, slowly and slowly this 'I' ness is being driven out of us. We take pleasure in merging and blending all our thoughts and will and desire in Him, rather than making Him bend to our dictates. We have to take our ego out of us—and that can only be done through meditation. Then we will automatically be drawn towards the Master, we will automatically be surrendering to Him. Actually, we can only unconditionally surrender when we reach the Radiant Form of the Master inside, and then merge ourself in Him and go ahead. That is real surrender.

"But for that real surrender, that sharan,* we may

---

*Unconditional surrender and submission.

strive at this stage, in the world, while living. For that we have to remain within the dictates and principles of Sant Mat explained to us at the time of initiation; we have to put forth our honest effort to remain on the Path and to give full time to meditation—all these things are in a way surrender to the Master. For they will lead us to that real surrender."

"Well, from all that you have said," concluded Peter, "the ego is a disease over the soul which bars it from the realization of that surrender and merging in the Lord."

"Yes," Maharaj Ji said, smiling. "But the ego is not a disease of only one or two years—it is a lifetime's disease. We are all victims of it. As one great Saint has written, 'In the whole world there is only one great disease and that is ego. Everywhere I look I find everybody suffering from the same disease.' The fact that we are here is clear evidence of the fact that we are victims of that disease of ego. Our attachment here is ego—attachment to worldly possessions and faces. We look at them and wish to possess them; we worry and work hard in order to possess them—but then we find that we are the slave of them. For example, the spider weaves happily its own web, and when he looks to see how beautiful it is, he suddenly discovers that he is a prisoner of his web and he cannot escape from it. That is what we are doing with our ego. We are weaving our own net, which is keeping us a prisoner and a slave to all the things which we create and possess. These things have now possessed us, and we have no more freedom left. Then we find it difficult to get out of this net when we want to. That is ego."

"How may this disease be best overcome, Master?" Peter spoke earnestly.

"We can only break that net by means of the Shabd or Nam. When, through the Grace of the Lord, we are attached to the Shabd, we will be rid of this disease of ego. That attachment, that love *drives* the ego out of us. Love is such that when it comes within us, all the good qualities in a human being come to the surface like cream on milk. No more will we have to fight with ourself to be good, to be honest, to be pure and humble and submissive—automatically these things will appear in us when we feel that devotion for the Lord. There is no other way," He concluded simply.

"Can we have that love for the Lord if it is not bestowed upon us?" Mrs. Mutter asked.

"It is His gift if He gives it," the Master said, turning to her. "We think that we love; but actually He gives us His love. He is within us, He creates that awareness of love within us. It begins with Him; and without His grace we can never love Him. We *feel* we love Him, actually *He* loves us. He has given us this bliss and this treasure. Without His grace, we can never *think* about Him even; we can never even wonder about how to achieve Him. All comes from Him; it is He who gives us love." Then He added, "But we have to be receptive to that love."

"What is the best way to be receptive?" she asked.

"Well," the Master said, taking a deep breath, "when He would like us to be receptive, we will become receptive."

At this the group broke into laughter.

"He knows the ways and means to make us receptive," He went on. "When His love comes, it just comes, to be very frank. You don't have to build it, you don't have to grow it—when it is His grace it just comes. But we may make an effort by reading literature, devoting time to our meditation every day, helping each other and attending group meetings—all these things help us in developing that love. But even still, all these help us only when His grace is there. Actually, even receptiveness to His love comes only when He wants that we should have it."

After a brief pause Peter asked, "Master, would you please speak to us about the nature of that love itself?"

The Master was silent for a moment with His eyes lowered. Then He looked up at all of us and said, "Love is something in which there is that complete surrender, that merging of our will, our love, into Him— just losing ourself in Him. We then find that we don't exist any more. We find only that the Lord exists, the Lord is acting, the Lord is speaking, the Lord is doing. We merge ourself in that Ocean, we are *lost* in that Ocean of Love." The Master spoke these words slowly, His expression was gentle yet strong. The group sat in rapt attention. And that sweetness seemed to increase and sweep us into itself. It was all I could do to keep my pen moving on the notebook page.

"Master," Peter spoke up again, "it seems that all we can do if we haven't made inner progress yet, is to do everything with the idea that the Master is doing it all".

"When we *merge* in the Master we feel that the Master is the doer. Only by that love do we merge in Him and when it happens, we always know that the Lord has done it, that the love is all His grace. Merely saying it intellectually won't solve the problem; for we *feel* that love, and we can feel it only when we lose our-self and we merge in the inner Master, when we absolu-tely blend ourself in the love of the Master. And when by His grace we are really in love, we *know* that we are nothing, that we are not doing anything, that we are not the lover. It is our *Beloved* who is giving us all.

"But there is no failure in this effort," He continued, smiling. "Our effort brings the grace of the Master, and this grace leads to more effort. This grace creates in us the longing and the yearning and the love which will enable us to see the Radiant Form of the Master within, which will enable us to merge in Him."

Again, we became silent, letting the love which the Master's words carried fill us. Then He glanced slowly from one to the other of us and said quietly, "If life is well lived, even one day spent in the love and meditation of the Lord is enough. If out of our whole life we give Him one complete day, just *merge* in Him, it is worth living the whole life."

The silence which followed continued so long that it seemed the discussion had drawn to a close. Deeply engrossed in the wisdom and beauty of the Master's words, it seemed that the desire to ask questions had suddenly fled from all of us. But Mrs. Hemming was the one who found her voice first, and the questions which finally followed were most unusual, and brought words from the Master's lips that one would rarely if ever hear Him speak.

"Maharaj Ji," Mrs. Hemming said, shifting in her seat before she spoke. "I don't quite know how to word this question." She sat very still for a moment with her eyes lowered as if caught up in a world we could not enter. Then she looked up at Him and asked, "Did you have to work and meditate like us?"

"Everybody has to work up to it," He replied, smiling. "Has worked or is working—everybody has to do it."

She nodded her head slowly. "We can only come to Nam in the human form, " she stated, looking at the

Master for affirmation. He nodded His head and she continued. "Were all of us here in this room linked together before through the Shabd?" Her voice gained a more deliberate, confident tone. "Did you have us with you in another life?"

"We must have been connected with the Shabd. Some have earned it by sincerity and devotion. Some are on their second, third or even fourth incarnation after first having received the seed of initiation." Maharaj Ji stopped speaking for a short minute. Then in a softened voice He said, "Whosoever follows the Shabd, with that rope we are linked together."

"And you are our savior, Maharaj Ji," Peter said in a deeply reverent tone.

"It is the Word, the Shabd, not the flesh and the human body," He said, slowly shaking His head.

Somehow we all became conscious of an indefinable quality in the room. Many in the group leaned forward in their chairs to listen even more attentively.

Then Mrs. Hemming said softly, "Your compassion and pity must have been very great to come back here for us."

As if He hadn't heard her words, Maharaj Ji continued speaking. "We have so many clouds over one sea. We can say that these clouds are linked together because they have come from the sea and are going back to that sea. As the drops of water from those clouds merge in the ocean, and become one with it, similarly, we can say that we are linked together by the Shabd."

"You are our redeemer," she finished slowly, looking directly into His face as she spoke. Her eyes were bright with unshed tears.

"The Lord is the Redeemer. He puts the Shabd

in everybody," the Master said. There was visible a
great kindness and humility in His face at that moment.

Then Manfred, the youngest of the South African
boys, asked, "Maharaj Ji, how much of the Master is
man, and how much is God ?"

The Master turned to him with a smile. "Could
you rephrase that question please?" He asked.

"I mean, when is the Master in the body, and when
is He with God?" Manfred restated after some thought,
smiling with us at his own boldness.

The Master said simply, "The Master is always in
and always out." There was a tone of humor in His
voice.

Now the questions really started to fly. Somehow
the atmosphere had changed to a lighter tone, and we
were all halfway into laughter. It seemed that Maharaj
Ji was purposefully drawing us away from the serious
approach to such questions.

Then Mrs. Hemming said, "I think the question
we all really want to ask is, do you always know our
thoughts and everything?"

We eagerly listened for His reply, but Khanna
Sahib answered for Him. "Why must you ask about
this and about that when the Lord knows everything
and the Lord Himself sits right here?" he asked us,
gesturing towards the Master.

But the group would not give up this question so
easily. We wanted to hear these words from the Master
Himself. Peter voiced the question asked by Mrs.
Hemming again, speaking directly to the Master.
Peter, too, was caught up by the humor that had crept
into the group.

Laughingly, the Master said to us, "I think we
might like it better if He didn't watch us, but unfortuna-

tely, He watches everything that we do."

These words completely destroyed our attempts at remaining serious and we broke into unrestrained laughter. I think our laughter stemmed from the joyful relief of having a question which is so often on the mind of every initiate answered by the Master Himself. And it seemed wonderful to find an excuse to express that joy which He had given us so abundantly that day.

When the laughter had ended, there was a pause, a suspension, for we all knew He would speak again. And then, reading our thoughts, He extended His hands towards us and said, "Don't you think that God is everywhere? And that He is within every one of us? And that He watches us, all that we do? The Master never leaves a disciple; He is always with us."

How simple He made it sound! His words echoed and added to those which He had spoken a month ago during another discussion when He had said, "The Lord will come to us anywhere. For Him, the universe is one." Slowly and slowly, through an increased awareness which He was developing in us, His teachings were beginning to take on reality, to bring into being an entirely new sphere of knowing which had very little to do with the words He spoke.

In fact, everything He had been saying seemed to culminate in the fact that we are, right now, and every moment, in the love of God. That the only barrier which keeps us from that full realization and awareness of Love is our *self*—a veil, nay a dream—which can be dissolved like morning mist in a noonday sun. It was as though He were teaching us in installments, giving us as much as we could assimilate at once, allowing enough time to pass for the meaning of each lesson to

be understood, preparing our minds and hearts for the
moment when we would be ready to comprehend a
fuller meaning. And now, incredibly so, it seemed
that one of those moments had come. A glimpse of
that understanding towards which He was leading us
burst forth like a veritable explosion within. I looked
into the Master's eyes and experienced that tremendous rush of power and love.... *He is within us, He
watches us, He guides us .... For us, He is forever and
He will remain for us, forever....*

CHAPTER SIXTEEN

THE MIRACLE

But where are the miracles, the reader may wonder? Already three-quarters of a book has been written on the experiences of a disciple with a spiritual Master—yet there has not been even a whisper about a miracle. Surely one such as He who is portrayed in these pages would have the power to move mountains if He wished! Surely the sick and the lame and the blind would find healing refuge at His feet! If the reader has previously opened the covers of a book about the yogis of the East, he has no doubt discovered reports and testimonies of astounding miracles and supernatural powers exhibited upon occasion by these yogis. Perhaps such reports have even become a necessary sign of divinity for many seekers when investigating a spiritual path.

Let us consider first the definition of "miracle" as it is given in *Webster's Collegiate Dictionary*:

> "An event or effect in the physical world deviating from the known laws of nature, or transcending our knowledge of these laws; an extraordinary, anomalous or abnormal event brought about by superhuman agency."

The Master's power is such that He could, as many thousands can testify, perform any manner of "miracle" transcending the known laws of nature as defined by Mr. Webster. Such would be less than child's play for Him.

Further, the disciple himself automatically acquires many higher powers when reaching only the first stage of the eight stages of the Path. In fact, when one begins to penetrate the astral planes, Kal, the negative power, will sometimes manifest to him and request that he employ the powers which have been newly awakened in him. In the Bible, we read the familiar story of how even Jesus was approached by this same negative power, the devil, and was tempted in innumerable ways to use the immense powers which were His. And His answering words were, "Get thee behind me, Satan: for it is written, Thou shalt worship the Lord thy God, and Him only shalt thou serve."*

On the inward Path, the disciple is under the protection and guidance of his Master at every step and is given the strength not to succumb to the temptations which the new powers over the physical world present. He avoids their use as he would avoid suicide. For such practice *is* suicide to one's spiritual progress. The release of this energy, not to speak of the ego which may grow into uncontrollable proportions, can only be destructive and harmful. In the first place, miracles are all performed in the realms of mind and matter where illusion and deception are ever present. "Miracles" as such simply do not nor cannot exist in pure spiritual regions where only love prevails and the deepest secrets themselves melt away into God-Consciousness.

Moreover, it is understandable that when one does not have adequate knowledge of a subject, he should not blindly exercise what limited knowledge he has. A first-year medical student with a new scalpel in hand cannot conceivably perform intricate brain surgery. Such responsibility is left to those who have had more than a decade of higher education and training plus

*Luke 4 :8.

the experience of at least another score of years. Similarly, it is unthinkable that a disciple could rightfully use the powers he has acquired when he is merely a beginner on the Path to full understanding and realization. Instead, the disciple pours forth this energy and power as Love at his Master's feet in the inner realms, and his spiritual ascent is accelerated beyond belief to higher and higher regions of consciousness.

But then, why do the *Masters* not use these powers? Certainly they would be able to employ them with full understanding and knowledge. The answer to this is that they *do* use their powers, but not for *public exhibition.* It is a fixed law among Masters that they never win disciples by displaying superhuman feats. When we turn again to a Master's real mission in coming to this world, we see that it is to redeem those souls whom He is pre-ordained to redeem. Therefore, He does not wish to draw unwanted crowds by publicly manipulating the forces of nature, for to be surrounded by curiosity seekers or those who have been awed, perhaps frightened, by superhuman feats is contrary to the very essence of His mission and would be no more than an encumbrance to His work.

If one's motive for following a Master is based only upon a show of supernatural powers, that motive has not stemmed from a truly yearning heart. For faith wrought only by miracles is as shaky and unstable as a palace of cards which is ready to collapse at a single careless touch. And as the Master is, in His inner being *one* with Supreme Lord and Creator, and *one* with the creation as well, His power is such that He does not *need* to demonstrate it openly in order to attract the ones who are truly ready for their spiritual journey. Those souls are known to the Master long before they even hear of Him. Wherever He goes, He has that special mission, that special purpose in view, of sorting them out and drawing them to His feet. By His love He calls them, and instils within their hearts a fervent desire for God-realization. And they are drawn towards Him as surely and inevitably as the river is drawn to the sea.

For, in the words of Dr. Johnson :*

"He is a God-man. A word from Him is a word from God. He has no need to teach. Even His presence alone is elevating, inspiring, stirring and life-giving. His very company is self-illumination—living in His company is spiritual education. His tender smile radiates light, bliss, joy, knowledge and peace. He is a blessing to suffering humanity. All agonies, miseries, tribulations, taints of worldliness etc., seem to vanish in His mere presence and one's doubts are removed. He can awaken through sight, touch, speech and mere thought. He can transmit spirituality to the student as easily as one offers fruit to another. He is an ever flowing fountain-head of the water of life. A thirsty man only drinks the water. A thirsty aspirant who has implicit faith in his Master and who is very eager to imbibe His teachings can only drink the nectar from Him. The student imbibes from his Master in proportion to the intensity and degree of his faith in Him and of his fervent receptive attitude."

And the Present Master Himself says : "This is a Path strictly of love. It is the sincere longing and yearning to meet the Lord which will compel one to follow it."

Becoming initiated and following a true Master is

---

*From *With a Great Master in India.*

for the sole purpose of returning to the bosom of the Lord, and from the very beginning emphasis is laid upon this ultimate desire to the exclusion of all else. As far as healing the sick is concerned, the Master works on the inner planes to lighten the karmic loads of His disciples. In fact, it is said that a disciple who works faithfully to carry out the Master's instructions has only to experience a fraction of the burden which he would otherwise have to bear. Again, as Dr. Johnson stated above, much depends upon the disciple's "intensity and degree of his faith.... and of his fervent receptive attitude."

The Present Master says further : "We should not become initiated because we wish to run away from our worldly responsibilities, nor does it mean that we escape from our bodily ills." For it is true, after all, that while we are here in the material cosmos we are clearing up our karmic debts and becoming purified and fitted for life in the higher regions. In fact sometimes, a disciple will have to take more "concentrated dosages," than a non-initiate. But he knows that all his experiences are administered by the Master, and he accepts whatever comes to him in life asking only for the Lord's love and grace.

But this is not to say that there are no miracles, for the Masters do sometimes use their powers in this plane of consciousness. These occasions are rare, however, and are never seen by the public—only being performed to fill a definite need of a disciple in certain emergencies and arising out of a Master's infinite grace. In most instances, only the disciple involved is aware of the miracle, and he usually keeps his experience a secret.

A question is raised here in the Western mind

which should not be overlooked—where do the miracles performed by Jesus Christ fit into this law? Let us first say that we cannot really presume to look back two thousand years ago through the study of reports made a century or two later. We don't know all the circumstances which may have surrounded many of the miraculous acts which Jesus performed. When Masters out of necessity or great compassion perform miracles of this kind, they ask those involved to keep them secret. Even in the Bible, we read of instances where Jesus asked some of those he healed to tell no one.* But always, when a Master has passed on, or even during His lifetime, these acts of mercy are circulated and become known. Though the Great Master Sawan Singh ministered as short a time ago as the first half of this century, more and more of the miracles He performed, kept secret during His life, are being told. In fact, miracles done by the Great Master that parallel nearly all of the ones Jesus performed could be written here. Though it is neither important nor appropriate to eleborate on some of these miracles, I would like to cite one small example :

It was late December; many thousands of people were expected at the Dera for Bhandara day on the 29th. But as it happened, a large number of people began to pour in through the Dera gates long before that date. Late one night, nearly a week before the actual Bhandara day itself, more than three hundred people, including many women and children, arrived quite unexpectedly. The bhandari (the manager of the langar kitchen) and his staff had already retired for the night after working a full day of double duty. When

---

*Matt. 8 :4; 9 :30, for example.

he was told that hundreds of hungry people had just arrived at the colony, all expecting a hearty meal before retiring, he was greatly distressed. Only a few chapatis were left in the kitchen, so great had been the numbers demanding food that day. The supply which remained was hardly enough to feed twenty people. How would it be possible to serve a veritable multitude? The ladies who cooked the chapatis, even if recalled from their beds, would easily require two hours to prepare an ample supply of the thin, unleavened wheatcakes. Perplexed and not knowing how to explain to those who waited to be fed that there was not enough bread, the bhandari went directly to the Great Master with the problem.

The Great Master smiled at the desperate expression on the bhandari's face. "Don't worry," He said, "We will feed them."

"But there are more than three hundred of them and the food in the kitchen is not even sufficient for twenty people," the bhandari lamented.

"That does not matter," the Great Master reassured him.

The bhandari, not wanting to contradict, was grateful when the Great Master accompanied him to the kitchen. There he showed the Great Master the basket from which even the previous number of chapatis had been reduced.

"Well," the Great Master said, "I think these will be quite sufficient; the number of the party is not so very large." Then He added, "But please put a white sheet over the basket, as it is no good to leave food uncovered." Immediately the bhandari followed the Great Master's instructions without question.

"These people do not observe ordinary rules of

hygiene," the Great Master told Professor Jagat Singh*
who was standing nearby. "Please sit here by the
chapatis yourself and supervise the serving of the food."
He cast a meaningful glance towards the Professor, the
meaning of which the Professor seemed to directly
understand.

The Great Master then left for His residence and
the Professor took charge of the small covered basket.
Immediately he and the bhandari began to serve the
food. And far into the late hours of the night they
continued to serve the hungry people, the Professor
taking pile after pile of chapatis from under the white
sheet and placing them on large brass serving plates for
the bhandari. And when the feeding was over and the
people had all retired, the level of chapatis had not gone
down at all under the white sheet—rather it seemed to
have increased.

Both the Professor and the bhandari knew without
a doubt that they had been instruments in the Master's
hands—instruments of one of those rare and wondrous
events which could only be called a miracle. Yet the
Great Master, when told of what had happened, said
simply, "I do not know a thing about it. This is all the
work of the bhandari and Jagat Singh."

As Jesus and other Masters who have lived in this
world, the Great Master Sawan Singh also performed
merciful acts of healing, but great care was always taken
to keep the matter secret. In fact, most of them
occurred in such a way that the Master attributed the
healing to someone or to something else, as was the case
with the chapatis. In the *Call of the Great Master*,
Daryai Lal writes of one of these miracles :

*Sardar Bahadur Jagat Singh who was the Great Master's
successor.

"The Great Master was once returning from His farm at Sikanderpur to Sirsa, from where He was to entrain for Beas. He was on horseback and Mian Shadi (a Mohammedan disciple of the Great Master), myself and a couple of other Satsangis were following Him on foot. Very venomous snakes abound in that district and as there were no regular roads in those days, we were passing through cultivated fields. Suddenly Shadi cried that a viper had bitten him. The reptile was still there and we killed it. The viper is said to be as deadly as the black cobra, its poison affecting the victim instantly. There is a saying among the people of that place that a viper says to its victim, 'Do not fall upon me. Fall on the other side.'

"Shadi's color changed immediately. He was unable to walk. I started towards the Great Master, who was a few yards ahead, to tell Him of the mishap, but Shadi cried in anguish, 'Please don't!'

" 'I must. Why shouldn't I?' I said. 'Where is the harm?'

" 'Is this the only gift that I can make to my Lord?' Shadi said. 'I do not want to present Him with a snake's venom.' I strongly disagreed with him, but he appealed to me so pathetically that I could not act against his wish. He fell down senseless, perhaps dead.

"We were left behind at a considerable distance, but the Great Master suddenly looked back and, seeing that we were in an agitated state, He turned His horse and came back to where we were standing around Shadi's body.

"He was very sorry to learn what had happened and asked us to try to put Shadi on the back of a horse so he could be taken to Sirsa hospital. But it was found

impracticable. Shadi could not remain on horseback
even with the support of two of us. So we spread a
sheet on the ground and laid him down on it. The
Great Master said that if a Neem tree could be found
somewhere near, its leaves were said to be very effective
in removing snake poison. But there was no tree of any
kind in sight. Seeing a small shrub standing at some
distance, the Great Master sent a man to bring a branch
of it. Waving this branch round the place of the wound,
He said, 'I have heard that passes like this made by a
shrub branch remove the poison.' But we all knew what
was removing the poison. After about ten minutes
Shadi came to his senses or, I would rather say, was
brought back to life, because he was practically dead.
His body had turned black from head to foot, and one
bitten by a viper was seldom known to have survived.

"Shadi, a few minutes after his recovery, when he
came to realize what had happened, began to weep
bitterly and said, 'My Lord! Why have you taken the
dark load of my heavy sins on your head. A dirty worm
like me was not fit for this Grace.' Then he asked me,
'Why did you tell my beloved Lord, you should not
have done that. Better that I had been crushed than
my lovely rose suffer any inconvenience.'

" 'I did not tell him, Shadi,' I replied.

" 'You should have let me die rather than cause
my Lord this trouble,' he said.

"The Great Master enjoined upon us not to talk
about it any more."

Our clearest angle of vision on the question of the
miracles performed by Saints and Masters is given by
our present Master. His words were prompted by a
disciple who had asked about miracles in general, and

particularly the miracles of healing performed by Jesus. He said :

"Jesus has healed the sick souls. He has not just healed the physically diseased people—that is a wrong interpretation. He gave eyes to the blind, ears to the deaf, and life to the dead. But we are *all* blind, for we do not see the Lord. We are *all* deaf, for we do not hear the Shabd, the Word. We are *all* dead as far as the Lord is concerned, for we have forgotten Him. So Jesus gave His disciples, His initiates, the eye to see the light of wisdom; He gave them the tongue to speak the language of love; He gave them ears to hear that silent music; He gave them that living water by which their souls rose from the grave of the physical body. These are not the physical, outside miracles, though He may have performed them too. But that was not His mission, that was not His purpose.

"If He meant only to cure the sick and heal the diseased, the world would not be as it is now. Are there no lepers now? Are there no blind people now? Are there no deaf people now? Has the poverty gone out of this world? Are there no jealousies, no wars, now? That is why Christ said, 'Think not that I am come to send peace on earth : I came not to send peace but a sword. For I am come to set a man at variance against his father, and the daughter against her mother, and the daughter-in-law against her mother-in-low.'* But we misinterpret those teachings. The object of a Saint is not to make this world a heaven on earth, but to *detach* us from each other and *attach* us to the Lord. If the purpose of the Saints had been to make this world a heaven, this world would have

---

*Matt. 10 : 34-35.

been heaven by now, for there has been no dearth of Saints who have visited us. Rather they, as Christ, came for their allotted sheep, their marked souls. They came, collected them, and took them to the Lord. Naturally, they wouldn't want to create miracles here, but because they are so soft, they are so kind, they are so loving, miracles do happen in the lives of the Saints. Then we just give them greatness by their miracles and not by their teachings. We give absolutely no importance to the spirituality they want to give us—we are only fascinated by the miracles they perform."

And yet, in another sense, miracles occur continually in the life of every disciple of a perfect Master as he watches his own metamorphosis take place and experiences the transformation of emerging from a lower way of existence towards God-realization. The instances where he can recognize the protecting and intervening hand of the Master in his daily life are showered upon him in abundance, though more often the Master works towards a disciple's evolvement without the disciple being consciously aware of it until he reaches the first stage of the inward Path. In the following paragraphs two experiences are related—experiences which are representative of these spiritual "miracles". Both these experiences tell of the ways in which the Master calls souls from within to the Path, for to every disciple, the way in which he was called seems to him a miracle—not because it is an outward display to attract the disciple or a "superhuman feat" for others to see, but because that call answers his deepest longing.

One seeker may hear the Master's call in the furthermost corners of the earth, while another may live in the next village and never know of His divinity. For example, in the summer of 1961 the Master went on His first tour of the Far East, during which He visited Hong Kong and was asked to give some discourses on the Spiritual Path. A Russian Lady, who was a professor in a college in Hong Kong, related the following story regarding her meeting with the Master.

A few days before the Master's arrival, she said, she began to have visions of Him. It was a most elating experience and she felt happy beyond words. But she could not recognize the person in her visions, try as she might. Was it her beloved Jesus who appeared to her? It was just possible. But the paintings of Jesus always showed Him with a short beard of auburn color, while the beard of the one in her vision was long and gray. And too, the figure in the vision wore a turban, a type of head covering never used by Jesus as far as she knew.

Then, in a newspaper one day, she saw a photograph of the Master with an announcement beneath it saying that Param Sant his Holiness Maharaj Charan Singh of India would hold a Satsang at the Sikh Shrine in Hong Kong. With photograph in hand, she went to the Satsang and there she saw the figure of her vision before her in physical form.

"You have been coming to me in visions for the past four days," she told the Master without any preliminaries.

"I do not know anything about it," replied the Master with a gentle smile.

"But I know! It has been no one else but You," said the lady intently.

"Well," the Master said, still smiling, "if you know, then that settles the matter."

Thereafter, the Russian lady attended all the Satsangs of the Master, not a word of which she could understand. But every moment she kept her gaze attentively fixed on His face. For it was a divine face, she knew. In the morning, at noontime, before Satsang, and in the evening after Satsang, she was always present where the Master was. She never asked any questions. She never made any request.

On the last day, when the Master was waiting for His plane to take off from the Hong Kong airport, she said:

"You are Jesus, no doubt."

"No, I am not fit to be the dust of His feet," replied the Master, as Masters always do.

"Then you are God, the Father," she said softly. Tears came to her eyes and streamed down her face as the plane took off.

Another experience of how the Master calls His souls to His feet was told by an Indian college professor of Vedanta Philosophy. His college was closed for two months' summer vacation and he planned to make a pilgrimage to the cave of Amarnath in Kashmir. The distance was more than 1500 miles, but the eighteen-thousand-foot height of Amarnath and the wonderful stories and legends told about the cave tempted him to undertake the long journey. He had always felt a longing to grow closer to the Lord, and perhaps at that cave he would realize that longing. No friend or associate agreed to accompany him, so he left alone one morning for Calcutta from where he boarded a train for Srinagar. At this beautiful spot, in the company of about five hundred others, under the charge of a government official, with doctors, an ambulance and all other paraphernalia of first aid, the journey to the cave began. The whole troop was led by a number of priests who claimed their hereditary right of presiding over the worship in the cave. A number of pilgrims and sadhus were travelling on foot, but some had hired horses or ponies. The professor took a horse.

"Our journey to Pahalgam and Chandanwari with its bridge of snow was quite without incident," the professor said when relating his story. "But after passing a couple of stages further on, we reached a height of sixteen thousand feet where the ground and the surrounding mountainsides were completely covered with snow. We were moving slowly, single file, and deep chasms yawned their depths at our side. Suddenly I felt a peculiar faintness creeping over me and found myself helplessly falling from the horse. The gorge swam mistily before my eyes, thousands of feet below, and I knew I was going to plunge downwards. But then I felt a strong arm, and in those few seconds of semi-consciousness, I saw the face of the one who saved me. I had never seen Him before, nor ever dreamed such a one existed, for there was a strange light, a radiance all around His figure.

"After that I do not know for how long I remained senseless. It might have been ten or fifteen minutes or more. When I regained consciousness I found my head in the lap of that figure. He was lightly touching my head with His right hand. 'Well, goodbye, my friend. We will meet again,' said He, and vanished.

"'Who was He? Where has He gone?" I enquired from the owner of the horse who had been travelling behind me. But he only looked at me as if I were raving. When I sat up and repeated my question he replied that he had not seen any person there. As soon as he had seen me fall, he ran in search of a doctor, but not being able to find one he quickly returned to my side, finding me alone.

"So my saviour that day was not a human being. No one else saw Him. I remember thinking that perhaps He was the Lord Shiva, who is worshipped in the cave. The face and figure of my saviour was certainly like Shiva's as painted by various artists. But He wore a princely turban on His head which almost resembled that of an Indian Raja.

"In the cave at Amarnath, I tried my very best to be devotionally minded, but at its eighteen-thousand-foot height I found no trace of God. I even enquired from everybody I met whether any holy man, sadhu or yogi lived anywhere in the vicinity. There was none.

"I remained in the beautiful valley of Kashmir for more than a month. But always that face remained in my mind. On my way back, I stopped at Amritsar to see the Golden Temple of the Sikhs and met a gentleman who offered to guide me around. He asked why I was visiting the Punjab, and I explained that I was merely a tourist.

" 'Well,' he said, 'if you are simply on a sight-seeing tour, I can take you to another place of interest nearby'. And in less than an hour we reached the banks of the River Beas, and the Radha Soami Colony. A Satsang was being held there in the open ground. Almost reluctantly I agreed to attend, for I thought I knew all there was to know about how I should seek the Lord from my Vedanta studies. But then I glanced up at the dais, and to my great joy, I saw the same figure who had saved me on the mountainside a month before. Our eyes met. He smiled, then love and light seemed to enter my heart through His eyes, melting me away. It became difficult for me to remain sitting in the

Satsang. I wanted to rush forward immediately and kiss His feet. That half an hour seemed to pass like an age, but when it was over, I ran towards the Master. He did not allow me to fall at His feet, but took me in His grasp.

" 'Well, well', He said, smiling in a way I had never seen before. It was not a smile, it was the Presence of God. 'You have come. We will have ample time to talk, but now you may take some rest. You must be tired.'

"At the Colony I remained for weeks afterward— until the opening of college. For I found my God there. All Vedanta and Yoga were forgotten in the delight of meeting my Lord."

In conclusion, let us always remember the words of the Master when He said, "We must always look to the Masters for their teachings, for their real mission in coming to this world—to take us back to our Father."

Should we then look to Him to juggle a few natural laws in front of our eyes in order to make us have faith in Him? One has only to spend a few days, a few moments in His presence to be aware of the other kind of miracle, the assurance that one has come to the feet of the Highest. There are no words which can adequately describe this miracle. It does not deal with the physical world. In fact, it cannot really be called a miracle in the definitive sense of the word, for no "event" or "effect" occurs in the order of the material cosmos which is "abnormal or deviates from the laws of nature." The material cosmos is *transcended,* is *understood,* is seen to be as illusory and unimportant as it really is in the infinite kingdom of God.

Perhaps we may even form a new definition of the word miracle. Once when I was telling a friend about

the spiritual journey, and was saying that the soul leaves
this plane of consciousness and rises upwards to the great
Ocean of Light and Love of God, she said to me, "Why,
that is a miracle!"

And so, let us tell of the other miracle, the real
miracle—the wonder of a spiritual journey on the Inner
Pathway to God-Realization.

CHAPTER SEVENTEEN

PRELUDE

The Prelude is death. Death of one's self, yet death unto new birth. Again and again we read, throughout all mystic literature, that only in death is there victory; only in death is there life.

And only through Love, can this death be won. From the immortal words of Christ we read:

"Whosoever will save his life shall lose it: and whosoever will lose his life for my sake shall find it."*

Expressing the same thought, the Great Master wrote in his book *Philosophy of the Masters*:

"A person who dies while living lives forever. If you wish to realize God, you must die while living..."

And this is no empty allegory. It is fact. One must die to one's self, one's limited ego-self, before one can awaken to the full consciousness of life in the love of God. It is an actual scientific process, this Prelude, this death. It may take decades of practice; it may be instantaneous. But it is absolutely necessary. It is the first step on the Path of the Masters, and it must be made before the threshold to the Infinite Pathway can be reached.

But death synonymous with birth? While yet living in the human body? A curious paradox, it would seem. But here is not meant, as the reader must be aware, the physical death which ends man's mortal journey through life, and which is not under the conscious control of the individual. That death which

---
*Matt. 16:25.

must precede a mystic's birth is one which is consciously achieved and controlled, and it does not mean the termination of earthly life. The natural death occurs only once in each incarnation, and occurs only at the pre-ordained instant in time governed by the karmic law when a particular soul must leave the mortal body. That moment is fixed and unalterable. Generally speaking, it is an experience which one anticipates with anxiety and dread, without knowledge of what may lie beyond the grave. Death in the mystical sense, however, can and does occur daily. We read in the Bible the words of Paul, who from his prison cell, wrote: "I die daily."*

Except for the fact that the body does not cease to function on a physical level, this experience of dying while living is exactly and precisely the same as the experience of real death. One actually leaves the confines of the material cosmos, of his physical body, and crosses the barrier which is otherwise removed only at the time of his natural death.

But is such a practice not dangerous, is a question often asked? What if one were not able to return to his physical body? What if one really died a mortal death? For an answer we turn to an incident which occurred during the life of the Great Master.**

A disciple of the Great Master found that immediately following his initiation, during meditation the pulling force of the Shabd became so strong that it quickly withdrew him from the body, and his whole body seemed to have become absolutely dead. He felt that his hour of mortal death had come for there

---

*I Cor. 15:31.

**Related by Ishwar Puri, a disciple of the Great Master, while on a tour of the United States.

was simply nothing left in the body. And he said, quickly recovering himself, 'I know that I have to die, everyone has to die, but I don't want to commit suicide. The moment I sit in meditation again, this terrible Shabd is going to pull me away."

He went directly to the Great Master with his fear. The Master laughed in His inimitable way. "Look here," He said, "Are you afraid of dying?"

"No, I am not," the disciple replied.

"Who do you think you will meet," the Master asked him, "if you were really to pass on?"

"I hope to meet you, Beloved Master."

"Then what is it you fear?"

"I shouldn't really be afraid, but I don't think that to die in meditation is the most appropriate way of dying."

"But you will never die a mortal death during meditation," the great Mater assured him. "As you know, mortal death can come at any time during your daily life; it is not in your hands. It may come while you are eating your food. People have lifted the spoon to their lips and died of heart failure before they could touch the food. Mortal death can come during sleep, or while walking, or while sitting in your office doing your daily work. It can come at any time—but does it not sound a little unusual to you that nobody has died a mortal death while sitting in meditation? Not in the known history of this very ancient spiritual teaching has anyone died during his meditation.

"The experience is exactly *like* that of death," He went on to explain, "but you are not really dying. You are still maintaining all your vital bodily energies here. In the practice of dying while living, breathing does not cease. The body may appear to be dead, because the gross senses are deprived of their motive energy and consciousness. Finer inner senses are awakened for functioning on the planes of higher consciousness, and the soul is free to rise to subtle regions and behold their glory. In fact, with the experience of dying while living, you are more *living* than ever before, the Great Master finished.

The disciple, his fears then removed, resumed his meditation with enthusiasm and learned from personal experience the truth of the great Master's words.

Further to these words, the Great Master has written :

"One who practices Surat Shabd Yoga leaves his body in the same manner during his lifetime as one does at the time of one's death. The only difference is that the 'Silver Cord' of life with the body is not broken. Therefore, a successful devotee has at his command the power to go to the Astral, the Causal, and even higher regions, and *to come back at will*."

Plutarch described the state at the time of death as follows :

"At the moment of death the soul experiences the same impressions, and passes through the same process as is experienced by those who are initiated into the Great Mysteries."

And the Present Master, when asked if one must die to realize the Lord, said :

"We have to die *daily* to go back to Him. That means that we daily practice withdrawal of the consciousness right from the soles of our feet to the Eye Center, in order to follow the Spiritual Path within. First our feet become numb; then our legs become numb; then our thighs and the lower portion of the body become numb. When we withdraw back to the Eye

Center, we are no longer conscious of the body and the senses. This is 'dying while living.' Then only will we be on our real Path within. We have not to leave this physical body permanently in order to go back and merge into Him. We are to meet Him while we are living."

Before beginning the practice which will enable one to die while living, it is essential to find a living Master and receive initiation and instruction from Him. At the time of initiation, the Master literally takes upon Himself the soul of the disciple; actually removes him from the realms of negativity by directly "linking" or "connecting" the initiate's soul from within to the Shabd. Though the Shabd sustains all creation, and all consciousness, one cannot be transported beyond the realms of negativity by its power unless this connection is made. In a conversation with the Master, a seeker brought out this very point, as follows :

Seeker : The Shabd sustains everything, is that correct?

Master : Yes.

Seeker : That means that the Shabd exists within everybody, yet we are told that we are "connected" to the Shabd Current by the Master at initiation. What does the word "connection" mean here if we are already sustained by it?

Master : At initiation you know the process of consciously coming in contact with the Shabd. You are internally in touch with the Shabd. The Shabd is within every one of us, that is true, but the Master *concentrates* it within us, so to say, so that it may pull us up.

For example, when a radio is connected with its battery of electricity, we hear a broadcast; but if that radio is not tuned to a particular focus or point, then you do not hear anything, even though everything is in the radio and the electric connections are made. The Master gives us the ability or power to receive.

Seeker: As if we are receiving sets and the Master turns on the switch. Can non-initiates hear it at all?

Master: Whosoever will concentrate will definitely hear the Shabd, due to their past Sanskaras (spiritual attainments and impressions from previous births). But he would not know what it is, nor would he be pulled up to the higher stages of consciousness by it. I have read of a yogi who said that he could go within and see the light, but some sort of sound disturbed him and distracted him from the light. If he had known that through initiation he could advance with that sound—that the Sound is very essential for the light—he would have listened to it.

The method of meditation which the Master imparts to the initiate is a method which is readily adaptable to the Western, modern world. It is one which any person of any age can understand and practice without having to withdraw from his domestic, professional or social life. It is, according to the Saints, the easiest and best means of achieving the state of dying while living. Only the innermost signs and specific instructions are kept for the guidance of the Initiated, instructions which would be of no use at all to others. But let us again turn to the words of the present Master for a description of this method. The following are a selected number of questions and answers which have been spotlighted from my notes of many group discussions with Him on the subject:

Seeker: What is the method of meditation?

Master: Meditation is a general word which

covers whatever practice we do to develop devotion for
the Lord, and includes everything concerning our actual
spiritual progress. The daily practice itself is divided
into three parts—simran, dhyan, and dhun. Simran
is repetition at the Eye Center of the five Holy Names*
given at Initiation, and its purpose is to withdraw our

---

*The 'five Holy Names," or "key-notes" as Dr. Johnson
termed them in *The Path of the Masters,* actually represent the five
stages of higher consciousness through which the disciple
ascends by the agency of the inner Master, the Shabd. Lekh Raj
Puri, in his book *Mysticism,* Vol. II, writes:

"As we have to go up into inner subtle planes, adepts generally
tell us to repeat the five names of the five manifestations of God on
the inner five stages from the Astral plane to Satta-Loka (i.e., Sach
Khand, literally the True or Imperishable Region; esoterically, the
fifth Spiritual Region, presided over by the Supreme Father.
Once the soul has reached this stage, the further stages of God-
consciousness are made within that consciousness.)

"When we repeat these names in our mind, our thought by
association goes to those inner stages. It helps us in collecting our
scattered mind inside, and preparing our soul for the upward
journey. The advantage of using these five names over other
names is that as these five are the inherent names of God connected
with inner spiritual Reality, they facilitate our work of inner concentration; whereas other names which are attributive, and given
to God for His various qualities, have no such association with inner
spiritual planes. For instance if we repeat a name which means
the omnipresence of God, it would be difficult to collect our mind
inside, for we shall try to think of a Being diffused all over, and
consequently our mind shall also have a tendency to spread over a
vast area. But if we repeat the five names connected with the inner
five stages, then our mind will naturally tend to come within.

"However, we must not forget that there is nothing very much
in a name... The chief power in Repetition is the power of the
mystic adept transferred to the disciple at the time of initiation; and
therefore whatever "Name" he tells the devotee, shall have power
for him.... Real power lies in resigning to His will, in loving
Him and following His instructions."

consciousness back to the Eye Center through concentration. Dhyan is contemplating on the form of the
Master at the Eye Center in order to hold the attention
at that point while doing simran. And Dhun, the last
part of our practice, is the listening to and merging into
the Shabd or Word which will pull us up from the Eye
Center to the higher realms of consciousness.

Seeker: I have heard of other methods of reaching
the Eye Center, such as hatha yoga and pranayama
and other forms of yoga. Can one use those breathing
methods and physical postures as a supplement to
dhyan and simran in order to speed up his progress to
the Eye Center?

Master: Yoga is that which unites the souls back
to the Lord. But the word "yoga" as it is used today
generally refers to the progress which is made in the
six centers or chakras of the physical body, located in the
spinal column. These centers are but poor reflections
of the stages above the Eye Center, yet yogis try to make
progress by concentrating on the lower centers one by
one upwards to the Eye Center. However, if we are
in the middle of a hill and want to reach the top,
we wouldn't go to the bottom and start again to reach
the top. Instead, we would make a start from the
middle and go upwards. Our center of consciousness,
the seat of the soul and mind knotted together is
between the eyes. So from here Saints say we should
try to go up, rather than first dropping our attention
to the lowest center and then slowly and slowly taking
the attention from the body again. Why not first
concentrate at the Eye Center and let the Shabd take
the soul up from there? When we will keep our
attention at that point, and try to hold our consciousness
there, automatically we will withdraw upwards.

Many Saints have given descriptions of those lower centers, so that yogis may not think that Saints do not know about the centers. Swami Ji, Kabir Sahib, Guru Nanak, the Great Master and many others, have described the lower centers, in their writings, but they advise us not to be concerned with those centers.

Moreover, to follow the yogi exercises is very difficult—we cannot do it in this modern age when we have hardly an hour or two a day to sit for meditation. And if we don't have a proper teacher to supervise those exercises, we can damage the body and the mind; we can lose our mental balance even. Sometimes people who have been practising pranayama and certain other breathing in the past try to mix the simran with their breathing. There are many schools of mysticism which teach that practice. A Satsangi, however, should not bother at all with the breathing. For example, while I am talking to you and you are listening to me, neither are you conscious of your breathing nor am I conscious of my breathing. Breathing is a normal function of the body. We are just to forget, about our breathing, forget about our posture, forget even about ourself. If we keep our attention at the Eye Center and practice simran and dhyan, we will withdraw our consciousness, hold it at the Eye Center, and go ahead.

Seeker: I understand that color is light, and the different rays are emanations of God. Can we meditate on colors?

Master: It is not the outside colors which we see in meditation. Colors automatically come to us within in the beginning. We will understand inside that they are the reflections of the five tattwas, the five elements.

Whatever we see, we should just keep our attention in simran.

Seeker: How does the method of simran, or repeating the Holy Names, **help** one to concentrate?

Master: From the Eye Center, our consciousness is pulled down by the five senses and scattered in the world. We are always thinking about worldly faces and worldly objects, and contemplating on them. Howsoever we may be confined to a room, still we are not there. When we close our eyes, our thoughts are moving about in the darkness before us—we are worrying about the problems of daily work, about the children, about the business—never is our mind still. So it is the *habit* of the mind to always think about some thing and to contemplate on what it thinks about. By the same type of process, we withdraw our consciousness from the world and back to the Eye Center where we start on our real spiritual journey. Only now we think about the Lord by repeating His name, and contemplating on the form of the Master.

Seeker: Should we repeat these names with the tongue, or only with the mind?

Master: Simran is done mentally. Mentally we repeat the Holy Names, keeping the whole of the attention at the Eye Center and holding the mind behind the eyes.

Seeker: How do we know exactly the point at which we should focus concentration?

Master: You should not try to find any particular point within yourself. You should not try to physically invert your eyes in order to focus on a particular point. This practice may rather harm or damage your eyes than help in concentration. When you close your eyes, you see darkness and feel you are in this darkness.

Mentally keep your attention in this darkness and do simran. Do not try to find the center of the forehead or the right or left of the forehead—the Eye Center cannot be found physically. It has nothing to do with the physical right or left or center. When you close your eyes, if you can eliminate the outside world from your thoughts and concentrate in simran, you will automatically be within yourself; you will not think "Now I am within."

Even if you see some visible spot of light moving about in the darkness, don't try to follow it. Don't try to pursue it. If the attention is kept in repetition, that light will automatically remain before you and will spread.

Seeker: Should the words be repeated quickly or slowly for best concentration?

Master: Whether the speed of repetition is slow or fast does not make any difference. We should try to do simran at that rate which is most natural for us. Fast repetition does not bring more results than slow repetition. It is the degree of concentration which matters.

Seeker: I have heard that the words themselves are so significant that a single simran erases many karmas.

Master: If mathematically we try to solve the problem it is impossible. By sirman we mean concentration. It doesn't mean that we have repeated so many words. No. We have to build exact concentration with the help of repetition. Concentration helps us in withdrawing our consciousness; it helps us in clearing our karmas. To attain this concentration, we should always keep ourself in simran; we should continuously meditate. We should build that fort around us of devotion and of love and of simran. Simran is not a mechanical process.

Seeker : Then simran should be carried on at all times? Not just during the time of meditation?

Master : We should never remain unconscious of our mind; we should always be alert. Repeating the Name of the Lord continuously has two advantages. The first advantage is that it saves us from mental worry and frustration, and from creating new karma. Our mind is usually engaged either in thinking about what has passed or what is in store for the future. If we think about the past, we carry a sense of guilt for what we have done. If we think about the future we are always worrying and bothering about what is to come. By constant simran, we will be saved from all these unnecessary worries and frustrations.

The second advantage is that we will at once be able to concentrate our attention at the Eye Center at the regular time of sitting for meditation, because we have not allowed our thoughts to scatter in the world during the day. If the whole day we are thinking about worldly faces and associations, we cannot possibly concentrate our thoughts at the Eye Center during the two or three hours allotted for daily meditation. But by constant simran, we will easily be detached from our worldly life and attached to the Shabd.

So Saints always advise us to keep our attention in simran throughout the day—when we are walking about, when we are meetng friends, when we are traveling, when we are working. We should so much be in the habit of simran that even when we are talking with someone, that simran will automatically go on within us. Simran is a dry process, but a very essential one. Without simran we will hear the Shabd, we will enjoy it, but we will not be pulled up by it. Unless we withdraw and concentrate at the Eye Center, we cannot begin to travel on the spiritual Path. And simran is the means to concentration. Once the first stage is crossed, simran ceases to exist.

Seeker: How does one keep one's mind from wandering when doing simran?

Master: We are in constant struggle with the mind, for it doesn't want to let us concentrate. The mind has multipurpose activities—it wants to take us in, it wants to draw us out. For ages and ages, eons and eons, the mind has been in the habit of scattering in the world and of thinking about the world and worldly objects. Now we have to make use of this habit by converting it into thinking about the Lord. In other words, simran should become our habit now. We already have the thinking habit; we have only to direct it into the right channel.

Seeker: How and when do we practice dhyan?

Master: Dhyan, or contemplating on the form of the Master, should be done at the same time as simran. By keeping the image of the Master at the Eye Center, we give the mind something to hold on to while we are repeating the Names, and concentration is easily attained. Otherwise, the mind may slip back down. This practice leads to the real dhyan, contemplation of the Master's Radiant Form within, which eventually merges into Shabd.

Seeker: While repeating the Names, do we contemplate on the entire form of the Master, or just the eyes?

Master: The face.

Seeker: What about those who have not seen the Master's physical form?

Master: For those who have seen the Master, dhyan is very essential. Those people who have not seen him do not have the advantage of dhyan in the initial stages, but they have another type of Grace from the Lord. It will take them a little longer to concentrate, but they will also contemplate on the Radiant Form within, whether they have seen the physical form of the Master or not.

Seeker: Can one contemplate on the Master's photograph and keep that image in his mind for dhyan in meditation?

Master: We should not try to contemplate on photographs. The pictures of our relatives and friends we keep just to refresh our memory of them. We never contemplate on them. The pictures serve only to remind us of our friends and relatives, of our affection for them, of their goodness to us and our obligation towards them. Certainly we do not worship those photographs. Similarly, we may keep a picture of our Master in the house so that we remain reminded of Him in the sense that we are reminded of His teachings, and of the principles of Sant Mat which He has taught us to follow.

For a long time the Great Master would not let himself be photographed. He did not want the people to start meditating on and worshipping the photo, as had been the practice with pictures of old Saints, for this is against the principles of Sant Mat. The first picture of the Great Master publicly was taken when an American Satsangi wrote persistently that he wanted to see what his Master looked like on the outside. So the first picture was taken just to be sent to the American Satsangis. From then on slowly and slowly, copies of that picture were given to others in India. I still remember it. It was a great problem for people to get a copy of that picture. But when cameras and photography became popular, the Master couldn't conceal himself and wherever He went His photograph was taken. But He always insisted that these photographs should never be used for meditation. We should never contemplate on photographs.

Seeker: The books tell me that the Shabd should be attended to only from the right side or center. Does it make any difference whether the Shabd comes from the left or right?

Master: Yes, it does make a difference, particularly when we are in touch with the actual Shabd. Then, whether we hear it from the right or from the left side definitely makes a difference. But in the beginning, we don't know whether the Shabd is coming from the right or left or Center so we have not to give any attention to either side.

In the initial stages we are in the habit of hearing through the ears, so we try hear the sound through the ears—the right ear. The more we concentrate our attention by simran at the Eye Center, we automatically know that ears have nothing to do with the Shabd. Actually, the power of the Shabd comes from the Eye Center, so concentration should be kept fixed at that Center. When we hear the Shabd of the first stage, we have to avoid going to the left side or negative side.

Seeker: What are the characteristics of the Shabd before we reach the Eye Center?

Master: In the beginning, we don't hear the pure Shabd of the first stage, only its echo—a mixed sound. For example, an orchestra is giving a concert. From a distance, if we were to try to hear that concert, we would not differentiate between the various types of musical instruments being played. We would hear a mixed, jumbled sound. But the closer we draw ourself to the concert, the more we would be able to distinguish what types of instruments are being played there. Similarly, the sound of the Shabd is at the Eye Center—but we are drawn out through the senses and are scattered away from it. When we try to hear that Shabd, we don't know what type of a sound it is. Therefore, we hear an echo, a mixed sound. With the help of simran, when we are able to increase our concentration, that very sound becomes distinct and clear, and we are drawn to the real Shabd, which will pull us up.

Seeker: Before one reaches the Eye Center, does one hear the Sound first or see the Light first?

Master: Some people begin with the Sound and then see the Light. Others begin with the Light and then hear the Sound. We shouldn't worry which will come first, because ultimately Light will merge into Sound and Sound will merge into Light. The power of seeing within is called nirat; the power of hearing is called surat,* and both these faculties are essential as we continue on the Path.

For example, if from your house in the evening you take a very long walk and stray from your familiar path, you may absolutely forget the direction you should take to return. Pitch darkness surrounds you on all sides. The logical thing to do would be to stand quietly in the darkness and listen for some sort of sound coming from the house. Perhaps a television set is turned on, may be someone is talking or laughing, perhaps the dog is barking. With the help of that sound you try to discover the direction of the house. But then another obstacle comes in your way—the darkness. There may

---

*also means "soul".

be some bushes, there may be trees, a stream or a pond to block your way. But if you have a flash-light or a torch in your hand, you will be able to see the path in front of you as you follow the sound leading to your home. Similarly, the Lord is within every one of us, but we have absolutely forgotten the Path leading to the Lord's kingdom. Therefore, He has kept Sound within us; He has kept Light within us. With the help of that Sound, we will know the direction which we have to follow in order to reach Him; with the help of that Light we can travel on the inward Path. These two fundamentals are absolutely essential for us to return to the Lord.

But there is no harm if we see the Light first and do not begin with the Sound, or if we hear the Sound and do not begin with the Light. When we will progress a little ahead, the Sound and the Light will both become the same and uniform.

Seeker: What particular postures are used for meditation?

Master: The postures which are suggested at initiation are mainly for reasons of health. Actually, posture in meditation has absolutely no relationship with inner progress itself. We in India are accustomed to sitting without the help of a chair or cushion, so we can easily sit cross-legged as I am sitting now. If you will sit in this way, your backbone will naturally be straight. With a straight backbone, you won't feel lazy nor have the tendency to sleep; there will be no physical cramp developing in the body. But you should never fight with your body to keep it rigid in a particular posture, for then you will not be able to concentrate at all. If your body is aching and strained and you are fighting to keep yourself in a particular posture, you're always *in* the body. But the fight in meditation is with the mind to gain concentration—therefore you should be absolutely unmindful of the body and should adopt the posture in which you are able to sit in a relaxed and comfortable manner.

Seeker: What is meant by the body becoming numb?

Master: When we say numbness, we mean that process of withdrawing the soul currents from the feet upwards to the Eye Center. We may not be conscious that our body has become numb, and still we have withdrawn. Even without feeling any numbness in the body we can be inside and see many visions, but these experiences are not within our control. When we have actually withdrawn consciously, we will find that the body has become absolutely numb. Then our withdrawal is in our control, and we can go within at will. Otherwise, before our actual withdrawal, we will have glimpses and experiences here and there.

Seeker: How much time should we allot to meditation every day?

Master: Normally we should devote one tenth of our time, or two and one-half hours, to meditation. But if, in the beginning we are not able to sit that long at a stretch, we can easily spread the time into two, three or even four sittings. We should, however, try to give more time in the morning, and slowly and slowly increase that time until it reaches a continuous two and one-half hours. But we should definitely give more than one tenth of our time to meditation if we can. Actually, every moment that we spend in His memory, in His Love, in meditation and devotion to Him, is accounted for and we receive its advantage in concentration. You see, it is not only the mechanical meditation which enables us to concentrate. It is not that particular time which matters, it is our whole *living* that matters. Day and night we have to live in the atmosphere of meditation and love.

Seeker : How much of that time should be devoted to simran and dhyan and how much time to dhun?

Master : The object of simran is to concentrate, to bring back our consciousness to this Eye Center, and to be in touch with the Shabd. The procedure is, especially for the beginner, to devote at least three quarters of the sitting time to simran and dhyan, and one quarter of the time to hearing of the Shabd. But if one is successful in concentration and in withdrawing his consciousness to the Eye Center, he can give less time to simran and more time to the Shabd. If the Shabd is forceful within and is attracting us, is pulling us, then we can easily switch over our attention from simran to dhun. There is no hard and fast timing that at the time of simran you must avoid the Shabd. These timings are observed in the beginning, when we have to start at A to arrive at Z. But the more we are able to concentrate, the more we can decrease our time for simran and increase our time for Shabd.

Ultimately the stage comes when we cease to do simran. We only are aware of Shabd, we merge into Shabd; we become Shabd; and Shabd takes us back to the Lord. We don't need simran at all then. The moment we close our eyes, we are there, we are in it, we are with it.

Seeker : I have heard it said that there is great benefit in getting up early in the morning for meditation. Why is this time better than day or evening time?

Master : There is no particular time for meditation, but the early morning hours definitely have advantages. At that time there is so much more quietness than during the day or evening time. And when we get up in the morning we are fresh, physically and mentally. We are not disturbed by traffic noises outside; we don't expect any guests or telephone calls at that time; our children are asleep. Sleep has come to our help to forget events and difficulties of the previous day. But during the evening hours, the body is tired from the day's work, and we are just liable to sleep if we try to meditate. All our thoughts which we have scattered during the day come before us as if on a cinema screen. So what concentration we may achieve in an hour of early morning meditation may require three or four hours in the evening. And as we are going to start the day, why not start it in the Name of the Lord so that we live in that bliss throughout the day?

But if we cannot adjust our schedule to meditation early in the morning, we shouldn't feel frustrated or unhappy about it. We may give whatever time during the day or evening which is convenient to us. Most important, we should be regular and punctual in our daily meditation.

Seeker: Is there a penalty if meditation is missed? Does one lose a great deal of concentration if a day is missed?

Master: Well, we have missed an opportunity, that is all. We should always attempt to sit in meditation every day, because the opportunity of this human form is given to us for that very purpose. If we do not make use of this opportunity, naturally we are missing something. But there are no penalties in Sant Mat; there are no penalties in devotion, in the way of Love. That we have missed meditation is the greatest penalty in itself. When a lover misses his beloved, what more penalty can he receive?

Seeker : What happens if we fall into a half sleep while doing meditation? Do we make any progress during that sleep?

Master : We make real progress only while sitting awake in meditation; not during sleep. That progress is made within, but is not in our control if we sleep.

Sometimes we are sitting in meditation and we go into a half sleep. We have certain visions—visions in the sense that the soul is flying because it gets released from the body. You see, in meditation we are training the mind to be still so that the soul can leave the body. So in this half sleep, we have dream-like experiences that we are flying over hills and mountains or we are flying over oceans. But we want to go by our *will*. And that we can only do when we are not asleep.

Seeker : What is the way to know that we are really attentive, and not in a state of sleep?

Master : We don't lose our awareness, yet we are so much absorbed inside that we become unconscious about the surroundings. When we sleep, the attention, which was centered at the Eye Focus, falls down to the throat center and our control is lost. But in meditation our attention is held at the Eye Center or goes upward and we become *more* conscious; we become unconscious of the body and our surroundings; but inside our consciousness becomes thousandfold.

Seeker : Is it possible to rise to the Eye Center while sleeping?

Master : No, it is not. Our attention remains below the Eye Center. But if your tendency is always towards meditation, and your devotion and your longing is always to go up and up but certain of your karmas will not let you leave the body and make much progress, then sometimes it happens that in sleep the soul leaves the body. The soul goes up. It passes through those regions, sees visions. But you have no control over these spiritual dreams and once you wake up, you are the same. You should not give any importance to those dreams at all, nor try to analyze them. They were pleasant, that is all.

Seeker: How, then, can we remedy the problem of falling asleep in meditation?

Master: When we go to sleep, we are at the throat center; when we meditate, we try to concentrate at the Eye Center. At the time of doing simran, our attention may slip down from the Eye Center to the throat center, and we go to sleep. The reasons for that slip are many, but the most fundamental one is that we don't give full sleep to the body. Nature has designed this body in such a way that at least seven to eight hours out of every twenty-four are necessary for its rest. In this modern life perhaps that is too much time to spare, but if we do give that time for sleep, and cut short our other engagements, then there is very little chance of sleep during meditation. In addition, we should try to take light food early in the evening, so that we are light when we retire.

Before meditation in the morning, we should move about in the room, wash the face with cold water, get rid of the "cobwebs" of sleep, and then meditate. If the body has had its required rest, the chances are much better that we will be able to stay awake and hold the attention at the Eye Center.

Seeker: Should one sleep *after* meditation in the morning? Someone told me that it helps in digesting the meditation.

Master: Generally, it is not good. Why lose that happiness of meditation? That bliss, that joy, that elevation you feel in meditation—why forget it by sleep? Let that atmosphere remain with you throughout the day.

Seeker. What is meant by destroying our karma in meditation? Can we reach a stage where we do not have to go through karma at all?

Master : We can always burn or destroy our karmas. By meditation, the karma which would otherwise take us one hundred lives to fulfill, can be cleared in one or two lives. To destroy those karmas so that we can merge in the Lord is the purpose and object of meditation. Kabir says that just as one matchstick can burn a large stack of dry hay, so the Shabd or Nam— one little portion or item of it—can burn and destroy thousands and millions of our karmas. Since these karmas all have a relation with our mind, we destroy them by rising above them. When through the Shabd our mind returns to its origin in Trikuti, the second stage, these karmas just drop down. Whatever rust may cover a knife, when we touch it to a grinding stone all rust is rubbed off. The knife shines and becomes pure. The same is the condition of the soul when it comes in touch with the Shabd.

Seeker : Why can't we share our internal experiences with others?

Master : There is always danger of ego coming in that sharing. When we describe our experiences to anybody else, we are apt to take on airs, and we always lose what we have. And sometimes, when others know that you are spiritually advanced, they may try to take advantage of your powers. You may lose in temptations.

Seeker : How is one to know that one is experiencing reality? He might be experiencing a thing of the imagination or of false power.

Master: Imagination might be for a day, for two days, for three days—but not for years, ages.   Imagination might exist with one or two or three persons—not with thousands.   We can only call our experiences imagination if they happen just with one person.   When the same experiences happen to everyone who goes within, we cannot call them imagination.

The experiences of the Saints born in Persia compared with those born in India or any other country are the same.   Those Saints who never had the chance to meet with each other in this world, who lived in different centuries, grew up on different cultures, spoke different languages—all have recorded the same experiences.   When we compare our experiences with those writings, we know our experiences are not just hallucination or imagination.

Moreover, we always automatically know whether an experience is imagination or reality.   These questions arise only when we have no real experience.   When we are making inner progress we know whether it is reality or imagination, for definite signs and methods to test our experiences are given to us.

Seeker: How do you know when you are going up?

Master: You feel it within.   When you read a map leading to New York and you are given an outline of what you will see on the way, you know you are going to New York when you see those sings and milestones appear as you drive.   Similarly, when all Saints explain to us that we are going to meet certain experiences when we are going up, and we do see those things, we know we are going up.   And then we will *feel* that we are going up.   We will experience a certain bliss, a certain happiness in those situations—we will feel a certain joy.

We dance within ourself in happiness when we are in those stages. We radiate happiness.

Seeker: How long does it take to reach the Eye Center once a person has started to withdraw?

Master: Once we have started to go within, we cannot generalize about how long it will take. There is no time limit that can be fixed for anybody. It may take a day or thirty years—it may even take a moment. Everyone carries his individual past sanskaras with him, so we can never put a time limit on progress. It depends on the individual.

Seeker: After one has successfully gone within once, does he have to start all over again the next time?

Master: Then withdrawal becomes instantaneous at will.

Seeker: For the non-initiate who wants to meditate, what do you suggest?

Master: The full and correct technique as well as the description of the internal Shabd at the five stages and the characteristic secrets of the five stages and beyond are revealed to the disciple at the time of Initiation. Prior to that time, however, one can concentrate his attention behind the eyes at the Eye Center and mentally repeat the words "Radha Soami."

Following his initiation, the disciple's first step on the real spiritual journey begins. It is now up to him to apply himself to the practice of daily meditation. It is now up to him to strive to withdraw from the body the currents of consciousness which have descended through the senses and have attached themselves to the world, and to gather up those currents and focus them at the Center of Consciousness from whence they have descended. It is up to the initiate to apply his sincere efforts; it is up to the Master to give the results. The process, in most instances, is a long one; but the initiate will be given glimpses of the inner threshold of light and sound and vision with ever-increasing intensity and awareness as he continues in his meditation. Never is he left to feel entirely alone, unguided or hopeless. Always he is given some proof, some sign by which he is led forward.

There may be times of discouragement during the endeavor to take this first step, times when it seems as if it will never be made. There may be new lines of thought, questions to provoke the beginner on the Path which had never even occurred to him before. Contradictions, which sometimes seem to appear in the study of the Path, may afflict the mind. There may be intervals when these doubts and afflictions are felt so keenly that one wonders how a solution could ever be found. There are, in the life of every disciple, those moments when he falls, when he feels he can never be forgiven for the countless mistakes and sins which he helplessly commits. Yet the disciple should never let the knowledge leave him that such thoughts are actually signs of his progress, actually encouraging guideposts that he is on the Way. For it is a quality of the mind in the beginning to inflict these waves of doubt and confusion into the consciousness of the aspirant. The deeper one penetrates into the Path of mysticism, the more the questions and contradictions smooth out and disappear from the mind entirely. For contradictions actually do not exist; they seem to arise only when one plane of consciousness is compared with another. The laws themselves do not differ, but their aspects do, as they are reflected down through denser and denser regions. As the Master has said, "When that realization of love

and devotion comes, we find that we have no question ...
For the answers come from within.''

As one sincerely continues in his meditation during
those early stages, though he may not at first even be
consciously aware of the changes which are taking place
within him, these waves will become less violent, less
upsetting, and finally still. Effortlessly, the questions
and doubts which had once painfully taken hold of his
thoughts, melt away as snow in the warmth of a summer
sun. He becomes unshakeable in his conviction
concerning the rightness of the Path. The whole
world's opinion could not shake him then.

And as these waves become still the intensity of
longing for spiritual progress, to meet the Beloved and
to merge into Him, enter more and more into one's
consciousness. It is the very force of that longing
which leaves no room for the play of the intellect. All
questions dissolve into triviality in the presence of that
longing. It possesses one's heart and mind and allows
no other desire to enter. So intense does it become
within the disciple's heart that he is constantly engrossed
in meditation and prayer to the Lord for mercy, for His
forgiveness, and for Himself. It is the sweetest yet
most painful state of being the disciple has ever known—
pain arising from the sharpened awareness of one's
separation from the Lord and one's own helplessness in
attaining Him, sweetness arising from the certainty that
the longing is the last step to the threshold of the inward
journey.

The Great Master writes: "Longing does not
necessarily create only pain and sorrow. It is a unique
intoxication of the mind, because one is not willing under
any circumstances to banish it, even at the cost of
innumerable hardships.''

One feels that that longing could not become more intense, more acute, more extreme. But it does. It grows and increases beyond all imagination. As the disciple continues in his meditation a glimpse is given him; a taste of the nectar of bliss which awaits him; a sudden, enrapturing moment when the veil is pulled aside, just a fraction, and the power of the Shabd pulls the soul from out of its bodily prison to soar high and free toward the regions of Light.

Longing is truly the offspring of God's Grace and Love. His love for His disciple exceeds that of the furthest imagination and the reflection of that Love is manifest in the disciple's yearning.

True longing for the Lord teaches the disciple many things. It creates the desire to live a life uncluttered with traces of self and ego and mind. When that longing is first born in the disciple's heart, he becomes more conscious of his actions and of his thoughts and intentions. He examines his motives and desires with more critical eyes; he becomes increasingly aware of his shortcomings and worthlessness, and feels that he cannot possibly hope for inward progress when the obstacle of his self is so strong. It is as if a clear, penetrating beacon light were focussed on him, revealing every speck of dirt within the mind and heart, every impediment, and giving them no place to which to escape. It is as if the deep layers of mud and silt which lie at the bottom of a lake were to be removed. The lake's surface would in the process, become disturbed and agitated. Waves would erupt upon its surface; the muddy silt hidden in its depths would darken its clear waters; and perhaps, if the lake were to have its own self-consciousness, there would be great unrest and alarm therein at the sudden appearance of so much undesirable material from within itself.

Once the present Master was asked : "Why is it that since I have come on the Path I seem to have more faults and sins than ever before?"

He replied : "You do not have more of them than before you started on the Path; you are simply becoming aware of these faults and sins within yourself now. It is a state of transition you are in, and you are looking at yourself with new eyes."

And at another time, when asked about how to overcome the pitfalls which come in the disciple's way as he strives toward the Light, He said :

"When making an earthen jar, a potter always keeps one hand inside the clay which he is shaping. From above he slaps and strikes the clay to expand and shape it. But always the guidig hand is inside to support and help to mould the clay into shape. Similarly, whatever comes to us comes from His hands; His guiding hand is always there. When we are eager to achieve some destination, we run to that destinaton. Sometimes we fall, but we fall with our faces always towards the light. Again we run, again we fall, and again get up to run. Though our footsteps may falter, their direction is ever pointing towards that destination.

"But on the other hand, if we don't make a start at all, of course there may not be any pitfalls, but we definitely are not going towards our destination. We are not covering any distance. If we run, we have a chance to fall, but we only fall to get up and run again. A seed once sown is never destroyed. It is a question of time before it sprouts. It may need one rain or it may need two or three rains; it may need watering and special care. But the seed must sprout.

"So we should never lose heart at all that we have run into pitfalls or we have fallen or we are being driven away from the Path. No. His guiding hand is always there to steer us through all those pitfalls and weaknesses which present themselves, whether we are conscious of it or not. He never leaves us. Momentarily we may feel we have left the Path; another moment we feel we are back on the Path. Actually we cannot leave the Path. We are so strongly bound that we really cannot go astray at all."

In the face of his shortcomings, the disciple tries harder, prays more earnestly, gives more time to meditation—and the longing grows. It keeps on growing, expanding, veritably conquering all of one's being even to the smallest fiber. For the Lord does not grant the bliss of reunion with Him until every last vestige, every last particle of worldly desire has been vanquished, until one becomes strong enough to digest and assimilate His majesty and power.

Again we read the words of the Great Master:

"It (longing) is actually a touchstone or test of love, and at the same time it purifies the devotee's love and devotion, as a goldsmith purifies a piece of gold by putting it in the fire...

"In order to meet the Beloved, intense longing comes first, in the same manner as flowers bud and bloom on a fruit tree before it can bear fruit. Where there are no flowers, there can be no fruit. Similarly, where there is no longing, there can be no meeting with the Beloved."

Strangely, with time, longing teaches patience and submission. One learns that the fulfillment of his longing for the Lord depends upon the Lord Himself, and not in the final analysis upon the disciple—that not of one's own demand can God-realization come. Yet, incredibly so, it has often been said that the Master is a hundred times more anxious to bring that realization to His disciples than they themselves are eager to receive it.   One learns that impatience is a crippling handicap on the gift of longing.   One learns that he must maintain an equilibrium of faithful patience with his longing.   The assertion "I am ready, why does the Lord withhold Himself?" has no place in the presence of true longing.

An incident occurred during the life of the Great Master which well illustrates this point:

One day a Muslim faquir or holy man came to the Great Master at the Dera and said to Him, "When I was searching for God, people even called me a son of God, and I have thus acquired a following.   But I have come to you for I know now that you are one with God; I want You to show me Your Glory."

"True, you have come to me," the Great Master said, "But coming to me here is just one step on the Path which you have to follow.   I will lead you to that Path, and you will realize the Lord in due time."

"Oh no, don't deceive me.   You cannot dupe me," the Muslim's tone was self-assured.   "I know You have all the powers right here and now.   I *know* that I can't do a single thing by myself to realize God.   I know that if You wish You can take me to the highest Truth in this moment; and that You will take me to that highest Truth whenever You want to.   What game are You trying to play with me—that I should start making an effort?"

The Master laughed and said, "But there must be a purpose to the game if I ask you to play it."

"There is no purpose. I know You are just fooling me.   If somebody has come with all his heart and with all his seeking to You, why don't You give? I have come

and I want You to give me all that You have. I am
absolutely ready to accept," he asserted.   "Why don't
You give?"

"How do you know you are ready?" the Great
Master asked him.

"Because of the very fact that I have found You.
I have found that You are one with God," he declared.
"I have found that there is a longing in me to meet God,
and I have come to You because I have found that
You can show me and give me God. This stage of
my journey is ended. What else do You want me
to do?"

"This is not enough preparation," the Great Master
shook his head slowly. "And the only way I can prove
this to you is to show you a little spark of God."

"Spark!" the Muslim retorted. "I want to meet
God right now. I am absolutely ready."

There was a meaningful pause. Then the Great
Master said quietly, "All right then. Come and sit
down here in front of me—if you are ready."

And so, the Muslim confidently sat on the ground
at the Master's feet. Oh, he was a beautiful, radiant
man. He had a big, bulky body, a glow on his face, and
a constant smile as he gazed expectantly upon the Great
Master. By this time a number of people had gathered
and they whispered among themselves, saying, "How
gracious the Master is—He is going to give him something."

The Great Master raised his hand and the
people were hushed. "Now close your eyes and give
your attention here, between the two eyebrows,"
He instructed the Muslim. "Withdraw all your
thoughts from every thing else and focus them on
this point."

Within a matter of moments, the Muslim fell back and rolled over three or four times.   Immediately he got up, with a surprised, stunned expression on his face. "Allah!"* he cried.   "I never knew it was like that."

The Great Master laughed. "Why? What has happened?"

"I got the experience as if a *million suns* had suddenly come upon me and broken loose on me." The tone of his voice was incredulous. "I can't stand that! I didn't know this thing was at all possible."

"But you said you were ready."

Laughter broke out in the group at the Great Master's words. Yet the faquir still could not contain himself. "But I had no notion at all that such a thing was possible!"

"This very thing," the Great Master told him, "that you have seen today is a minor spark—just a small reflected light from a very tiny speck on the Face of God. How will you face Him squarely, and see His entire face? We believe that we have become prepared, but we haven't really become prepared at all. If this very experience had come to you step by step, stage by stage, and you had seen it growing from day to day, you would have taken it in your natural stride. That preparation is necessary for the experience you have received today. Now you may start again—but from the beginning this time...."

And the Great Master initiated him. For years that man practised before experiencing anything in the nature of his experience that day. Slowly and steadily he made progress and cleared his karmas so that his experiences came just at the right time and

---

*Allah is an Arabic name for God.

in the appropriate way in which he could digest and appreciate them. A real and earnest longing for the Lord grew in him—a longing which bore with it resignation and humility—the "blossom before the fruit."

It is a strange paradox, but true, that the greater and more intense the longing, the less the disciple feels that he is "ready" for spiritual progress, for the more one longs, the more one becomes faced with his faults and shortcomings which shield him from the Lord. Yet this very feeling is actually a sign of one's readiness for spiritual progress, and he should not become discouraged and give up his longing as hopeless. As the present Master has said, "When we think we are not able to make much visible progress, we don't know how thin a veil we may have yet to pierce through before the Light will dawn in us. If a man is boring through a wall that is four or five feet thick, we who sit on the other side will never know how much progress has been made until the wall is bored through. Even if only a thin, small layer is left, we may feel that nothing has yet been done. Similarly, we have certain layers of karma which have to be cleared before we can go ahead. By whatever time we have devoted and are devoting to meditation, we are clearing a great deal of karma; we are making definite progress. So we should never feel discouraged and lose heart, for there are absolutely no failures in Sant Mat. We always go ahead, and never back. We pierce through, and we do come to the Light."

So from the time of initiation until the disciple merges from the cocoon of the human body into that higher Light, he daily grows purer of heart and more fit for conscious, spiritual ascent. He is led without fail through the darkest night, and always he knows that the dawn of daybreak is just ahead. He has only to reach out his hand, if he stumbles, to know that the guiding and loving hand of his Beloved Master is there.

And when the course of his first step of Love has been fulfilled, this Prelude, the disciple knows the miracle of a second birth...

CHAPTER EIGHTEEN

MANSIONS OF THE SOUL

There are no words sweet enough to write this chapter. There is no way of comparison, of association. Is it possible to describe the Aurora Borealis to a creature who dwells beneath the earth? Ridiculous, it seems. But no more so than an attempt to relate the experiences of higher consciousness. The most gifted of authors may search through the height and breadth and depth of language for words sweet enough—but it would be of no avail. The pen is dumb, helpless. Those who have had a taste of the bliss of realms on high can only cry out, "Love is the one word which gathers within it all the words I may be able to write."

Yet attempts have been made; descriptions have been given to us by Saints and Masters of the past. Perhaps if it were possible to bring forth on these pages all the inspired portrayals of the inner realms which have sprung from the hearts of these God-men throughout all time, we might be able to catch a fractional glimpse of what we may expect to experience in those higher worlds. But even then, the multiplication of words would serve only to further limit the imagination of the reader. For words cannot be used to portray that which transcends their very nature. Neither can the bark of a dog nor the song of a bird convey to their kind the knowledge of material science which man has discovered for himself in this present day. Such knowledge is open only to the mind of man. Similarly, even at the first stage of higher consciousness words and allegories and symbols do not exist. How is it possible to use them to accurately convey that which is experienced within? It is only futility to apply language where language itself is a barrier.

To illustrate this helplessness of language, let us look at the word "path". Here is a word which is repeatedly used in mystical literature, being a basic word used to denote any procedure or method which an aspirant adopts to reach the goal of God-realization. Yet Kabir, a great Indian saint of the sixteenth-century, once said :

"Path assumes distance. But if the Lord be near, thou needest no path at all. Verily, it maketh me smile to learn that a fish in water can thirst."

Of the difficulty of communicating the nature of the Shabd to mortal ears, the present Master, when asked if the sound of the Shabd resembles "Om" or various musical instruments, said :

"Our imagination plays a trick on us when we try to explain the Shabd with words. In fact, imitative words or musical instruments are very poor substitutes to explain the Shabd which is within us. But since there is no other way for Saints to describe it to us than by suggesting outside instruments and symbols, they try to find the nearest approximation to that Shabd. But it is very difficult even to say what it sounds *like* or looks like. A dumb man eating honey, when asked what the honey tastes like, won't be able to explain it. If he were able, he may say, "sweet". But the word "sweet" doesn't convey the taste of the honey itself.

"We can say that the Shabd we feel or hear is like "Om". But that again is our imagination. One may be able to invent another word and capture the likeness, and then say "This word is like that Sound". But you see, a word or the sound of an instrument may suggest the Shabd, but it is not the *Shabd* itself."

Perhaps it is well, then, at the beginning of this chapter, to emphasize these limitations of expression, and impress upon the reader's mind the confining nature of the symbolism of words. They can do no more than hint, suggest. Yet suggestion is their only purpose here, for it is up to the reader himself to explore the hidden Path which lies above these words, himself to rise above the limited media of language and experience the sweet reality, himself to withdraw the heavy curtains of his intellect and advance to that Understanding that exists within consciousness itself.

So let us, with these thoughts in mind, take that limited, imaginary journey to the heights of mystic revelation. We have explored the methods, and the practice of meditation—those technical aspects of the Path which have been permitted into these pages. What follows are descriptions of those stages through which the disciple passes on his way to ultimate God-realization. These descriptions are derived from the writings of the Saints of the past, from the Sant Mat literature, and from the teachings of and conversations with the present living Master.

At his first awakening into higher consciousness, the disciple steps into a world which he had only dreamed could exist—a world which is a real Utopia, the world of ideas of Plato, the paradise of Dante, the Eden of the Bible, the Shangri-la of one's most treasured hopes.

"Seeing without eyes, hearing without ears, walking without feet, working without hands, speaking without tongue....", in the words of Guru Nanak, does the newly awakened initiate enter this world. Yet in his astral form, now unhindered by the physical senses, the disciple has finer faculties of perception. He now has "ears to hear that silent music, eyes to see that light of wisdom, a tongue to speak the language of love," as it is beautifully expressed by the present Master.

These finer, heightened senses convey such pleasurable sweetness to him that all that went before seems shadowy, dreamlike; the world which he had once regarded as his home now appears to him as a dark prison; the body which he had once thought of as himself he now sees as a cloak of ignorance which had covered a higher self.

And at this awakening, at the moment when his efforts have reached fruition, the disciple of a sudden becomes aware that his every step was guided, was in fact administered, by his Master. For now, the real threshhold to the Infinite Pathway to God-Realization has been reached. For it is here that the aspirant meets the beloved Master in His Radiant Form. The disciple becomes aware that all the flashes of light which he had experienced earlier in his meditation, all the swirling, whirling colors and ripples of light which he had seen, all the entrancing suggestions of the Shabd which he had heard, were but emanations from the grandeur and glory of this Form.

Such a meeting can never be fore-visualized, can never be imagined even in the furthest stretching of the word. Of this experience Dr. Johnson says:

"Any one who has had that experience will tell you that there is no joy in this world so great as that which the disciple experiences when he first beholds the Radiant Master. It is the culmination of ages of struggle. It is the signal of victory in his long battle with mind and matter....From here on, the disciple can see the Master on the inner planes as well as the outer."

The disciple is transformed by the joy of that vision, that transcending Glory which he recognizes as his Master. He is enraptured by the all-enveloping, pure strains of the Shabd which emanate in flowing power from that Form. On beholding that Form, the disciple comprehends the meaning of knowledge without thought, beauty without senses, love without emotion. Steeped in ecstasy, his soul is filled with the wisdom that he is in the presence of the King of kings. Irresistibly, effortlessly, he is drawn to and given to that Light and that Shabd, which are now not manifested separately but as One infused in the Master's Radiant Form. The longing which we have described leaps into new, intoxicating dimensions—its very fulfillment now a deeper, more noble, more sublime expression of longing.

It is an expression of being which is new to him, for love unites itself with longing in an entirely new way, bringing forth a bliss which knoweth no description. It is a love that obliviates space and action and self, a love that sweeps the disciple into itself to fulfill itself, swirling, expanding, dissolving, creating untold rapture of the soul. Thought itself becomes ashes in the burning fire of that love.

One cannot discern, and it does not occur to him to try, whether that love is the result of longing or if longing is the result of that love. Rising spiralwise, born on the wings of that love and longing, the soul soars upwards, ever upwards; as it is drawn to and led by the Radiant Form of the Master.

As he ascends, the disciple is shown the lower planes, and all the secrets of creation and the material cosmos become part of his consciousness. These revelations have been likened to standing on the summit of a lofty mountain peak and thus at once surveying all that

lies below in every direction.   He is led through multi-
tudinous spheres of color and light, and beholds scenery
unimaginable.

He finds these planes not to be without forms, but
forms which are not as they appeared to the mortal
mind—forms which are so exquisite that they are seen to
be "essences" rather than things, thoughts instead of
languages, ideas instead of structures.   The workings of
how these essences are manifested in the material
cosmos of the consciousness of each expression in creation,
is clearly seen.   It is a world of colors and light, yet
colors of a new medium and light of a greater fullness or
substance of understanding.

He recognizes those who have reached the same
stage as he, and those who have passed from earth life.
But he now sees them as expressions of rainbow-like
hues of varying degrees, recognizable because these expressions are more a likeness to their true nature than
their physical forms had been.   He can converse with
those from every nation of the earth, for there, language
as we know it does not exist.

When the present Master was asked what the
activities of the disciple are as he progresses upwards
through those regions, He replied.

"There is no activity as we know it here.   Activity
for the disciple there, if we must so call it, is that of
love."

And incredibly so, as he progresses, the disciple
beholds the Radiant Form of the Master in ever-increasing splendor and power and light.   As he draws nearer
to the apex of the first stage of consciousness, the disciple becomes aware of the formlessness of the Master,
that His real being is manifest by the Shabd itself—
nay, is the Shabd.   The splendor and radiance of the

Master, even at this lowly stage of the disciple's development, has been beheld "as a mass of most brilliant light,
as if crores (tens of millions) of morning suns were
rising. . . ."

But the joy, the wonder most sublime, the bliss
which is the essence of the disciple's rapture, is the
shedding of his limited self as his soul begins to dance in
pure clear brightness itself—the Master's Radiant
Love.

After having traversed the spheres of the astral
heavens,* the disciple enters the height of the first stage.
Of this experience, Joseph Leeming writes.**

"Guided by the Master in his Radiant Form, the
disciple now enters the Capital, the indescribably
beautiful Sahansdal Kanwal, meaning the Thousand
Petalled Lotus; a marvellous region of light and beauty,
indescribable in human language. Here are one
thousand and one glowing lights—one large center light
surrounded by a thousand smaller ones. Each light is
of a different tint or color, and all are clustered together
somewhat in the form of an immense celestial lotus
flower.

"This radiant group of brilliant but softly glowing
lights is sometimes called Koh-i-Noor, or the 'Mountain
of Light'. It is in fact the power house of the physical
universe. From it, as from a giant dynamo, goes forth
the power that creates, sustains and controls the entire
creation below the astral world, all the millions of suns,

---

*It should be noted here that the astral regions are so vast and
so greatly vary as to the degree of spirituality within them that the
higher astral realms have often been mistaken for the causal or
mental realms, while only the lower astral heavens—those in
closest proximity to earthly life—are said to be "astral".

**In *Yoga and the Bible*.

stars and galaxies each moving in its appointed orbit, that make up the incredible vastness of the physical universe.

"And from this first stage of consciousness onward,, the disciple is never consciously left to feel alone again. As he moves in this world and performs his worldly duties, he is ever aware of the presence of his Master, of the uplifting and transforming strains of the Shabd. He sees the Lord manifest and revealed in every phase of life—not just with his imagination, but by direct vision. Now he understands the motives and attitudes of those around him; now he is conscious of a new compassion and selfess love as he sees the Lord indwelling in all the things of the earth and within every person. No more does he differentiate between color or caste or creed or nation. Without effort, he radiates the Master's love wherever he moves.

"The amount of time which the disciple spends in his astral form depends upon his previous karmas and his spiritual attainments, and upon the force of his longing coupled with the Master's Grace. When he leaves this form, he is taken by the Master to the second stage of the spiritual journey, that of Universal Mind, or Brahm. The disciple functions in his causal or mental body as he passes through the planes of this stage. It is here that he becomes conscious of the record of his sojourn through millions, perhaps billions, of lives in the material and astral cosmos. It is here that all the residual or stored karmas which he had been accumulating throughout the course of those lives is destroyed by the unimaginable power of the Shabd. And it is upon leaving this region, that the final veil, that of the mind, is cast off and the disciple's consciousness increases in understanding and power far beyond our comprehension."

As the disciple passes from the first to the second stage, he is aware of a change in the manifestation of the Shabd, for as has been described earlier, at each stage of the first five stages of the inward journey, the Shabd reverberates in a different expression, each increasing in wonder and purity and strength. Of these manifestations, the present Master has said:

"The Sound or Shabd is one, coming from the top to the Eye Center. Generally, the spiritual journey has been explained by the Saints as having five regions.* Since the Shabd passes through these regions as it descends, we feel that it changes at each stage—but the Shabd is One. For example, a river leaves its source and travels on its course to merge into the sea. At the source the river gives a particular sound; when it becomes a waterfall it gives another, different sound; when it passes through rocks, when it spreads on the plains, and when it merges back into the sea—each time it gives a different sound. Yet all the same the river is one.

"In the same way the Audible Life Stream or Shabd is just one, descending from the highest stage to the Eye Center. But since it passes through many stages of

---

*when asked if there are regions above Sach Khand, the Fifth Stage, the Master said, "Sach Kand is the last stage, though by some it is further divided into three more stages—Alakh, Agam and Anami or Radha Soami. Some name only two regions, one below Universal Mind and one above it. But we become just lost in the understanding of these regions with words. You see, to merge back into the Lord is the object. We may call it one journey; we may call it two stages or eight stages or five stages. This is just quibbling with words. But generally, for the purpose of explanation, Saints have divided the fifth stage into Sach Khand and three further stages."

consciousness, Saints have tried to explain to us that there are different sounds at the different stages. Actually the Shabd is One."

The stage of Brahm is the apex of reality, the very height of spiritual attainment, to one who has not a perfect Master who has gone beyond the reach of Brahm. With the blending of the self into Universal Mind and the expanded consciousness which embraces the furthest reach of the cosmos of the Universal Mind, it seems that no stage can be further attained. For how is it possible even to conceive of a stage above and beyond Universal Mind, often called Unity itself? To merge into that which interpenetrates the entire universe would seem to constitute the furthest limit of spiritual ascent.

Yet for the one initiated by a perfect Master, the now purer and far more powerful force of the Shabd lifts the disciple out of this appearance of Unity and transports him to the stage of Parbrahm—"beyond" Brahm. And here a greater, more glorious dimension of consciousness is met. For each stage reflects the higher, and a reflection—no matter how real and pure and beautiful it may seem—cannot but distort and vaguely hint at that which it reflects. Thus the appearances vanish and the Oneness of Brahm is known to be but a part of the Whole. In fact, the sojourner directly comprehends that there is not only *one* Brahm, but others as well—that within each of these Brahmandi regions revolves the same vast, seemingly limitless cosmic scheme, each with its own cycle of birth and death and liberation, each with its own Universal Mind and Astral and material creations.

At the third stage of the spiritual journey, the soul is pure, completely unfettered and free. The once

slumbering spirit realizes its true identity as a drop of
the Supreme Ocean and for the first time wakens to the
full wonder and glory of God.   From this region the soul
needs to return no more to be born in the flesh.*   All
downward tendencies have been left behind, all coverings
have been removed, the soul rejoices in its new revelation
and knows an ecstasy inexpressible.   So great is the
radiance and illumination of the soul at this stage that
it is equal to the light and radiance of twelve suns.   It
is only here that the soul becomes truly worthy of its
power of God-realization.   Of the soul's awareness at
this stage the present Master has said :

"Then only does it realize its own beauty, its own
radiance, its own love and affection for the Lord.   And
only that pure love and affection takes the soul back to
the Lord."

Consumed by a great and overwhelming attraction,
the soul rises rapidly to the purely spiritual regions above
and crosses the threshold of the Regions of the Supreme
Lord, the fourth stage.   Now the soul is in the majestic
realm of pure spirit-consciousness, and awe and joy and
wonder become increased beyond imagination.   At
each threshold of the stages of consciousness we have
described, the soul is flooded with the awareness that
glory of a greater dimension lies beyond.   And at the
awakening to the Golden Shores of Eternal Life, human
language and ideas have been left so far behind that
description of any length and detail are impossible.
Suffice it to say that at these higher realms of spirit the
soul's consciousness transcends all earthly imagery and
penetrates deeper and deeper into the heart of the

---

*The only exception to this law is when a soul is sent to a
lower world on a mission of redemption,

Shabd, the Master, and love and joy and rapture mount in ever-increasing, higher and more purely spiritual consciousness.

When the disciple has crossed the fourth region, he enters the regions of eternal, everlasting life—the first plane of which is the fifth stage on the Inner Pathway. Here the soul merges into the first degree of God-consciousness, but has yet to travel through the most sublime and beautiful part of its journey. For by the great Love and Light of the True Lord Himself, the soul, united with God-consciousness, expands and advances to the three remaining regions.

But to these, the highest and most exalted realms of all, no names or descriptions can be given which convey even the least idea of their nature. Those Masters and Saints who have become united with the very essence or Lord of these realms have limited their descriptions to one or two words. They have called the first plane, or fifth region, Sach Khand, meaning True Home; the second plane they have named Alakh Lok, meaning the Invisible Place; the Third Plane is Agam Lok, meaning the Inaccessible Place; and the ultimate and final, absolute Region is Radha Soami Dham, meaning Home of the Spiritual Lord, also called Anami Lok, meaning the Nameless Region. When reaching this stage, the soul has at last reunited with its Origin, its beginning and its eternity. It has returned to the Bosom of the Supreme Father, the all-pervading, all-sustaining, impersonal Lord; the One who is the fathomless Ocean of Light which knows no boundaries, no limits. Naught can surpass Him, naught can embrace Him nor subsist beside Him, for He is within all, and is all, and is beyond all.

From the tiniest atom to the grandest Spiritual

Realm, He is the lifebreath and sustenance of all that is, and was, and ever will be. Deathless, He has neither beginning nor end, but is everlasting, omnipresent, and omnipotent. Perfection is too limiting a word to use in His description; infinite and eternal serve only to constrict Him. Can a small human mind comprehend the combined light of a trillion suns multiplied by itself? If this were possible, the thoughts of the mind would not yet come close to comprehending the magnitude and splendor of His Light. If the light of all the suns of all the galaxies were combined in a single cluster, that light, unfathomable as it is, would appear as no more than a few small, darksome specks floating in an ocean.

He is limitless, boundless, unconfinable to dimensions of the most inconceivable magnitude, so declare the Saints. All realms of consciousness, all regions of light and grandeur, all cycles of every manner of creation, spiritual and astral and material, all joy, all darkness, all light, all love—all are sustained within the heart of Him. All is His reflection; all is His projection; all is the expression of that limitlessness, that boundlessness.

And of this, the highest region of God-Consciousness, the great Saint Soami Ji writes :

"Love plays the supreme part—*It is all love.*"

The soul has now reached the terminus of the Inner Pathway of the Masters, has now passed through the mansions of the soul. Freed from its burden of mortal flesh, its astral and causal coverings, the soul has ascended stage by stage to the utmost height of God-realization, the true Kingdom of Glory. Through the Grace of the Master and the spiritual power of the Shabd, the soul has risen from the prison-like confinement of the human form and blended and merged into that Love—nay, has become that Love Itself. The candle flame has merged in the sun; the drop has become the ocean; the soul, long estranged, has returned to the Father.

And this is the promise of the Pathway of the Masters. . . .

EPILOGUE

The rain poured thunderously on the terrace outside my room. It was late in the day, and it had been storming for many hours. The wind tore leaves from the trees and flung them along the ground. The sky moved in shades of darkness, and the distant rolling of thunder echoed through the whine of the wind. The wooden windows and doors of my room were tightly bolted as the storm shook them as if to tear them loose and carry them away.

There were only a few days left for me at the Dera and the fury of the storm seemed to be shaking me into this realization. Would I ever reach the stage where I would feel the same contentment and peace in any other corner of the world—no matter how distant from the Dera? For without really being aware of how it has happened, one finds on this spiritual pilgrimage that the Master has become his predominating thought at all times, even one's desire to reach the spiritual heights becomes secondary to this new, incredible love, the overwhelming desire to serve and please Him, and to be near His physical form. One may even call it "painful," but this strange brand of pain brings with it such unutterable joy.

But then suddenly, one finds that the time has come when one must leave the Dera and his Master's feet, to be separated by oceans for one knows not how long. The experiences of all disciples in these last moments vary greatly. There are those who leave quietly, with a sadness at leaving His physical form but with an aura of joy stemming from their conscious knowledge that the

Master is eternally with them.   And there are those who weep without restraint when it comes time to leave Him—but always He gives them the strength and under-standing they need before they depart through the Dera gates for the last time.   I can never forget when He once said on tour, "We part only to meet."

The following personal experience is told here because it so clearly indicates the unlimited grace and strength—imparting kindness which flow from the Master to His disciples at this time.

The storm that had raged a few days before my departure subsided, but its message remained in my mind during the remainder of my stay.   Always I had put that inevitable moment of leaving the Dera into the back of my mind until those last few days.   And then, there were only three hours remaining.   We were scheduled to leave at night, 8:30 p.m.,   after the English discussion period with the Master in His drawing room. Those of us who were leaving, Mr. Leeming, Mr. Perez, and myself,   were to have our last, private interviews with the Master following the discussion.

With a heavy heart I walked into the drawing room at 6:30 with the other foreign guests.   This time I did not bring my shorthand notebook; it seemed far more important never to take my eyes from His face, for the last few moments were slipping by far too quickly. How long would it be before I again would behold that glorious face, when those kind and powerful eyes would once more meet mine and probe every corner of my soul?   The time left was not to be wasted—not a tiny second of it.

I cannot clearly remember what was said during the last discussion, but it came to an end shortly before seven—much earlier than usual.   We all filed out of the drawing room, and the three of us who were about to leave were asked to wait on the terrace outside. Mr. Leeming and Mr. Perez were called first, and they together entered the drawing room. Outside I sat and waited as it grew dark. And as the darkness increased, my heart grew heavier. But my eyes were dry—it seemed that the pain of leaving could in no way find release, and if the tears were allowed to escape even for an instant they would never stop flowing.

An age seemed to pass before the others said "Radha Soami" to the Master and left the drawing room. Khanna Sahib then motioned to me to enter the room. At that moment I was suddenly reminded of my first night at the Dera—curiously parallel to this one—only this time the words were to be of parting rather than of meeting.

Then suddenly, I was sitting next to Him, the room being empty save for us, and somehow the tears had a will of their own as they involuntarily began to escape from my eyes. Oh that beautiful face—how could one bear life without seeing it every day? For a moment He let me weep while He remained silent. But then I heard Him say, "Why cry, now that we have become closer together? There is no need to cry."

We talked for some time—it seemed necessary to keep talking, to make those last moments stretch out as long as possible. I remember asking Him to reassure me that He would never leave me wherever I might go. And He said, "The Master never leaves His disciples."

But then, as if an instant, there was no more to say. The Master called Khanna Sahib to bring in the parshad, as it was customary to give each guest a packet of sweets personally blessed by Maharaj Ji during the last interview. I watched Him as He closed His eyes and held the small packet in His hands, but my mind seemed to be running away with itself. This was it! The thought kept repeating itself over and over again. And He knew. He knew the storm that was in my heart, for He hardly looked at me then and did not meet my eyes when the interview was over. Having exchanged the last Radha Soami with Him, I stumbled onto the terrace, not knowing what was to come nor how the future could be endured. I could not breathe; I knew not where to turn. Finally my feet started carrying themselves to the office of our dear friend, Mr. Ahluwalia, after they had wandered aimlessly, without direction, over the familiar Dera land. The real tears had finally let loose, just as the clouds had let forth their torrents of rain in the storm that had raged a few days before. I believe that all the tears shed throughout all the years of my life could not equal the force of those shed that night. How long did this last? I do not know. But I do remember that Mr. Ahluwalia said something to the effect that perhaps I might see the Master once more before finally leaving the Dera.

Still the tears would not stop as I left for the Guest House, and there met the jeep which was to take us to the Beas Railway Station. My memory of those moments is not entirely clear, but I do recall that after we had climbed into the jeep and started on our way to leave the Dera, Khanna Sahib asked the driver to stop in front of the Master's gate. And he motioned us to follow him, as he walked through the gate into that blessed garden.

In the darkness I stood there on the terrace, the remnants of sobs still catching my breath. The mind was exhausted, unable to reason. I felt engulfed by the

darkness of night, and ashamed at my lack of understanding and calm. Had I not understood a tiny
particle of the essence of His teachings so freely
given? Had not even a glimpse of the revelation of
His love impressed itself upon my consciousness?
What was troubling me so deeply? What was the
matter with me? Had it all been in vain?

And then, in a flash, a floodtide of memories washed
over me—memories of those many precious moments
during the past six months when those glimpses of sub-
limity had been given—yet somehow the stark reality
of leaving the security of the Master's physical form
overrode the consolation which those memories afforded.
There was, it seemed, nothing that could remove
the pain and sense of desolation which overwhelmed
me.

The door of the Master's house which opened onto
the terrace opened after a moment, and He appeared.
He crossed the few yards which separated us. I
remember hearing the sound of His footsteps on the flat
stones of the patio; I remember how the light breezes
gently moved His white garments and His beard; I
remember how He first looked into my eyes with an
ocean of gentleness. And I remember His words,
"I think you just don't want to leave us." But when
I looked deeply into His eyes as so many times before,
suddenly all thought ceased, the surroundings, everything dissolved and melted away. There was only Him—
there was only that wondrous, indescribable sea of
love and joy. And He was God. I knew it then and
for all time. All existence, the world, melted away and
drifted into nothingness, merged into love. That
measureless pain which had held me in its grip for so
many hours dissolved like mist in the morning sun, and

a strange, powerful, exhilarating joy took its stead within the heart....

"*The Master never leaves His disciples*"... For love knows not the boundaries of time or space and He is Love itself.

INFORMATION AND BOOKS ON THIS SCIENCE ARE AVAILABLE FROM:

The Secretary
Radha Soami Satsang Beas
P.O. Dera Baba Jaimal Singh 143204
District Amritsar, Punjab, India and from:

U.S.A.:

Col. E.R. Berg,
U.S. Air Force (Retd)
4001 Mavelle Drive
Minneapolis, Minn. 55435

Mr. Henry F. Weekley, Apt. 611
4600 Connecticut Avenue
Washington, D.C. 20008

Mr. Roland G. deVries
2922 Las Flores Avenue
Riverside, Calif. 92503

Mr. Roy Ricks
651 Davis Street
Melrose Park, Ill. 60160

MEXICO:

Mr. James L. McMellon
Calle Bruselas 247
Guadalajara, Jalisco

CANADA:

Dr. J. Khanna
2740 Jones Avenue
North Vancouver, B.C.

ENGLAND:

Mrs. F E. Wood
Willow Cottage, Worple Road
Leatherhead, Surrey

SWITZERLAND:

Dr. Pierre Schmidt
17, Rue Toepffer
1206, Geneva

WEST GERMANY:	Mr. Rudolf Walberg D-6232, Bad Soden/Taunus Falkenstr. 18.
SWEDEN:	Mr. T. Gunther Ostadkulle 6018 44100 Alingsas Stockholm
HOLLAND:	Mr. L.G. Metz Trompstraat 7, Flat 5 Zandvoort
GREECE:	Mr. Thr. K. Androulidakis 17 Lemessos Str. ATHENS-821
ITALY:	Mr. John W. Abel Centro Avila Via Cassia 1170 00189 Rome
SPAIN:	Mr. S.W. Balani P.O. Box 2058, Las Palmas, Grand Canary Island
FRANCE:	Mr. Theophile Perron 179 rue du Plessis Bouchard 95130, Franconville
ISRAEL:	Mr. E.A. Mandelbaum P.O. Box 2815 Tel Aviv
U.A.R.:	Mr. Zaki Awad 1, Kurra Ibn Shureck Str. Giza, Egypt

SOUTH AFRICA:	Mr. Sam Busa P.O. Box 9513 Johannesburg
CENTRAL AFRICA:	Mr. E.L. Dawson Anchris House, Room No. 20 Post Box 852 Kitwe, Zambia
EAST AFRICA:	Mr. Joseph Kyagambiddwa P.O. Box 20012 Kampala, Uganda
WEST AFRICA:	Mr. Lakhi Nebhani P.O. Box 400 Kumasi, Ghana
NEW ZEALAND:	Mr. Henry Hill P.O. Box 5331 Wellesley Street Auckland 1
AUSTRALIA:	Mr. A.J. Walker 3 Bayview 26 North Esplanade North Glenelg, 5045
FIJI:	Mr. R.M. Prasad Victoria Arcade, Suite 2-A Box 319, G.P.O. Suva
PHILIPPINES:	Mr. Deepchand Dayaldas Room 314, Garcia Bldg., 3rd Floor 636 Rizal Avenue Manila

HONG KONG:	Mr. Gobind Sabnani, c/o Monico Enterprises (H.K.) Ltd., P.O. Box 13906
THAILAND:	S. Mohinder Singh Sethi "Siri Sawan" 95/71, Triphet Road Bangkok
SINGAPORE:	Mr. Shankardas Nanwani 12 Broadrick Road Singapore-15
INDONESIA:	Mr Krishin T. Vasandani Gunung Sahari XI No. 8 DJAKARTA
WEST INDIES:	Mr.Thakurdas Chatlani 2A,Gittins Avenue Maraval, Trinidad(W.I.)
For all foreign orders write to:	Mr. Krishin Babani Buona Casa Bldg., 2nd floor Sir P.M. Road Fort, Bombay-400 001, INDIA

BOOKS ON THIS SCIENCE

1. **Sar Bachan**—By Swami Ji Maharaj Shiv Dayal Singh, Translated by Sewa Singh, Distt. & Sessions Judge
2. **The Path of the Masters**—By Dr. Julian P. Johnson, M.A., M.D.
3. **The Path of the Masters—Abridged**—By Dr. Julian P. Johnson, M.A., M.D.
4. **With A Great Master in India**—By Dr. Julian P. Johnson, M.A., M.D.
5. **Mysticism, the Spiritual Path, Vol. I and Vol. II**—By Professor Lekh Raj Puri, M.A., P.E.S.
6. **Teachings of the Gurus, Series 1 to 4 (as given in Adi-Granth Sahib)**—By Professor Lekh Raj Puri, M.A., P.E.S.
7. **The Mystic Bible**—By Dr. Randolph Stone
8. **Sant Mat and the Bible**—By Narain Das, B.A., C.E.
9. **The Inner Voice**—By Colonel C.W. Sanders
10. **Spiritual Gems**—Letters from the Great Master, Huzur Maharaj Sawan Singh Ji (1919-1948)
11. **Light on Sant Mat**—By Maharaj Charan Singh Ji (Discourses and Excerpts from letters—1952-1958)
12. **The Science of the Soul**—By Sardar Bahadur Jagat Singh Ji Maharaj, M.Sc.,P.E.S.—(Discourses, Dialogues, Sayings and Excerpts from letters—1948-1951)
13. **Tales of the Mystic East**—As narrated in Satsangs by Huzur Maharaj Sawan Singh Ji
14. **Discourses on Sant Mat**—By Huzur Maharaj Sawan Singh Ji
15. **Philosophy of the Masters (Gurmat Sidhant), Series I to V**—By Huzur Maharaj Sawan Singh Ji (An Encyclopedia on the Teachings of the Saints)
16. **Call of the Great Master**—By Diwan Daryai Lal, Retired Judge
17. **Yoga and the Bible**—By Joseph Leeming, published by George Allen & Unwin Ltd., England
18. **The Mystic Way**—By Eleanora Jepp (A brief glimpse of the teachings of the Masters on Sant Mat, the Science of God-Realization)
19. **Prayer**—By Kathryn Windress
20. **My Submission, Part I and Part II**—By Huzur Maharaj Sawan Singh Ji

21. **Spiritual Discourses**—By Maharaj Charan Singh Ji

22. **The Mystic Philosophy of Sant Mat**—By Peter Fripp, with fully illustrated plates, published by Neville Spearman Ltd., England

23. **Radha Swami Teachings**—By Professor Lekh Raj Puri, M.A., P.E.S.

24. **Divine Light**—By Maharaj Charan Singh Ji (An explanation of the Teachings of the Saints, and Excerpts from letters—1959-1964)

25. **Sarmad—Jewish Saint of India**—By Isaac A. Ezekiel

26. **In Search of the Way**—By Flora E. Wood

27. **The Master Answers**—By Maharaj Charan Singh Ji to Audiences in America

28. **Kabir, the Great Mystic**—By Isaac A. Ezekiel

29. **The Living Master**—By Katherine Wason

30. **Spiritual Letters**—From Baba Jaimal Singh Ji to Huzur Maharaj Sawan Singh Ji—1896 to 1903

31. **St. John, The Great Mystic**—By Maharaj Charan Siingh Ji

32. **With the Three Masters Vols. I, II and III**—From the Dairy of Rai Sahib Munshi Ram

33. **Ringing Radiance**—By Sir Colin Garbett, K.C.I.E., C.S.I., C.M.G., D.Sc.J., M.A., LL.B., F.R.G.S., F.R.S.A.

34. **Liberation of the Soul**—By J. Stanley White, M.A.,

35. **Message Divine**—By Mrs. Shanti Sethi

36. **Quest for Light**—By Maharaj Charan Singh Ji

37. **Philosophy of the Masters (abridged)**—By Huzur Maharaj Sawan Singh Ji.

38. **Radha Soami Satsang Beas**—Origin and Growth

39. **Thus Saith the Master**—By Radha Soami Satsang Beas Society

2.90